Dear Reader,

People have spent thousands of years exploring human nature through art, religion, philosophy, literature, and poetry, but it has only been fairly recently in history that we've begun to study the science behind the human mind and behavior. If you're like most people (including myself), your first foray into psychology was a required course during your first year of college. I didn't expect to fall in love with the subject, but from that very first lecture I was utterly captivated.

No matter where you are in your education, my hope is that this book will inspire you to learn more about yourself and the people around you. Psychology is a remarkably rich subject, and studying it can spark both philosophical questions and provide practical uses in your daily life. Whether you have a casual interest in the subject or plan on one day becoming a psychologist, the goal of this book is to provide a solid foundation and to increase your appreciation of the wide world of psychology.

Kendra Cherry

Essentials of
PSYCHOLOGY

Essentials of
PSYCHOLOGY

AN INTRODUCTORY GUIDE TO THE SCIENCE OF HUMAN BEHAVIOR

KENDRA CHERRY

Foreword by Paul G. Mattiuzzi, PhD

FALL RIVER PRESS

New York

This book is dedicated to my family.
Your support, dedication, and love mean so much.

FALL RIVER PRESS

New York

An Imprint of Sterling Publishing
1166 Avenue of the Americas
New York, NY 10036

Cover design by David Ter-Avanesyan
Interior design by Maria Mann

ISBN 978-1-4351-5441-4

For information about custom editions, special sales, and premium and corporate purchases,
please contact Sterling Special Sales at 800-805-5489 or specialsales@sterlingpublishing.com.

Manufactured in China

2 4 6 8 10 9 7 5 3

www.sterlingpublishing.com

Contents

FOREWORD

In a 2008 article, a national news magazine included psychology on a list of "overrated" careers. At my blog and in correspondence with the author, I wrote that psychology is not just about helping people, and that we pursue this field of work because we are deeply fascinated by our profession's rich knowledge base.

Reading *The Essentials of Psychology,* you will find that our field is expansive and that psychologists are intensely curious. Mental illness and psychotherapy are common topics of interest, but what should truly capture your imagination is how ordinary people think, feel, and behave.

Psychological understanding depends on answering the question of epistemology: How do we know what we know? Can watching violent TV shows encourage violence? The answer happens to be yes, but to understand the answer, you have to understand how the research was done and how the knowledge was acquired. In this book, you will read about a famous experiment in which kids imitated aggressive behavior they saw on TV. Maybe it is common sense, but that is not where we get the answer.

Very little of what we know in psychology is as simple as common sense. Our most fascinating insights are *counterintuitive*: not what you would expect. It seems obvious that if kidnap victims have a chance to run, they will escape. In reality, they often don't. From *cognitive dissonance* theory, we learn that many of our ordinary, everyday decisions are irrational and that we often act without really knowing why. Yes, some things do happen in the unconscious. Freud is famous for having seen this and for having seen it in how we dream.

In a sense, learning and conditioning are also about unconscious processes. As a kid, I once watched a chicken play a piano. In psychology courses, I learned how the chicken's behavior had been shaped and that we can be shaped as well, even against our will. We happen to learn in ways similar to Skinner's rats and Pavlov's dog, sometimes equally unaware of how we have been influenced.

We are not always aware of what is happening in our minds, and perception research tells us that the world we experience is not necessarily the same as reality. Every piece of sensory information we receive from the outside has to be analyzed and interpreted. Everything you see depends on a psychological process that can be influenced by expectations and experience.

Sometimes our minds fool us and sometimes psychological processes fail. An optical illusion is an example of how we can be fooled. Mental illness is an example of how our minds can fail us.

The Essentials of Psychology takes note of the fact that without thoughts and without consciousness, "we would instead be plants." You need a brain to have a thought, and so of course we study the biological underpinnings of behavior. Still, what makes psychology of enduring interest are the curious, perplexing, and often elegant ways in which our minds form ideas, beliefs, feelings, and behaviors. Our minds and our psychology define us as humans.

Paul G. Mattiuzzi, PhD

What do your dreams mean? Can we change people's attitudes? Can animals learn sign language? Psychology strives to answer these questions and many more. Everyone has an interest in psychology, whether they realize it or not. If you've ever wondered what causes people to behave in certain ways or questioned why you have particular personality characteristics, then you've expressed an interest in psychology. It's natural that we feel such a strong interest in psychology, because it is such a crucial part of who we are as individuals and the role we play in a larger society. Psychology helps us answer the questions that make us who we are and helps us understand where we are going.

Psychology is such a broad and diverse subject, encompassing nearly every aspect of human nature, that it would be impossible to cover it all in one book. Even an entire stack of books could not truly do justice to the complexities of the mind and behavior. Instead, the focus of this book is to set the foundation for a solid understanding of psychology. By laying this groundwork, you'll gain a better understanding of yourself as well as develop insight into the behavior of those around you.

You might not realize it, but you've probably studied psychology on a very informal basis by asking questions about why people do the things they do. You probably think about the motivations of others, explore your own feelings, and discuss the actions of people in your environment on a fairly regular basis. All of these things are a central part of psychology.

As you begin this book, you'll start by learning about some of the major areas within psychology and how each one has contributed to the growth and development of psychology as a whole. You may be surprised to learn that psychology is actually a very young discipline when compared to some of the other life and social sciences, and you'll learn more about this fascinating history by reading about some of the major thinkers and their theories. While some of these ideas are outdated or even downright shocking, understanding psychology's past is a great way to discover how the subject came to be what it is today. Psychology is always evolving and our understanding is constantly growing as researchers find new ways to investigate the human mind.

Of course, we'll also talk the symptoms, causes, and treatments of psychological disorders. Mental illness is quite common, and yet it is something that many people know relatively little about. While popular movies, television, and books often present a very stereotyped and exaggerated view of mental disorders, this book focuses on presenting facts and a realistic view of these frequently misunderstood illnesses. In order to fully understand human psychology, it is essential to understand the roots of mental illness and how psychologists work to help people suffering from psychological distress.

In addition to helping you gain a better understanding of other people, psychology can give you personal insight into your own thoughts, emotions, and behaviors. As you read through these pages, think about how the information relates to your own life and experiences. Welcome to the wide world of psychology!

PSYCHOLOGY—
Yesterday and Today

IT'S LIKELY THAT PSYCHOLOGY is more than you think it is. Just about every aspect of human behavior has been or is being studied by psychologists, often from more than one perspective. If not, it's on the list. Psychology's goal is to understand human behavior objectively and in its entirety.

What Is Psychology?

While psychology is one of the most popular courses on college campuses throughout the world, it is actually a relatively young discipline. "Psychology has a long past, but a short history," explained pioneering thinker Hermann Ebbinghaus (1850–1909). Since emerging as a distinct subject in the early nineteenth century, psychology has evolved into a broad discipline that touches on almost every aspect of your daily life. Modern psychology reflects a rich and varied history along with a wide variety of influences, including philosophy, biology, and neuroscience. There is no such thing as "the psychologist," and it's unlikely that any two psychologists will give you the same definition of their discipline. In order to gain a full understanding of the depth, breadth, and diversity in psychology, you need to learn more about the history and many subjects that psychologists study.

People often confuse psychology with psychiatry. They are not the same. While psychology comes from the Greek for "study of the soul," psychiatry derives from the Greek for "soul healing." Psychiatrists are medical doctors who focus exclusively on understanding and treating psychiatric disorders. Many psychologists also study and treat mental illnesses, but psychology is a much broader discipline.

While it is difficult to pin down psychology with one short and simple description, it is helpful to have some type of working definition. Psychology is often defined as the scientific study of the mind and behavior of humans and animals. You can understand this definition better by taking a closer look at some of the key elements:

- The term *psychology* originates from the Greek words *psyche* (for "soul" or "self") and *logia* (for "the study of").

- Psychology *is* a science, which means that scientific methods, experiments, and statistics are used to find objective evidence to back up its claims.

- Behavior refers to anything an organism does, whether it can be observed directly or must be inferred.

- Observing behavior includes measuring it with increasingly sophisticated techniques and equipment.

- Behaviors that can only be inferred—so far—include thinking, feeling, being motivated, and the many other "unseeable" activities that go on in your mind; but in studying these behaviors, psychologists must back up what they say with directly observable evidence.

- Psychologists have been known to study plants, and certain areas of psychology study nonhuman animals in their own right, but the goals are most often to understand humans and put this understanding to good use.

What Do Psychologists Do?

In the past, there was a distinction between psychologists who did "basic" research that focused on gaining knowledge and advancing theories—like a physicist seeking to understand the mechanics of the universe—and those who did applied research oriented toward solving individual and societal problems—like a chemist trying to develop a more effective drug for pharmaceutical company to market. Those who did basic research were known as "experimental psychologists" and those who did applied research were typically called "clinical psychologists."

In recent decades, however, this distinction has become somewhat blurred. While there are many distinct specialty areas within psychology, an individual working in any one of these areas might be found doing basic research, applied research, or a mix of the two. Approximately half of all psychologists fall into the first category. The remaining half consists of small percentages of other subdisciplines including:

- Clinical psychologists assess, diagnose, and treat mental and behavioral disorders. These professionals often work in medical settings and usually work with people suffering from severe mental disorders. Clinicians frequently specialize in working with people of a particular age range or who have specific disorders. A large part of their work involves conducting psychological tests and performing psychotherapy.

- Counseling psychologists usually work with individuals who have less severe psychological disturbances, such as people who are having marital difficulties or those who are struggling to cope with a specific area of their lives.

- Cognitive psychologists are interested in the mental process underlying thinking, learning, memory, attention, language, problem solving, and decision-making.

- Developmental psychologists study how people grow and change throughout the entire life span, from conception through death. They often specialize in a specific age range or focus on a certain aspect of development such as intelligence, language development, or personality.

- Personality psychologists are interested in the influences that shape personality and often use experimental methods, case studies, and clinical research to study stable personality characteristics that do not tend to change much from one situation to the next.

- School psychologists and educational psychologists work in school settings to help children with emotional, academic, social, and psychological problems. They may focus on individual adjustment problems or may work to improve the educational process as a whole.

- Social psychologists study social influence, social interaction, and social perception, including how people behave in groups and how a person's behavior may vary from one situation to the next.

- Forensic psychologists work on a variety of issues involving the judicial and criminal justice system. They are often involved in child custody disputes, mental competence evaluations, and child abuse investigations.

- Industrial/organizational psychologists utilize their research and understanding of human psychology to improve employee performance, make workplaces safer, and improve product design.

- Comparative psychologists study animal behavior, often in the hopes of improving the understanding of human actions. It is a multidisciplinary field that incorporates research from psychology, biology, anthropology, and ecology.

- Biopsychologists (sometimes known as behavioral neuroscientists or physiological psychologists) are the newest on the scene. They study relationships between the brain, mind, and behavior and are trained extensively in both psychology and physiology. They often use tools such as magnetic resonance imaging (MRI) or positron emission tomography (PET) scans to look at how brain abnormalities impact behavior.

As you may have noticed, there are many psychological areas that overlap. Developmental psychology, for example, cuts across almost every discipline listed, as do certain elements of social and cognitive psychology. Modern psychology is indeed a complex network of specialties and interests, although a trend worth noting is that over the last few decades, psychologists have increasingly focused on understanding individuals as a "whole" person, rather than concentrating on specific aspects of development or behavior. However, putting it all together is still very much a work in progress.

Ethics in the Practice of Psychology

In the United States, psychologists must be licensed to practice psychotherapy with individuals or to work with organizations. Licensing ensures that they are properly trained and up-to-date on their particular discipline, and also ensures that they adhere to a strict code of ethics when working with their clients. The code of ethics is specified by the American Psychological Association (APA), the largest organization of U.S. psychologists, and it spells out in detail what psychologists should and should not do in order to maintain their professional obligations and to safeguard their clients' rights and dignity as human beings.

> The APA code also specifies that sexual intimacy between a client and a psychologist is strictly forbidden. So if your therapist "comes on" to you, only two possibilities exist. Your psychologist is violating the code, or your therapist is not really a psychologist or other legitimate therapist. In either case, contact your state psychological association.

Aside from the ethical requirement that a psychologist be competent to perform the services and not misrepresent this, perhaps the most important ethical consideration in the practice of psychology is confidentiality. For example, if you're in psychotherapy, your psychologist cannot divulge any of your personal information without your written consent. To do so would be grounds for a lawsuit and loss of licensure at the very least.

There are a few exceptions. One is if, for example, a judge issues a court order overriding your confidentiality, such as in a criminal case. Another instance is if you make a statement suggesting that you might hurt yourself or others, in which case your therapist has an ethical and legal duty to warn those who may be in danger. A third is the sharing of scientific knowledge. Your psychologist can write about or otherwise share information about your case, as long as it is done in a manner that in no way identifies you personally. But for the most part, your privacy is a cornerstone of your relationship with a psychologist. Different states have different exceptions to confidentiality; for instance, in Massachusetts, psychologists must break confidentiality if a client tells them about the abuse of a child or an elderly person.

The Influence of Philosophy and Physiology

As you learned earlier, psychology has not always been a distinct subject in its own right. While people have been interested in how and why people think and behave as they do since the very beginning of time, such observations were part of philosophy and physiology. Why is it important to study the early history of psychology? While contemporary psychology focuses on an enormous range of topics, from cognition to animal behavior, studying the past influences that have shaped the discipline into what it is today provides a richer understanding of what psychologists now know about the mind and behavior.

Some of the oldest influences on psychology date back to the time of the ancient Greeks, when philosophers such as Aristotle and Plato contemplated the dynamic between the mind and body. In the seventeenth century, thinker René Descartes suggested the concept of dualism in which the mind and body exist as two separate entities. Descartes believed that the interaction between the mind and body created the experience of reality.

Psychology today is still concerned with many of the basic philosophical questions that thinkers were contemplating thousands of years ago. Does nature or nurture have a greater influence on development? How do biological states influence behavior? So if psychology is still focused on these age-old questions, what separates it from the field of philosophy? The answer lies in the use of scientific methodology, systematic observation, and empirical evidence to support the claims made by psychology.

Psychology in the Early Years

It is generally agreed that Wilhelm Wundt (1832–1920) founded psychology in 1879 when he established the first "psychological" laboratory at the University of Leipzig in Germany. Wundt started out as a professor of physiology before setting out to study the human mind using a method called introspection. In this approach, specially trained individuals attempted to look inside their own minds and describe what went on in response to events they were exposed to, such as lights and sounds.

What's wrong with this method? Although introspection as a research method survived for a few decades and was briefly popular in the United States, it was far too subjective. The introspectors often reported conflicting information and there was no way to verify what any of them said.

> While it is no longer used as a research technique, introspection has survived in a different form. In some versions of psychotherapy, clients or patients are asked to report their innermost thoughts and feelings, which you will learn more about in Chapter 20.

American psychologist William James (1842–1910) also used introspection in writing his *Principles of Psychology* (1890)—a highly influential text that marked the beginning of modern psychology. James went into great detail in describing his thoughts and feelings and relating them to psychological processes such as perceiving, emotionality, and memory. Though subjective, many of James's observations held up reasonably well when later verified by scientific research.

James firmly believed that psychology should be the "study of mental life." He also proposed—in accord with the views of Charles Darwin (1809–1882) on physical evolution—that the human mind as it is today evolved as a result of successive adaptations by our distant ancestors. This view, which was called *functionalism,* would soon fall into disfavor, but it resurfaced in the later twentieth century as an increasingly popular line of theory and research now known as *evolutionary psychology.* Evolutionary psychology and other biological approaches to understanding behavior will be discussed in Chapter 3.

Psychoanalysis

Meanwhile in Austria, an Austrian physician named Sigmund Freud (1856–1939) was developing his psychoanalytic theory, a work that would span some forty years. Freud will be discussed in detail at various points in this book, but an overview of his theory here is helpful in understanding where psychology went next.

Up to this point in psychology's brief history, most research was focused on the conscious human experience. Freud's theory instead focused on the impact of the unconscious mind, a reservoir of thought, emotions, desires, and feelings that are outside of conscious awareness. You can think of the conscious and unconscious mind like an iceberg. The tip of the iceberg that lies above the surface represents the conscious mind, while the largest part of the iceberg that lies underneath the water represents the unconscious. The unconscious mind often contains thoughts or wishes that are unacceptable or unpleasant, including feelings that are painful, conflicted, or shameful.

The prevailing view in the late nineteenth century was that humans are rational beings, removed from other animals because of logic and morality. To Freud, humans were anything but rational, but were instead driven by selfish "animal" impulses (such as desires for nourishment and sex, and what Freud thought was a built-in aggressive impulse). Freud alleged that these impulses are biological in origin, and they demand satisfaction even though they are part of what he called the unconscious mind. Freud's views were considered hedonistic, suggesting that people exist to seek pleasure and avoid pain—making his theories particularly controversial in Victorian Europe.

So what happens when these impulses are repressed, restrained, or thwarted? According to Freud, it is the denial or suppression of these urges and desires that lead to emotional distress. Along with the fears and guilt over misdeeds—real and imagined—that you accumulate and that become unconscious because they are too painful to think about, they cause people to behave in maladaptive ways. This is especially the case with desires and guilt of a sexual nature, which Freud saw as primary determinants of behavior. Thus, life is a constant struggle to satisfy, or more often to try to contain, your impulses and guilt if you are to give the appearance of being rational and moral and able to live in relative harmony.

Freud developed his theory through his treatment of typically mildly disordered patients, which eventually yielded the treatment approach he called *psychoanalysis*. Some of Freud's ideas have survived, but much of his theorizing—especially the notion that sex is the primary motivator of human behavior—has been discounted. However, he is still regarded as one of the most influential figures in all of psychology, and he was the first to attempt a comprehensive theory of personality.

> Humans do have "animal" needs that must be satisfied just to survive. These include needs for oxygen, food, and liquids. We also need sex. Although some people might rank this right up there with survival needs, sex has more to do with reproducing our species. Many people manage to get by without being preoccupied with it, contrary to what Freud thought.

Have you ever referred to someone as "anal"? If so, you probably meant that the person is stubborn, demanding, and very picky. It's a Freudian term to describe personality characteristics that supposedly result from faulty toilet training. Other Freudian terms and concepts are also still used today. Some make sense; more don't.

Behaviorism

Psychology went through a dramatic change early in the twentieth century as a new school of thought known as behaviorism became a dominant force. Behaviorists rejected the idea of the unconscious and conscious mind and focused instead on making psychology a more scientific discipline that studied only observable behaviors. Strict behaviorism was a reaction against both introspection and psychoanalytic theory, each of which attempted to deal with the inner and unobservable workings of the mind.

In the early 1920s, an American psychologist named J. B. Watson (1878–1958) was a strong advocate of behaviorism and helped establish it as a major school of thought, but it was the work of two other researchers who truly deserve credit for the ideas and principles that served as the basis for behaviorism: Ivan Pavlov (1849–1936) in Russia and Edward L. Thorndike (1874–1949) in the United States.

Pavlov's Dogs

Ivan Pavlov, the man who played such an important role in behaviorism, actually wasn't a psychologist at all. He was a Russian physiologist who accidentally discovered what is now known as classical conditioning during his research on the digestive systems of dogs. As the famous story goes, he became distracted by the observation that his dogs developed a tendency to salivate before food was placed in their mouths. That is, they learned to anticipate food, in much the same way that you might salivate a bit when you approach a restaurant that you like.

Thorndike's Cats

Thorndike's most noteworthy contribution was his "law of effect," which he derived from work with laboratory animals—primarily cats. In brief, he proposed that any behavior that is followed by a satisfying state of affairs (such as getting food) tends to be repeated, and any behavior that is followed by an unsatisfying or unpleasant state of affairs (such as experiencing pain) tends not to be repeated. *Satisfying* and *unsatisfying* may not sound like terms a strict behaviorist would use, but Thorndike got around that by defining satisfying as something an animal typically approaches and unsatisfying as something an animal typically avoids—a nicely behavioral solution. Thorndike's work laid the groundwork for the operant conditioning approach of B. F. Skinner (1904–1990), who ranks alongside Freud among the most influential psychologists of all time and whose work is discussed in Chapter 7.

Behaviorism Today

Strict behaviorism, or the belief that psychology should only focus on observable behaviors, has largely fallen out of favor and very few psychologists today would identify themselves as strict behaviorists. Critics of behaviorism note that this approach to psychology failed to address factors such as free will, internal thoughts, and other methods of learning. Nevertheless, behaviorists had a major impact on psychology with their emphasis on scientific method. As opposed to shunning behavior that cannot be directly observed, psychologists now embrace it. But the bottom line is still observable, verifiable evidence.

Behaviorism may not be a dominant perspective in psychology, but many of basic techniques and principles from behavioral psychology are still widely used today in behavior modification, psychotherapy, education, and parenting.

> Strict behaviorism was a reaction to the nonscientific approaches that preceded it. In turn, the approaches that followed were in large measure reactions to strict behaviorism, psychoanalytic theory, or both. And added to that is the impact of modern technology, which allows for measuring behavior at a level of precision that the early theorists could only dream about.

Humanistic Psychology and Positive Psychology

By the middle of the twentieth century, there were a number of personality theorists who argued that there is more to being human than simply satisfying or controlling animal desires, or seeking pleasure and avoiding pain. Both psychoanalytic theory and strict behaviorism were limited to these factors in explaining human behavior. They had little to say about positive and uniquely human desires such as helping others, belonging to family and society, and becoming all that you can become as a person.

Enter the humanistic psychologists, the best known of whom were Carl Rogers (1902–1987) and Abraham Maslow (1908–1970). Their credo was that humans are different from other animals in important ways. Although humans certainly have needs in common with other animals and can be quite selfish at times, there's more to being human that simply striving to satisfy the basic drives. Humans have goals in life, a need to grow and fulfill themselves psychologically and feel good about it all, and humans have a need to find happiness that goes beyond satisfaction of basic needs. To the humanists, the positive thinking and hoping that both the psychoanalysts and strict behaviorists ignored are the most important aspects of human behavior.

> **Are humans basically just selfish animals or are we more?**
> The answer depends on your observations as well as those of the theorists. If you believe that people are hedonistic at the core, we're basically just animals. If you believe that people have concerns that go beyond their own needs, we're more. Give it some thought.

Then came positive psychology, which is an approach that runs parallel to that of the humanists but has a different emphasis. In the view of Martin Seligman, a prominent proponent of positive psychology, far too much emphasis has been placed on understanding undesirable and maladaptive aspects of human behavior—such as disorders and criminal behavior—and far too little has involved understanding the good things that people do—the things that lead to happiness, well-being, and being functional members of society. It isn't that undesirable behaviors aren't important; it's just that desirable ones are too. The details and impact of humanistic psychology and positive psychology are discussed further in Chapter 15.

Cognitive Psychology

Cognitive psychology took off in the 1960s, having been launched by the information-processing model developed by Allen Newell (1927–1992) and Herbert Simon (1916–2001) some years earlier. During this period, psychology once again turned its interest to the study of how internal states, such as thoughts, feelings, and moods influence behavior. As noted, cognitive psychology and its scientific approaches to studying mental processes have now been incorporated into virtually all areas of psychology.

Newell and Simon did indeed launch a "cognitive revolution" with their model, which is based on computer analogies. Simply put, human information-processing begins with input from the external environment, which is then stored temporarily in the conscious mind—for immediate use, such as when you look up a number and make a phone call—or is processed further and stored permanently for future use—such as making the call again from memory. The stages involved are thus encoding, storage, and retrieval. The complexities of how you accomplish this are the subject of Chapter 9.

Biological Psychology

Other areas of psychology that are having increasingly broad impact across the major psychological disciplines fall under the umbrella term biological psychology. This refers in general to researchers who study relationships between behavior and any aspects of bodily functioning, but foremost among them nowadays are those who search for direct links between behavior and the brain or behavior and the mind. Those who stay fairly close to observable brain-behavior relationships are called behavioral neuroscientists. Those who extend their study to the as-yet unobservable processes of the mind are called cognitive neuroscientists.

Both utilize highly sophisticated brain scanning and monitoring equipment to study what goes on in the brain in response to external events or while certain tasks are being performed. Their research includes accurately assessing which areas of the brain are active in a given situation and how the flow of information through the brain takes place. Their approach is being applied to areas such as understanding the physiological bases for learning and memory, emotionality, and mental and behavioral disorders.

Culture, Ethnicity, and Diversity in Modern Psychology

In the early years of psychology and continuing into the latter part of the twentieth century, it was mostly taken for granted that all human beings are the same where psychological functioning is concerned. At the same time, almost all psychologists were white North Americans or Europeans, and they mostly studied white people like themselves. There were some exceptions, such as research that compared whites and blacks or females and males, but even this was narrowly focused on topics such as intelligence.

By and large, psychology ignored the effects of culture, which is the aggregate of the practices and the beliefs and generally the heritage of differing groups of people. They likewise paid little attention to ethnicity, which includes a person's culture but traditionally adds biological heritage and considerations such as "race." The same went for diversity, which emphasizes ethnicity as well as gender, sexual orientation, age, and anything else that might consistently distinguish people psychologically.

> Many scientists now believe that "race" has no scientific basis whatsoever. One important reason is that all modern humans appear to have originated in Africa, which means that all humans have the same ancestors. Another is that so-called racial characteristics aren't clear-cut—you'll find almost every imaginable combination of skin color, facial features, and so on. In all, there is only one human race.

People often use the terms *culture* and *society* interchangeably, but there is a distinct difference. As noted, culture consists of beliefs, heritage, and the like—largely abstract things. In contrast, a society is an organized group of people—a physical thing. Thus, it has been observed that culture is to a society as personality is to an individual.

In the last couple of decades, psychologists have come to appreciate the potential impact of these considerations and a flood of research on cultural differences in particular has ensued. Psychologists have discovered that some of the basic psychological findings are actually not as universal as they once believed. Indeed, there has been such an overwhelming abundance of cross-cultural findings that researchers are still grappling with how to sort it out. A major finding, however, is that there are consistent psychological differences between people who live in individualist cultures, such as Western societies in which individual accomplishments are emphasized, versus collectivist cultures, such as Asian societies in which the emphasis is on group accomplishments. Research comparing the two has had its greatest impact on social psychology, as you'll see in Chapters 16 and 17.

HOW PSYCHOLOGISTS
Know What They Know

LIKE OTHER SCIENTISTS, psychologists prefer experiments that assess the causes of behaviors and other psychological phenomena, and they conduct and publish thousands of these each year. However, experiments aren't always possible. Fortunately, psychologists have various methods that rely either on observation or on self-reports of people's thoughts and feelings. Where necessary, psychologists also conduct experiments with laboratory animals.

The Scientific Method

As a part of the overall empirical process that psychologists use when conducting research, whether they are using true experiments or another type of research method, researchers follow the five basic steps of the scientific method. The scientific method is a set of procedures used by researchers to create questions, gather data, and arrive at conclusions. Briefly put, these steps are:

Formulate a testable hypothesis. A hypothesis is basically an educated guess about the possible relationship between two or more variables.

Design a study and collect the data. In this step, psychologists decide which research methods they will use to conduct their experiment. Next, they will collect the data by performing the experiment or study.

Analyze the data and arrive at conclusions. After all of the data has been collected from the study participants, it is time to evaluate the findings and determine what the results mean.

Share the findings with the scientific community. Research is often shared by writing up the results in an article format and publishing the findings in a professional psychology journal. By sharing the knowledge gained from the study, researchers add one more piece of valuable information to what psychologists know about a particular topic.

Descriptive Research Methods

Descriptive research methods such as naturalistic observation and case studies are often used in situations where performing an experiment is not realistic or is downright impossible. After the data has been collected, psychologists utilize statistical analysis to look at the relationships between the variables.

Observational Studies

Careful, accurate observation is essential to experiments and most psychological research, but sometimes it is conducted for its own sake—perhaps simply to detail what people and other animals normally do. Naturalistic observation means observing behavior in everyday settings, which could be a school playground, a shopping mall, a freeway, a remote village, a jungle, etc. For example, a researcher might gain insight into what factors are involved in people helping and cooperating with each other simply by observing situations in which they do and comparing these to situations in which they don't. The researcher also would then be in a better position to design experiments to determine what produces helping and cooperating or interferes with it.

Laboratory observation is also a useful tool. Laboratory settings can be either simulations of natural settings or completely artificial. The advantages of observation in a laboratory setting are that a researcher has much more control over what behaviors occur and, as applicable, can use sophisticated instrumentation. A classic example of laboratory observation using instrumentation is the 1960s research of William Masters and Virginia Johnson on the sexual arousal cycles of men and women, in which the researchers took physiological measurements while their participants were having sexual intercourse. Their basic findings about differences between men and women in this respect are still relevant today.

A question remains about whether the participants in the Masters and Johnson studies were representative of all adult human beings. They probably were, because basic physiology differs little from one woman or one man to the next. But ask yourself: Would you be willing to have sex while being hooked up to electrodes and watched? Might the participants have been "different" in some important way?

Case Histories and Interviews

A case history is an in-depth study of an individual or small group. Freud based his psychoanalytic theory in part on the case histories of his patients, and they are still used as a prelude to clinical diagnosis and treatment. Case histories consist of interviews with the person, perhaps also with the person's family, and sometimes a combing-through of the person's academic records, legal records, and work history—with the person's permission, of course. Case histories are also at times the method of choice in studying the origins of relatively rare mental and behavioral disorders.

Either way, the goal is to construct a thorough and rich picture of the person's life history and past and present functioning, and a case history's thoroughness is its advantage. The advantage of a case history is that it allows researchers to gain valuable information that would otherwise be impossible to obtain through traditional experiments. For example, psychologists have done case histories with feral children who have been raised in extremely deprived, neglectful environments. Obviously, actually conducting this type of experiment would be completely unethical, so case histories give researchers a unique opportunity to learn how severe deprivation impacts mental and physical development. The main disadvantage of a case history is that—like all psychological research methods except experiments—it cannot determine cause and effect.

> Researchers have found that people with "multiple" personality disorder (currently called dissociative identity disorder) were often abused as children, which makes it tempting to conclude that abuse is the cause. But there is no way to be sure. This demonstrates one of the most principles of psychology research—correlation does not equal causation. Just because two variables are correlated does not mean that the one variable is causing the other to occur. In reality, an unknown third variable could have had influence as well.

Interviews can be part of a case history or they can serve more immediate purposes in clinical practice. A mental status exam is one; its purpose is to determine a client's current functioning, and it includes relatively informal questions that assess things like bodily functions (Do you sleep well? How's your appetite? Any problems with your sex life?), emotional state (Have you been feeling depressed or anxious lately?), cognitive functioning (Count backward from 100 by 7s. What did you have for breakfast this morning?), and general orientation (What day is it? Where are you and why are you here?). Your general practitioner probably uses some of these questions during your checkup as a screen both for physical complaints and mental problems.

Self-Report Questionnaires and Surveys

Interviews are a form of self-report, but the term more often refers to "paper-and-pencil" questionnaires that researchers have people fill out. They take various forms, such as a simple Yes, No, or a more sophisticated Strongly Agree, Agree, No Opinion, Disagree, Strongly Disagree in response to statements designed to tap your beliefs, attitudes, preferences, habits, mood, and more. Psychological researchers often use questionnaires to screen experiment participants and also to assess the results of experiments. Questionnaires have the advantage that the answers can easily be turned into numbers for computer analysis—for individuals, or in the case of surveys, for large numbers of people. They also allow researchers to gather data from a large number of people relatively quickly and cheaply.

Questionnaires do of course have their disadvantages as a research tool. Where sensitive topics such as a person's use of drugs, sexual behavior, or attitudes toward his employer are concerned, participants may not risk answering truthfully for fear that the responses won't really be kept confidential. A more general problem is that people may not be able to remember their behavior accurately even if they want to respond truthfully. Assuming that it's a number larger than zero or one or so, can you remember exactly how many times you've had sex in the past year? Some people would have difficulty remembering even the past month.

Experiments—The Cornerstone of Psychology

The basic idea of psychological experimentation is that researchers manipulate certain aspects of a situation to see what happens to the behavior of participants or subjects as a result. What the researcher manipulates is called experimental conditions. If the experiment is conducted according to proper procedures, and if the participants' or subjects' behavior differs as a result of the experimental conditions, the researcher can conclude that the manipulation caused the difference.

An Example Experiment

Here's a classic experiment on children and how they learn aggressive behavior, conducted in the 1960s by Albert Bandura (1925–), a prominent social-learning theorist. Three groups of young children saw a film in which an adult "model" beat up and shouted at a Bobo doll in highly specific ways. The film was the same for all the children except for the ending: one group saw the model rewarded (praised) for doing a good job of beating up Bobo, one group instead saw the model punished (scolded) for beating up Bobo, and one group saw the model experience no consequences.

Next came what was called the performance phase of the experiment. Each child was allowed to play with a Bobo alone and the question was how many of the model's behaviors the children would imitate. So far, no surprises. Children who had seen the model punished imitated few behaviors; children who had seen the model either be rewarded or experience no consequences imitated significantly more.

Finally came the learning phase, in which each child was offered rewards for imitating the model's behaviors. Surprise: the differences between the groups disappeared and the children all imitated the behaviors at a high level. That is, all the children had learned how to mistreat Bobo in detail; the ones who saw the model punished simply didn't display this learning until the right time, when there was an incentive for doing so instead of—in their minds—the possibility of punishment. An important implication of this experiment and many related ones that followed is that when children watch violent television shows and movies, it doesn't much matter if the "bad guys" get it in the end. Children (and adults) still learn how to commit violence and aggression. Later, they may use this learning if the occasion seems to warrant it, especially if they don't think they will be caught and punished.

Elements of a Good Experiment

Psychological experimenters must attend to certain principles and adhere to fairly specific procedures. Otherwise, the results may be difficult if not impossible to interpret or may not be meaningful. The following is a partial list of important considerations in conducting experiments, using Bandura's experiment for reference:

- Participants are typically randomly assigned to experimental conditions in the hope that each group will be equivalent in any important respects. Bandura randomly assigned children in the hope that the groups, overall, would be equivalent in aggressiveness.

- Each group has exactly the same experiences except for differences in the experimental conditions. In Bandura's experiment, all the children saw the same film except for the ending.

- If the groups aren't equivalent and treated the same except for experimental conditions, the result is confounding—something other than the conditions might instead be responsible for the results. For example, Bandura's experiment might have been confounded if one group saw the film in the morning and the others in the afternoon, because the afternoon groups might be tired and pay less attention.

- What happens in an experiment must be relevant to the topic under study. The term for this is *operational definition*, and it was reasonable for Bandura—in studying aggressive behavior and imitation—to define these as exposure to an aggressive model and the extent to which the children beat up Bobo.

- Operational definitions also determine the extent to which an experiment reflects what happens in the real world, which is called *external validity*. Most would agree that Bandura's definitions and results shed light on children's observational learning of aggression that might apply to many real-world settings.

> Even when these considerations are followed, no researcher should make sweeping generalizations based on a single experiment. We can only say that children learn aggressive behavior through observing it because many others have replicated Bandura's experiments. That is, similar studies have been conducted with different children, in different settings, with different procedures, and with various other forms of aggressive behavior.

Psychological Tests

Some psychological tests are also self-reports. This time, however, the distinction is that the term applies to inventories of items that have been given to large numbers of people and carefully polished. They are also subjected to statistical analysis so that when they are given to an individual, the researcher or clinician has a much better idea of what the results mean.

There are two general types of psychological tests: those that assess one or another type of ability and those that assess personality. Ability tests come in two varieties: intelligence tests assess your intellectual/cognitive functioning and achievement tests assess the progress you've made in acquiring academic or other skills. Clinicians often include intelligence tests in diagnosis; researchers use them the same way that they use self-reports as noted earlier. Achievement tests assess progress during grade school, and some are intended to predict success in college or other advanced training. Personality tests assess relatively stable personality characteristics, using various forms of self-reports. They also are used in diagnosing and researching mental and behavioral disorders. Popular personality tests are discussed in Chapter 15.

The Essential Role of Statistics

Modern psychology couldn't get by without statistics. Some of these simply describe research data and stop there. An example is correlation, which yields a single number that indicates the extent to which two variables are "related." Another example is the set of often-complex statistical computations that help researchers decide whether the results of their experiments are likely to be "real."

A variable is literally anything in the environment or about a person that can be modified and have an influence on his or her particular thoughts, reactions, or behaviors. The amount of light or noise in a room is a variable—it differs from one room to the next. Height and weight are variables, as are intelligence, personality characteristics, and a host of observable behaviors, because these differ from one person to the next.

Correlation

In correlation, the resulting number can range from 0 to +1.00 or 0 to −1.00. Where it falls indicates the strength of the correlation. The sign of the correlation indicates its direction. A correlation of 0 is nonexistent; a correlation of either +1.00 or −1.00 is perfect.

For example, to assess the correlation between height and weight, a researcher would measure the height and weight of each of a group of individuals and then plug the numbers into a mathematical formula. This correlation will usually turn out to be noticeable, perhaps about +.63. The ".63" tells us that it is a relatively strong correlation, and the "+" tells us that height and weight tend to vary in the same direction—taller people tend to weigh more, shorter people less. But the correlation is far from perfect and there are many exceptions.

What the correlations you encounter in this book mean vary somewhat according to the application, but here's a rule of thumb: A correlation between 0 and about +.20 (or 0 and −.20) is weak, one between +.20 and +.60 (or −.20 and −.60) is moderate, and one between +.60 and +1.00 (or −.60 and −1.00) is strong.

As another example, a researcher might assess the extent to which people's blood alcohol content (BAC) is related to their ability to drive. The participants might be asked to drink and then attempt to operate a driving simulator. Their BACs would then be compared with their scores on the simulator, and the researcher might find a correlation of −.68. This is again a relatively strong correlation, but the "−" tells us that BAC and driving ability vary in an opposite direction—the higher the BAC, the lower the driving ability.

Inferential Statistics

For descriptive statistics such as correlation, the "mean," or average, and some others that will be considered in context later in the book, the purpose is to describe or summarize aspects of behavior to understand them better. Inferential statistics start with descriptive ones and go further in allowing researchers to draw meaningful conclusions—especially in experiments. These procedures are beyond the scope of this book, but the basic logic is helpful in understanding how psychologists know what they know.

Again recalling Bandura's experiment of observational learning of aggression, consider just the model-punished and model-rewarded groups. It was stated that the former children imitated few behaviors and the latter significantly more. What this really means is that, based on statistical analysis, the difference between the two groups was large enough and consistent enough to be unlikely to have occurred simply by "chance." That is, it would have been a long shot to obtain the observed difference if what happened to the model wasn't a factor. Thus, Bandura and colleagues discounted the possibility of chance alone and concluded that what the children saw happen to the model was the cause of the difference in their behavior.

This logic may seem puzzling to you, and it isn't important that you grasp it to understand the many experiments that are noted throughout this book. Indeed, it isn't mentioned again. The point of mentioning it at all is to underscore that people are far less predictable than chemical reactions and the like, and therefore have to be studied somewhat differently—usually without formulas.

Psychologists study what people tend to do in a given situation, recognizing that not all people will behave as predicted—just as the children in the model-rewarded group did not all imitate all the behaviors. In a nutshell, the question is simply whether a tendency is strong enough—as assessed by statistics—to warrant a conclusion about cause and effect.

Ethics in Psychological Research

Just as there is a tight code of ethics that governs how psychologists practice their profession with clients (see Chapter 1), there is a code that governs how they conduct their research that is mandated by the APA and public law. This applies to research both with humans and laboratory animals. The following is a list of primary ethical considerations in psychological research with humans:

- Psychologists must never knowingly conduct research that has the potential for immediate, significant harm or lasting harm of any kind; they can make their participants uncomfortable or upset, but only mildly and only if the research question justifies it.

- Research participants always take part entirely voluntarily, without coercion, and they can stop participating at any point without penalty—they don't even have to say why.

- A major aspect of voluntary participation is informed consent. Participants must be told in advance what to expect in experiments or other research efforts, and it must be made clear to them that they can stop participating at any time.

- Although participants must be told what to expect, they don't necessarily have to be told the true nature of the experiment; they can be deceived in this respect, because people may behave quite differently if they know what an experimenter is really interested in.

- When deception is used—as it often is in research with humans—participants must be thoroughly debriefed afterward, which means that they are told the true nature of the experiment and are allowed to ask questions and express any concerns they have.

- As in psychological practice, all information about a particular participant's behavior is strictly confidential and every effort must be made to keep it that way.

- Institutional review boards (IRBs), comprised of professionals, evaluate all proposed research to determine if there are potential ethical problems with any of the research practices. IRBs may suggest changes and they can withhold approval for the research to be conducted.

In accord with these ethical principles, by far most psychological research with human participants is benign. It is possible, however, for psychologists to conduct approved research with the best of intentions and inadvertently have things turn out differently than they had planned.

Should you find yourself in a psychological experiment, say, in response to an ad in your local media, remember the part about quitting at any point without penalty. Participants are usually paid, and in keeping with the ethical principles, you must be paid in full if you begin an experiment—whether or not you complete it. Withholding payment would be coercion.

In research with animals, the principles regarding the potential for harm are of course not as strict. Important research—particularly that of an experimental nature and that risks significant harm—can be conducted only with nonhumans. Nowadays, however, the question is always whether it is truly warranted. The main consideration in using laboratory animals for research is that they must be treated humanely, which includes caring for them responsibly and attending to their health and needs.

Identifying Pseudoscience

When you hear the word pseudoscience, obvious examples of "fake science" such as palm reading, astrology, and numerology might immediately spring to mind. However, there are also examples of pseudoscience that exist within psychology such as rebirthing therapy or primal scream therapy. A pseudoscience can be defined as a theory, practice, or method that is presented in a way that appears scientific but is not supported by real empirical evidence.

During the early nineteenth century, a German physician named Francis Joseph Gall (1758–1828) introduced a discipline known as phrenology, which suggested that personality, character, and intelligence could be determined by assessing the bumps on a person's skull. While it became quite popular, phrenology was discredited as a pseudoscience.

During the twentieth century, philosopher Karl Popper (1902–1994) suggested that *falsifiability* could be used to distinguish between science and pseudoscience. For example, the claim that God created the universe may or may not be true, but it is impossible to design a test to prove the claim false; the subject simply lies outside of the realm of science. So, in order for a claim to be proved, you must be able to present evidence that could possibly refute or disprove the idea.

Some of the classic signs of a pseudoscience include:

- The use of testimonials or anecdotes in place of empirical evidence—This type of "proof" lends a highly personal aspect to a claim, but the results may actually be due to other factors entirely or purely coincidental.

- A lack of peer review—As mentioned earlier, many psychological studies are published in professional journals. Prior to publication, research undergoes an intensive peer review process in which the methods and procedures are closely scrutinized. Pseudoscientific claims typically lack testing from outside sources; that is, only the individuals making the claims review them.

As you continue to learn more about psychology and explore further psychological research, consider some of the classic hallmarks of pseudoscience and analyze the scientific methodologies used in the research. By learning how to separate "junk science" from the good stuff, you will become a better-informed consumer of psychology research.

—◆—

THE BIOLOGY
of Psychology

YOUR BIOLOGICAL FUNCTIONING is a constant hum of activity, most of which occurs automatically without your awareness. Biological psychology is the specialty area that studies the brain and other biological processes that impact the mind and behavior. This chapter will take a look at the role of the nervous system, the role genes play, and some ideas about where it all came from in an evolutionary sense.

Neurons and What They Do

Neurons are the building blocks of the human nervous system. These highly specialized cells are responsible for communication throughout the nervous system, sending and receiving information from one part of the body to another. The nervous system is comprised of many billions of neurons—some estimates suggest the brain contains over 100 billion—and they come in many varieties, each with a highly specialized function.

There are three basic types of neurons. Sensory neurons are those specialized to communicate environmental information about such things as heat, sound, and light. Motor neurons are those that convey information to the muscles and glands. Interneurons represent the large group of neurons within the body, and they transmit information between other neurons. While these neurons may differ in function, they do have some essential things in common.

The Basic Structure of a Neuron

Like other cells, neurons have a cell body with a nucleus and other structures that keep them alive. Also like other cells, the nucleus contains genes that cause a neuron to become what it is in the first place. Early in life—mostly during the prenatal period—these genes also cause neurons to reproduce as the nervous system matures.

The remaining structures are involved in processing information. A neuron receives signals from other neurons at branches called *dendrites* and at smaller receptor sites on the cell body. It sends signals to other neurons via its axon terminals. In between is the axon, which, when conditions are right, generates a signal to its terminals. Many axons also have a myelin sheath, which serves a purpose similar to that of the insulation on an electrical wire.

Neural Transmission

So how exactly do neurons send information? Messages are usually received by the dendrites and then propagated down the axon via an electrical impulse known as an action potential. In some cases, such as when neurons are very close together, this electrical signal can pass almost instantaneously from one neuron to the next. While some neural communication occurs electrically, approximately 99 percent of all neural transmission happens chemically. Remember that neurons aren't directly connected to other neurons. A neuron's axon terminal and another's dendrite or receptor site "connect" via a synapse, which contains a minuscule gap across which chemical messengers, known as *neurotransmitters*, flow. Within the human brain in particular, a given neuron may synapse with thousands of other neurons, giving rise to many trillions of such interconnections—a level of complexity that staggers the imagination and helps you see why unraveling the workings of the nervous system is such a formidable task.

Neurotransmitters are minute biochemicals; scientists have identified more than 100 different neurotransmitters, but some estimate that there are perhaps several hundred different kinds. Some neurotransmitters stimulate the next neuron in line, while others inhibit it.

A "nervous breakdown" is not what it might seem. If your central nervous system were to break down like a car engine, you wouldn't run at all, and that would be the end of things. Instead, typically because of extreme stress, you lose the ability to think clearly and control your emotions; with proper care, this usually lasts for only a few days or weeks.

On a larger scale, an abundance or shortage of certain neurotransmitters in different areas of the brain affects our thought processes, emotionality, and overall level of arousal. One way psychologists know this is that alcohol and other "psychoactive" drugs—including medicinal ones—affect the brain through altering the levels of specific neurotransmitters. For example, "depressant" drugs alter certain neurotransmitter levels with the general effect of slowing down brain functioning, whereas "stimulant" drugs alter certain levels and speed it up. Another way neurotransmitters are implicated is through their association with certain disorders. For example, Parkinson's disease is associated with the degeneration of neurons that produce dopamine, a neurotransmitter that is essential to normal brain function.

The Central Nervous System

The central nervous system consists of the spinal column and the brain. The spinal column primarily houses a "cable" of nerves (bundles of neurons) through which the brain communicates with the rest of the body; this cable is called the spinal cord. The brain is best thought of as the "executor" of the nervous system as a whole. The brain and spinal cord are surrounded by protective structures including bone (the skull and spine), membrane tissue (the meninges) and liquid (the cerebrospinal fluid).

The Spinal Cord

The spinal cord consists of neurons that (1) relay sensory information to the brain, keeping the brain aware of external stimulation and internal bodily functioning, and (2) transmit information from the brain eventually to muscles that generate movement and to internal organs to control their functioning. The spinal cord also contains tiny interneurons (which link the sensory and motor neurons) that can bypass the brain. The knee-jerk reflex is an example: A doctor's tap to the patellar tendon of the knee causes it to jerk, and the connection is a direct one through the spine. The jerk tells the doctor that the connection is intact.

The Brain

The vast number of interneurons of the brain itself constitutes the center of the entire nervous system. They receive and transmit information through the spinal cord and in other ways, but by far the greater part of their activity is processing information through their myriad synapses. Somehow, this constant and incredibly intricate activity gives rise to consciousness and "mind."

> It may seem obvious to say that the brain is the location of mental activity, but this was not always thought to be the case. For example, some of the ancient Greek philosophers attributed mind and "soul" to the liver. And at various points in history, the location was thought to be the heart. The ancient Egyptians even threw away the brain of a mummy, assuming it would not be important in the afterlife!

The brain consists of a number of areas that are now known to be involved in specific functions, both physical and mental. Although the brain always works as a whole, certain areas are more active than others when different activities are taking place. Chapter 4 will return to the complexities of what these areas are and what they do.

The Peripheral Nervous System

Through their connections with the spinal cord and in some cases directly, the neurons of the peripheral nervous system are the rest of the chain that carries information to and from the brain. In contrast to interneurons, these can be quite long—extending much of the length of the body. Those that relay information to the central nervous system are called afferent neurons and those that relay information from the central nervous system are called efferent neurons. Based on function, the peripheral nervous system is subdivided into the somatic nervous system and the autonomic nervous system.

The Somatic Nervous System

The afferent neurons of the somatic nervous system relay signals from sensory receptors in the eyes and ears, plus those involved in taste, smell, touch, and certain internal sensations. The somatic nervous system's efferent neurons relay signals to the many skeletal muscles, ranging from those that produce "gross motor" activity such as walking, running, and jumping, to those that produce "fine motor" activity such as manipulating objects with the fingers. The brain coordinates the somatic nervous system and, for example, enables you to hear something, turn to look at it, and perhaps reach out and touch or grasp it.

The Autonomic Nervous System

The afferent and efferent neurons of the autonomic nervous system monitor and help regulate the internal workings of the body, such as breathing, heart rate, and the many other activities necessary to life. It is also important to your overall level of arousal and your emotional state: feeling up, feeling down, feeling "wired," feeling "laid back." An extreme example is the fight-or-flight reaction.

Given the appropriate signals from the brain and working in concert with the endocrine system (discussed in the following section), its sympathetic division initiates a variety of changes that help prepare the body to cope. When the danger is over, the parasympathetic division counteracts these effects and brings the body back to a normal state.

Most of the time, the interplay between the sympathetic and parasympathetic divisions helps maintain homeostasis, a sort of "steady state" within the limits necessary for the body to stay alive. Much like the way a thermostat tries to maintain a constant temperature in a house; homeostatic reactions try to maintain vital bodily states. For example, if your temperature starts to become too high, you perspire and the liquid cools your body a bit. If your temperature starts to become too low, you shiver and the heat generated by the muscle activity warms you up a bit.

The Endocrine System

The endocrine system works very closely with the nervous system, although it is not classified as part of it. Endocrine glands secrete a variety of hormones, which are biochemicals that travel through the bloodstream. The endocrine system is connected to the nervous system by a gland known as the hypothalamus. This tiny structure is responsible for regulating an enormous chunk of behavior, including sleep, stress responses, eating, thirst, and hunger.

The hypothalamus also controls the pituitary gland, sometimes referred to as the *master gland*, which secretes some hormones that directly affect emotionality and arousal, and some that stimulate other glands to secrete theirs. The onset of puberty and menopause are examples of complex processes that are governed by hormone levels.

> The effects of hormones take a while to wear off. Thus, if you get whiplash in a traffic accident, you initially don't feel much pain, but it becomes excruciating later when the endorphins subside. If you have a terrifying near miss, your "adrenaline rush" may produce so much arousal that you have to pull over for a while to get yourself under control.

During the fight-or-flight reaction, the pituitary releases endorphins, which are natural painkillers that work at the synaptic level and reduce the sensation of pain—a highly adaptive reaction if someone or some thing is assaulting you. The pituitary also stimulates the adrenal glands to secrete epinephrine (also called *adrenaline*), a hormone that is the agent by which the sympathetic nervous system increases heart rate, blood sugar level and red blood cells, in each case providing you with more energy—highly adaptive if you decide to run or fight back.

Genes and What They Do

Genes are segments of the deoxyribonucleic acid (DNA) that is present in the nucleus of each of the roughly 200 different kinds of cells in the body. Your first reaction to the term genes is perhaps to think of them as being involved in sexual reproduction and heredity, or that genes help determine what we look like. Both are true, but these aren't their only functions or necessarily their most important ones. A small but significant number of genes synthesize the proteins that make life possible in the first place. That is, they make it possible for humans to live and then reproduce.

> **What is DNA?**
> DNA is a number of "clusters" of six specific molecules, where molecules are compounds one step above atoms. In turn, a gene is a segment of DNA that can contain from hundreds to millions of these clusters.

Proteins

Proteins are molecules that perform a multitude of crucial functions both within cells and throughout the body. Humans have over 200,000 known proteins, with more undoubtedly waiting to be discovered. All are important, and an absence or malformation of a single kind can cause severe physical and mental disorders. Here are a few commonly occurring proteins and what they do:

- Enzymes, the most common, break down or otherwise process biochemicals; this occurs within cells, and also within internal organs; the enzymes in your digestive tract break down the food you eat into molecules that your body can use.

- Red blood cells contain the protein hemoglobin, which binds with oxygen and transports it through the bloodstream to cells and especially the brain.

- Collagen is a protein essential to the formation of skin, bones, blood vessels, and the walls of a number of internal organs.

- Actin and myosin are specialized proteins that enable your muscles to move.

- Hair is made of a specialized protein called *keratin*, as are fingernails and toenails.

Genes and Chromosomes

Genes exist in larger collections called *chromosomes*. These are distinctly visible under a microscope, but only when their genes come together during cell division and reproduction. Humans normally have twenty-three pairs of chromosomes with thousands of genes each, where—with some notable exceptions—one member of each pair comes from the mother and the other from the father. All of the chromosomes on the first twenty-two pairs (called *autosomes*) are alternates with regard to their genetic contents. That is, for each gene on one chromosome there is a counterpart on the other that can perform the same function. The members of the pairs are called *alleles*.

The twenty-third and smallest pair determines sex, so these are called *sex chromosomes*. In females, who are said to be XX for this pair, the arrangement is the same as with the autosomes—there are corresponding alleles on each chromosome. However, males are XY, denoting that the Y chromosome is different. It is much smaller than the X and contains far fewer genes, so that many of the X chromosome genes have no corresponding allele on the Y chromosome.

Gene Expression

Many genes play an important role in what you look like, how intelligent you may become, and perhaps even aspects of your personality. Increasingly, as work on the human genome continues, researchers are linking specific genes to psychological functioning and behavior. "Linking," however, is an important qualifier. In many cases, your genotype, which is your genetic makeup, does not entirely determine your phenotype, which is who and what you actually are. The link between genotype and phenotype can range from simple to exceedingly complex.

Simple Dominance-Recessiveness

Some characteristics are determined by a single gene and are affected little if at all by the environment of an individual. An example is the texture of your hair, which is directly determined by a single gene. The allele for curly hair—let's call it C—is dominant over the recessive allele for straight hair—call this S. This means that whenever either or both of the alleles for hair texture are C, the person will have curly hair, and only when both alleles are S will a person have straight hair.

> Suppose both parents are CS for hair texture. Thus, their child can be CC, CS, SC, or SS for these alleles. The child will then have a 75 percent chance of having curly hair (3 combinations out of 4) and only a 25 percent chance of straight hair (1 out of 4). If either parent is CC, no SS combination is possible.

Partial Dominance-Recessiveness

Allele combinations can also display partial dominance and recessiveness. A classic example is the sickle-cell trait, which occurs primarily among people of African ancestry and is believed to have developed originally because it enhanced the chances of survival. Here, the partially recessive gene that produces "sickle-shaped" red blood cells—which are less efficient than normal ones at transporting oxygen—are at the same time highly resistant to the mosquito-transmitted malaria that is rampant in Africa's wet regions. Thus, a person in these regions who has one allele for normal red blood cells and the other for sickled ones has a better chance of survival than does a person who has all normal blood cells. A mix of the two works best in an environment where malaria is a strong possibility.

> Alleles that fall in the category of codominance are neither dominant nor recessive. The result is a blend of the two, which happens in certain blood types. If a person has one allele for A positive and the other for B positive, the person's blood type will be AB positive.

People with the mix of red blood cells tend to experience joint pains from time to time and need to avoid high altitudes where the oxygen content of the air is low. But they survive. In contrast, those who have all sickled cells as a result of both alleles being the recessive for the trait have much more severe symptoms and cannot survive without regular transfusions of normal blood.

Genotype, Phenotype, and Polygenic Expression

Even where one pair of genes is concerned, genotype doesn't always determine phenotype. Hair type, blood traits, and blood type aren't affected by environmental factors, but many other physical characteristics are. For example, genes may set the stage for how tall or heavy or muscular a person may be, but environmental considerations such as nutrition and exercise are important factors too. Malnutrition, especially during early childhood, can make the phenotype much less than what it was genetically set to be. Exceptionally good nutrition, exercise, and so on can instead enhance the phenotype.

An additional complication is polygenic expression, which is characteristic of psychological traits such as intelligence and personality. The prevailing view is that a multitude of yet-to-be identified genes are responsible for complex characteristics such as these, and in turn that these are strongly affected by the environment in which a person grows up. The interaction between heredity and environment will be further examined at various points in this book.

Evolution and Humans

The scientific view is that "modern humans" evolved in much the same way as other forms of life did. But from there, much remains to be explained about why and how humans developed their proclivity for walking upright, thinking abstractly, using language, manipulating objects to make increasingly sophisticated tools, and—jumping to the present—developing technology that until fairly recently would have defied anyone's imagination. In addition, the story often changes with new "finds" by paleontologists and physical anthropologists who study fossil records and by biogeneticists who attempt to trace the evolution of human DNA. Following is a look at factors in evolution with emphasis on humans.

> Humans belong to a family called Hominidae, a line that began some 5 to 7 million years ago when our ancestors diverged from those of chimpanzees. The exact line of descent isn't known, but it appears that humans emerged relatively recently—some 150,000 years ago, more or less. Homo sapiens sapiens distinguishes modern humans from Homo sapiens neanderthalensis (the Neanderthals), who preceded us but "vanished" about 35,000 years ago.

Darwin's Survival of the Fittest

Darwin explained evolution in terms of natural selection, in which the fittest have the best chance to survive and reproduce. This is called *direct fitness*. But as profound as the concept was, Darwin had no biological basis for how this might happen—an understanding of the operation of genes was still decades away.

In the modern and more complete view of Darwin's survival of the fittest, hominids across the millennia either were subjected to changing environments or they migrated and subjected themselves to change. Change is the key. It often meant living in different environments such as jungles versus open savannahs and dealing with radically different climates. It meant finding different plant and animal food sources—plus catching or scavenging the latter. And it meant coping with different predators, of which there were many.

Thus, those of our ancestors who were best able to adapt and survive long enough to reproduce were more likely to pass along their genes to future generations. Those who were least able were less likely to reproduce their genes. Across generations, then, the gene pool would gradually change to favor adaptive characteristics in a given population, in accord with the environment in which they had to live.

Why would some individuals be more fit than others? As noted earlier, children aren't exact genetic blends of their parents. Chapter 12 will discuss several ways that this happens when it looks at the reproductive cycle, but one important way is mutation. At times and seemingly at random, the DNA that makes up genes changes in subtle ways, some of which are adaptive. Chance is again the key. If a person happens to inherit a mutation that is highly adaptive for a given environment, the odds are that the individual will have more children and likewise more successful ones—thus having a major impact on the gene pool down the line.

Indirect Fitness and Inclusive Fitness

Lacking information about the role of genes, Darwin couldn't see another important way that some characteristics get passed along and others don't. In addition to direct fitness, there is the concept of indirect fitness, and the two taken together constitute inclusive fitness. As elaborated by modern geneticists and evolutionary psychologists, indirect fitness works as follows. Anything you do that increases the survival chances of your offspring, or of relatives such as your sisters and brothers and their offspring, passes along at least part of your genes—the ones that you and they have in common. To a lesser but still significant sense, this also applies to members of your tribe or clan, who—at least in prehistoric times—would also share some of your genes.

Thus, for example, whatever genes might be involved in a tendency to help and cooperate with others can also be passed along. Indirect fitness therefore explains how a tendency toward altruism—helping others without regard to yourself, perhaps to the point of self-sacrifice—could have evolved in humans. More generally, it helps explain how humans have evolved to be the highly social creatures that they are.

———◆———

BRAIN AND MIND—
What Makes Us Human

THE HUMAN BRAIN has been described as one of the most complex, confounding, and astonishing features of the entire universe. The brain is the center of the nervous system and initiates activities that range from regulating bodily functioning to somehow allowing you to think, feel, plan, and dream. The tour of the human brain in this chapter is a general overview; a complete look at the brain would take stacks of books. First, you'll learn some of the ideas about where it came from; then you'll learn about its structures and functions. Finally you'll see how consciousness and mind might best be conceptualized in scientific terms.

Origins of the Human Brain

Why the early hominids walked upright—which is associated with their divergence from chimpanzees' ancestors—remains a matter of debate. It certainly was convenient, in that it allowed hominids to use their hands for manipulating tools and wielding weapons instead of simply for getting around. They could also carry things while they traveled. Travel and migration may have been necessary because of environmental change that sent early hominids out of dense jungles and into open savannahs, and therein lies another advantage of being upright as opposed to down on all fours: They could see both food sources and threats a lot farther away on the horizon.

How this relates to the evolutionary growth of the human brain remains unclear, except that theorists generally agree that walking upright came first. Something about that was accompanied by growth of the brain. Tool use may have been involved, although the fossil record indicates that increases in brain size and complexity don't correspond to the development of truly sophisticated tools—these didn't start appearing until around the time of Homo sapiens.

Do humans really only use 10 percent of their brain?
While this message if often repeated by motivational speakers and coaches, it simply isn't true. If it were, people who suffer from strokes would experience almost no detrimental effects. Brain imaging reveals activity throughout the brain, and there isn't a single area of the brain that can suffer damage without leading to some type of consequence.

A better candidate is the early formation of social hierarchies and the increasing intelligence necessary to survive and prosper in social interactions. It may be that as some hominids became smarter in developing social skills and "climbing the social ladder," others had to become smarter, too, just to keep up and not be less fit and have their genes drop out of the pool. As generations passed and natural selection exerted itself, there may have been an ever-escalating trend toward higher intelligence and therefore pressures that led to the development of a brain capable of this intelligence. We may, of course, never know.

The Hindbrain

Regardless of what drove human brain structures to their present state of development, the order in which this took place is reasonably well understood. The most primitive and earliest-to-develop part of the human brain is the hindbrain, which is involved in heart rate, breathing, digestion, and other basic activities ultimately administered by the autonomic nervous system, plus reflexes such as sneezing and those involved in balance and motor coordination. Such activities are necessary to the life of many animals, including some relatively low on the scale that have a hindbrain comparable to that of humans.

The Midbrain

Next came the midbrain, which is intimately involved in transmitting visual and auditory information to a portion of the hindbrain as well as controlling eye movements. As discussed in the next chapter, vision is our primary sense. Other animals that also are primarily visually oriented show a corresponding development of the structures of the midbrain. Last came the structures of the forebrain, much of which is what makes us distinctly human. As hominids developed into our present form, the fossil record indicates a steadily increasing growth of the size of the forebrain.

The Forebrain's Structures and Functions

As you continue to work upward in the brain, you encounter the thalamus, which sits on top of the midbrain. The thalamus is involved in sleep and arousal (as are the hindbrain and midbrain to an extent), and it also processes visual and auditory sensory information—as well as much of the information that reaches the brain from the nervous system as a whole. Closely intertwined with the thalamus is the hypothalamus, a particularly interesting structure because it processes information regarding bodily needs, sex, and emotionality. The hypothalamus "controls" the autonomic nervous system and the endocrine system, so it plays an important role in homeostasis.

Above and around those structures is the limbic region, which works along with the hypothalamus. It also contains the hippocampus, a structure that is intimately involved in the formation of memories. And above this is the cerebrum, the area of the brain that is most highly developed in modern humans. You'll learn more about specific functions of the brain at various points in this text.

The Cerebrum

The cerebrum comprises about 80 percent of the human brain, and it is wrinkled and folded, which allows much more of it to fit in the skull than would otherwise be the case. The outer cerebral cortex, or "bark," of the cerebrum is grayish in color and contains about two-thirds of the neurons of the nervous system. The inner layer is whitish and consists of the myelinated axons of these neurons as well as glia—cells that sustain them and play various roles in neural transmission. Like neurons, glia come in a wide variety of types.

A blow to the brain or an infection can cause irreparable damage. The neurons of the central nervous system don't regenerate, and when damaged, whatever function they served is lost. However, the human brain does display considerable plasticity—the ability to shift functions to other areas and recover them to an extent.

The cerebrum consists of a left hemisphere and a right hemisphere, which are connected by a set of neural pathways called the *corpus callosum*. The brain is essentially symmetrical down its middle. The areas toward the rear of the cerebrum are the occipital lobes, where visual information enters the higher areas of the brain.

Along the middle and sides are the temporal lobes, which process auditory information, and the parietal lobes, which include the somatosensory area. The latter receives bodily sensations, such as from our sense of touch, and it transmits signals that make bodily movement occur. Interestingly, the left side of the body is "mapped" to the right parietal lobe and the right side to the left. This is true of all motor control and all the senses except vision, which is a partial exception.

Much of the lobes, however, consist of higher-association areas. Association areas throughout the brain—especially in the frontal lobes, which consist entirely of association areas—are the most highly developed in humans. These are the areas that are responsible for distinctly human brain activity such as complex and abstract thinking, reasoning, and remembering.

The frontal lobes are associated with higher thought processes, including executive functions such as recognizing cause-and-effect relationships and detecting similarities between events. One obvious line of evidence is that as hominids evolved, the size and shape of the front part of the skull and therefore the frontal lobes increased the most. Even the Neanderthals had a more "sloping" forehead than modern humans.

Traditional Approaches to Studying the Brain

Neuroscientists have been "mapping" the brain's functions since the nineteenth century. The major challenge faced by scientists who studied the brain in the past is that they had no real way to "look" at the brain. Instead, researchers were forced to rely on their observations of behavior and inferences based upon those observations. Much of this research was performed by studying loss of behaviors as a result of accidental damage to people's brains. For example, a railroad foreman named Phineas Gage survived an astonishing accident in which an iron rod was driven through his head, destroying much of his frontal lobe. While he survived, he experienced personality changes, leading researchers to attribute damage to certain areas of the brain to changes in his behavior.

Specialization of the Cerebral Hemispheres

If you were to hold the human brain in your hands, the two sides would appear remarkably similar. In addition to the basic anatomical similarities, some of the basic functions of each hemisphere are mirrored in the opposite side as well. However, each of the cerebral hemispheres is specialized for certain abilities or functions.

For example, Paul Broca (1824–1880) helped determine that the brain's language centers are primarily in the left hemisphere by studying patients with damage to relatively specific areas of the brain—damage that resulted in speech problems. Patients with damage to the lower left frontal lobe, or what is now known as *Broca's area,* are able to understand written or spoken language, but they have difficulty speaking or writing.

Carl Wernicke (1848–1905) discovered that when another area in the left hemisphere was damaged, patients were still able to speak fluently—but what they said often made little or no sense. Today, this area of the left temporal lobe is known as Wernicke's area.

Wilder Penfield (1891–1976) took a more sophisticated approach called electrical brain stimulation, in which tiny and harmless electrical currents are sent through areas of the brain to see what thoughts or other behaviors result. His participants were people who were undergoing necessary brain surgery.

Roger Sperry (1913–1994) utilized a different approach. His participants were people who had their corpus callosum severed as a treatment for severe epilepsy, which has the effect of isolating the hemispheres. Sperry then presented various types of stimuli to only one hemisphere at a time, demonstrating that the hemispheres aren't exactly mirror images. Each side of the brain performs some functions better than the other.

Research on hemisphere specialization led some to speculate that differences in ability might result from being predominantly a "left-brain" or "right-brain" person. For example, a left-brain person was said to be better at logical reasoning, a right-brain person at artistic or creative endeavors. However, research generally has not borne out this notion.

In the years since, numerous researchers also have used systematic brain lesions (tiny cuts) to study changes produced in laboratory animals such as rats. This research, for example, yielded evidence that areas of the hypothalamus are involved in homeostatic behaviors such as eating. Rats with lesions to one area won't stop eating even when they become obese. Rats with lesions to another area won't eat at all. Still other lesions to the hypothalamus increase or decrease sexual interest.

Neuroscience and Brain Imaging—The Modern Approach

The development of computerized tomography (CT), or "cat scans," heralded a major change in the way neuroscientists study the brain. CT is basically an x-ray procedure that produces pictures of "slices" of the brain taken from rotated angles. The pictures have limited resolution, but CT can be highly effective in spotting brain damage and tumors. Magnetic resonance imaging (MRI) is better: here, higher-resolution pictures are produced by sending pulses of radio waves through the brain to a magnetic coil.

However, neither approach can provide information about ongoing brain activity and functions. The truly remarkable breakthroughs came with the advent of more sophisticated techniques and computers capable of imaging brain activity as it occurs. Brain imaging has become such a common part of popular culture—often discussed on television crime programs and in magazine articles—that it is easy to overlook how important and revolutionary this technology really is.

Positron Emission Tomography

In addition to oxygen, the brain runs on a steady supply of glucose (blood sugar), and positron emission tomography (PET) takes advantage of this by the injection of glucose treated with harmless amounts of radioactivity. As neural cells metabolize this glucose, special detectors placed on the head record the activity, and computer enhancement yields color images of the level of the activity in different areas of the brain. As a simple example, different areas might be more active when participants are looking at an object, thinking about it, or talking about it. However, the time required for metabolism produces delays of a minute or more between when the brain activity occurs and when it is displayed, which limits the accuracy of PET. Given the speed at which neural impulses travel—about 100 miles per hour—the researcher is always looking at the past instead of the present.

Functional Magnetic Resonance Imaging

Functional magnetic resonance imaging (fMRI) is much better and is the current method of choice. Here, precision detectors transmit information about areas of naturally occurring oxygen metabolism in the brain for computer enhancement, and the delay is seconds instead of a minute or more. Researchers are able to get a much clearer look at the brain and evaluate much smaller structures than they can using a PET scan.

It appears that brain-imaging technology will provide the basis for the lie detectors of the not-so-distant future. If specific areas of the brain are consistently active or certain types of ERPs (event-related potentials) appear when people lie, brain-imaging techniques could be much more reliable than today's polygraphs.

Because no "invasive" radioactive substances are involved, fMRI can also be used with any kind of participants—including infants. And the resolution is much finer, although the precision is still on the order of at least a few hundred thousand neurons that might or might not be doing the same thing. It's a safe bet, however, that researchers will continue to refine this method.

Quantitative Electroencephalography

Electroencephalography has been around for a long time. Originally, it consisted of placing two or three electrodes on the skull to measure overall brain electrical activity, such as during wakefulness or varying levels of sleep. In its present form, called *quantitative electroencephalography* (QEEG), the number of electrodes has greatly increased, a skullcap standardizes their location, and the much more localized measurements are subjected to computer analysis. This yields event-related potentials (ERPs), that is, minute electrical changes that are studied to localize brain activity—with only milliseconds of delay. This speed also allows QEEG to be used to mark timing as a cross-reference for fMRI, thus increasing its accuracy.

What Is Mind—Earlier Views

Throughout the ages, philosophers have pondered the nature of "mind" and especially its relationship to physiology. The issue has likewise been debated within psychology since the discipline's inception—except for the strict behaviorists who simply dismissed mind altogether as inappropriate for scientific study. First this section will look at some historical notes on what is known as the mind-body problem, then at what modern psychologists and neuroscientists have to say.

René Descartes (1596–1650), the first modern philosopher and also a good candidate for the founder of modern physiology, took what came to be a well-known position called *dualism:* mind, or "soul," and body are distinct, separate entities, but they interconnect at some physical point in the brain. Descartes took this to be the smallish pineal gland in the midbrain, whose function in humans remains poorly understood even today. Through this gland, he decided, the inborn "animal" spirits of the body—plus sensory experience—enter the thought processes of the mind, which in turn sends commands for motor activity and the like outward. Thus, mind took on an existence all its own, as did "consciousness."

> Descartes coined the famous expression ***Cogito, ergo sum*** (I think, therefore I am), which he took as the starting point in his philosophy. A less known but quite insightful quote from his writings is, in translation, "It is not enough to have a good mind. The main thing is to use it well."

William James later had a good bit to say about mind and consciousness—along with where the latter in particular came from both in humans and other animals. Basically, his view was that it enhanced fitness. As humans, we think about the events we experience, we make decisions, we make things, we change things—in each case enhancing our chances of survival by allowing us to adapt. In James's view, then, consciousness is essential to survival. Without it, we would instead be plants.

What Is Mind—Views Based on Neuroscience

Early researchers sought the "location" of consciousness in the brain, but they didn't get far because they lacked the necessary equipment and methods to study brain activities. It appears that their approach was also misguided. Virtually all psychologists and neuroscientists now agree that mind and consciousness have a purely physical basis in the brain. They take the form of neural pathways, that is, intricately interconnected networks of neurons that vary in their activity levels in accord with the kind of mental activity that is occurring.

Brain imaging is, of course, the means by which theorists and researchers have arrived at this conclusion. The phenomal experience of the mind, which means the subjective and personal experience that occurs when you think about things or engage in other conscious processes, has neural correlates in the electrochemical processes of the brain and its many billions of neurons. "Neural network theory," which attempts to pull together mental events with corresponding brain activity, has a long way to go in presenting a coherent picture of mind and conscious processes. One problem is achieving the necessary level of resolution, as noted earlier; fMRI, for example, as yet can only look at bundles of hundreds of thousands of neurons at a time. But the basis is a sound one and most agree that a coherent picture will eventually emerge.

So mind and consciousness are the constant hum of neural activity that becomes discernible during the prenatal period and continues uninterrupted until you die. Soul is another matter. If you equate soul with mind, then death brings a halt to soul as well. But if you separate soul as some special kind of matter that exists beyond brain activity—as Descartes did—then soul in some form might live on.

HOW YOU
Experience Your World

PSYCHOLOGISTS HAVE LONG STUDIED principles of how humans become aware of and interpret events in the world around them. This chapter will explore vision, audition, and the other senses, each of which plays an important role in daily functioning and survival.

Sensation and Perception

Take a moment to think about all of the sensory information surrounding you at this very moment. Focus on the colors of the room, the feel of your clothing, the sounds coming in from the street outside, and the scents wafting through the air. In a matter of seconds, you have gained information from four major senses: vision, touch, hearing, and smell. Your sensory system serves as an entrance for information about your environment, transmitting it to the brain so that you may then take action.

Sensation is the process by which the sensory receptors detect and then transduce, or "transform," incoming stimulation from the external world—or from within the body—into neural impulses. These are then relayed to various areas of the central nervous system for further processing, which constitutes perception. Perception includes higher cognitive processes such as discriminating, recognizing, interpreting, and understanding the incoming information and it is closely integrated with other cognitive processes such as learning and memory. In other words, perception is how you "make sense" of the ongoing events in your world so you can function in it as well as acquire and accumulate knowledge about it.

Sensory Thresholds

Each of your senses responds to a different and specific kind of stimulation, but the senses do have some things in common. In addition to transduction, they have absolute thresholds—minimum levels of stimulation necessary to trigger them in a given situation. In order for something to be sensed, it must first be strong enough to be detected. For you to hear a sound, for example, it has to occur at some minimum intensity that will trigger the receptors in your ears. The senses also have difference thresholds, which refers to the amount of change in stimulation necessary for the change to be discernible. In order to notice alterations in a stimulus or changes in intensity, they must also occur at a minimum threshold that is different enough to detect—that is, there must be a noticeable difference.

Sensory Adaptation

Sensory adaptation is another process that is characteristic of all the senses. As receptors are continually exposed to the same stimuli, their thresholds increase and you become less aware of the stimulation—or perhaps entirely unaware of it. For example, as you sit in your chair and read this, you are unaware of the chair and the clothing in between pressing against your body—unless something calls your attention to it, such as this sentence. This characteristic of the senses is extremely important in allowing you to focus your attention. You couldn't function if you were constantly distracted by sensations such as the feel of shoes or a wristwatch, the drone of an air conditioner, sounds from outside, and so on.

> It may occur to you that as you stare at something, your field of vision doesn't dim or go blank as sensory adaptation would predict. But vision is no exception. The receptors of the eyes never receive the same stimulation for long because of their automatic and rapid back-and-forth movements of which you are entirely unaware.

From a different perspective, what the senses also have in common is that how they work at the receptor level, where the information they transmit goes, and what perceptions they ultimately produce are relatively well understood. However, what goes on in the brain in between is not. Neuroscientists are in hot pursuit of how the specialized areas of the cortex process incoming stimulation from the senses, but they are only beginning to unravel these mysteries.

Of course, if sensory stimulation is too intense, relatively little adaptation takes place and you can't ignore it. The sound of a jackhammer on a sidewalk just outside your window is unlikely to "go away." Similarly, the loud and steady thumping bass of someone's stereo in an apartment next door can be impossible to adapt to and ignore.

The Eyes and Visual Sensation

Light is one type of electromagnetic energy that travels via waves. Other examples of electromagnetic energy include x-rays, ultraviolet rays, and radio waves. The human eye is capable of seeing only a tiny portion of the electromagnetic spectrum, a portion known as visible light. The eye is a highly intricate structure with over 100 million receptors that emit neural impulses when stimulated by light. More specifically, they respond to the "wavelengths" of light. A wavelength is exactly what it implies: a measurement of the distance from the peak of one wave to the next. It is measured in nanometers (billionths of a meter), and what is called the visible spectrum is the range from about 400 to 700 nanometers. What you see as purples and violets are the shorter wavelengths; below that are the ultraviolets that you can't see without special equipment. The reds you see are the longer wavelengths, above which are the infrareds that you again normally can't see.

After some additional processing by other neurons in the eye, impulses from the receptors travel out the back of the eye via the optic nerve and eventually to the occipital lobes of the brain. In between is the optic chiasm, which is responsible for the partial exception to the opposite-side brain mapping noted in Chapter 4. Here, vision is "split" so that the left visual field of each eye is sent to the right occipital lobe and the right visual field to the left. The evolutionary significance of this may be that if one eye is lost, the entire visual field will still be projected to both occipital lobes from the other eye.

How the Eye Works

Light enters the fluid-filled eye through an outer surface called the *cornea*, which is like the outer glass of a camera lens. Next it passes through an aperture called the *pupil*, which is expanded or contracted by the iris to allow for the intensity of the light— again, much the way a camera works. The lens of the eye, however, works differently. The ciliary muscles control the lens, causing it to "accommodate" and thicken or flatten to bring objects near or far into focus—something that the glass lens of a camera can't do. Finally, the retina is the rear of the eye where the visual receptors are located. Problems with the eye's structures cause many correctable visual problems, including the following:

- A cataract is a visible clouding of the cornea that limits the amount of light that can enter the eye, which greatly interferes with vision.

- An irregularly shaped cornea constitutes an astigmatism, which interferes with focusing.

- Myopia, or "nearsightedness," occurs when the focal point is in front of the retina instead of directly on it; distant objects appear fuzzy.

- Hyperopia, or "farsightedness," occurs when the focal point is behind the retina; nearby objects appear blurred.

- Presbyopia is a stiffening of the lenses that interferes with accommodation.

- Glaucoma is a severe disorder in which the pressure of the fluid within the eye becomes too high and can cause damage to the retina.

The Retina and Its Light Receptors

The retina consists of several layers of interconnected neurons. The deepest layer contains the rods and cones that are the actual light receptors, and the mostly transparent layers above combine signals from these and pass them along to the optic nerve. Rods and cones are named in accord with their shape, and they perform quite different functions.

Rods are by far the most abundant of the 100 million or so receptors and they are sensitive to the intensity (brightness) of the incoming light. Thus, rods are predominantly active in low light, such as on a moonlit night, when you see things mainly in black and white and shades of gray. If you go from a brightly lit area to a dark one, such as when you enter a dark movie theater, you may have to fumble for a seat because it can take up to thirty minutes for your rods to adapt and reach their maximum sensitivity.

The time that is normally required for dark adaptation is why many vehicles—including military ones—have reddish or orange panel lighting. Rods aren't activated by the longer wavelengths of this light, so your eyes remain dark adapted, say, when you're driving down a lonely road at night.

The eye contains only a few million cones, which are concentrated in the fovea—the area of the retina that is the main focal point of the lens. Cones have a much higher threshold for light than rods do, so they are inactive in the dark. Given sufficient light, however, cones have the ability to differentiate wavelengths and are therefore responsible for color vision. There are three kinds of cones, each of which emits signals in response to different wavelengths of light; the interplay between these sets the stage for the experience of color.

You probably know that in low light, you can see an object more clearly if you look just to the side of it. This is because the center of the human fovea contains no rods—only cones. So when you look slightly away, more of the low-light detecting rods that surround the fovea are stimulated and your vision improves.

There is one part of the eye that completely lacks rods and cones. This area is known as the *optic disk* and it is where the fibers composing the optic nerve leave the back of the eye. Because there are no visual receptors on the optic disk, there is actually a very small hole known as a *blind spot* in your field of vision. So why don't you notice this miniscule hole in your vision? Researchers have suggested that the brain actually "fills in" the missing information by using visual clues such as pattern and color from the surrounding environment.

Color Vision

Light waves have three properties that are involved in all visual sensation and perception. Wavelength, as discussed earlier, determines hue, the technical term for color. Intensity determines brightness. And the "blend" of wavelengths determines saturation—relatively pure colors such as vivid greens or reds contain a narrow band of wavelengths, whereas softer colors such as pastels contain a broader mix. Each of these properties of light interacts to influence the colors you perceive.

The rudiments of how you experience color have been understood reasonably well since the nineteenth century. In essence, the three types of cones and the cells in the eye that they synapse with generate different rates and combinations of neural impulses. Via the optic nerve, these impulses go next to the thalamus for further processing and recombination by several kinds of specialized cells, and from there they enter the brain through the visual cortex for even more processing, which researchers are still trying to figure out.

> Objects don't actually have color in a real sense. What you experience is wavelengths that are reflected from objects instead of being absorbed by them. The pigmentation of a bright yellow canary, for example, absorbs all wavelengths of light except those for yellow, which bounce off and enter your eyes.

Each cone in the eye is sensitive to certain wavelengths of light—some cones sense short wavelengths (blue), some detect medium wavelengths (green), and others detect long wavelengths (red). When a color other than blue, green, or red strikes the retina, it stimulates a combination of cones in order to produce the experience of that color. The most common form of color blindness, known as red-green color blindness, occurs when people have the normal blue sensitive cones, but only have either red or green cones instead of both. As a result, red and green appear to be the same color.

It is known, however, that the processing is based on complementary colors, which are pairs that when combined produce white or gray. According to the opponent-processing theory of color vision, there are four basic colors and two pairs of color-sensing neurons—a red-green pair and a yellow-blue pair. The two members of each pair oppose each other, so if the red-sensing neurons are stimulated, then the green-sensing ones are inhibited. Thus, the myriad colors we experience are not neurologically "canceled out" down the line.

The Ears and Auditory Sensation

The apparatus for the ears is mechanical up to the point where sounds are transduced into neural impulses. The sound waves that stimulate our ears are produced when, for example, something in the world around you clicks, rings, vibrates, or scrapes against or hits something else. Each produces cyclical displacements of molecules in the air—that is, contractions and expansions of the air. Although you can't see these waves, you can get a clear idea of how sound is produced if you remove the front cover of a speaker system, turn up the volume, and watch what the bass and midrange speakers do.

One instance of expansion and contraction is a cycle, and sound waves are measured in cycles per second called *hertz* (Hz)—in honor of a prominent physicist. People vary considerably in the levels and the range of sound waves they can detect, but the typical range is 20 to 20,000 Hz. This is also the range that home electronics manufacturers try to cover as faithfully as possible, although modern systems often go below and above this range just to make sure that everything on a CD is reproduced.

> Repeated exposure to extremely loud sounds can cause permanent damage to the structures of the ear and diminish hearing in certain ranges. Think about this the next time you're tempted to stand in front of the speakers at a rock concert.

How the Ear Works

Sound waves enter through the pinna—the outer part of the ear that you can see—and travel through the auditory canal to the tympanic membrane, or eardrum, which then vibrates as a result. The vibrations are amplified by several bony structures called the *ossicles* and transmitted to the cochlea (which, because of its coiled shape, derives from the Greek word for "snail"). While the cochlea is an incredibly complex structure, it is only about the size of a pea. Within the fluid-filled cochlea the vestibular canal carries the vibrations in the form of ripples to the basilar membrane, where thousands of tiny hair cells move in response to the ripples and transform the transduction into neural impulses. From there, the thousands of receptor neurons of the auditory nerve relay the signals to the thalamus and eventually to the auditory cortex of the temporal lobes. Partial or complete hearing loss can occur anywhere along the way, such as through the following:

Obstruction of the auditory canal

Inflammation of the auditory canal because of infection

Puncturing of the eardrum

Fusion or other damage to the ossicles

Less-efficient hearing associated with aging

Damage to the hair cells of the basilar membrane by viral infections or exposure to very loud sounds

Damage to the auditory nerve

Most of these conditions are correctible either through medical intervention or use of a hearing aid. The last two are not. Damage anywhere from the basilar membrane on is irreversible.

Auditory Perception

Three qualities of the sound waves that enter the ear interact to determine what you hear. The first is frequency in Hz, which determines pitch—from bass sounds, which have the slowest frequency and therefore the longest waves, to treble sounds, with the highest frequencies and the shortest waves. The second is the amplitude, or strength, of the wave, which determines loudness. The third is complexity, or timbre, which accounts for the "richness" of what you hear. For example, most musical instruments produce multiple frequencies of sound called harmonics even when only a single note is played.

> Timbre accounts in large part for how you tell the difference between a guitar and a violin when the same note is plucked. In turn, the richness of the harmonics generated and resonated by such instruments determines their quality. Each human voice has a unique timber, which is why you immediately recognize a close friend's voice after hearing just a few words on the telephone.

Discriminating Sounds

Your perception of loudness depends mainly on how many of the hairs on the basilar membrane are being stimulated, but your perception of pitch is more complex. One long-standing observation—called *place theory*—is that different areas of the basilar membrane are maximally sensitive to different frequencies. You therefore experience pitch in accord with which receptors are being stimulated and sending signals to the auditory cortex.

However, more recent research indicates that the timing of the neural impulses being generated is important as well. That is, different tones produce different patterns, or "bursts," of neural impulses independently of the area of the basilar membrane being stimulated, thus also providing information about frequency to the auditory cortex. The auditory cortex then somehow combines this information to determine your perception of pitch in response to frequency.

Localizing Sounds

How you determine where sounds are coming from is straightforward, at least at the level of the auditory receptors. Any sound that isn't precisely centered in front of or behind the ears stimulates the receptors differently in two ways. One is intensity: a sound to the right, for example, will be louder in the right ear than in the left. The other is timing: a sound to the right will reach the right ear slightly sooner than the left. Again, however, how this information is processed in the auditory cortex remains under investigation.

Smell and Taste—The Chemical Senses

Olfaction (smell) and gustation (taste) are senses that respond to minute traces of chemical molecules that foods and many other substances emit. These two senses are closely linked. If you've ever had a bad cold that made it difficult to smell, you may have noticed that your sense of taste was suppressed as well. In humans, there are perhaps 10 million olfactory receptors in the nasal cavities that respond to specific odorants or combinations of them when they enter the nasal tracts from the surrounding air. The number of receptors stimulated determines the strength of the smell. The particular combination stimulated determines the quality of the smell, which of course can range from pleasant and enticing to thoroughly obnoxious.

Signals from the olfactory receptors fan out to a number of areas of the brain, and compared to the other senses, they take a much shorter route. They also go to an area deep in the cortex called the *amygdala,* which is intimately involved with emotional responses—you therefore very quickly feel pleasure or disgust in response to an odor. All of this is consistent with the view that smell is the oldest and most basic sense in terms of evolution, and it is likely that your ancient ancestors had a much keener sense of smell than you do—as do dogs, cats, and many other animals that rely more on smell than on vision or hearing.

In gustation, chemical molecules from substances you eat enter the saliva and stimulate taste buds concealed in small bumps on the tongue and also fan out to areas of the brain. You have about 10,000 taste buds, which are maximally responsive to molecules that give rise to "sweet," "salty," "sour," or "bitter" tastes. But the delicate experiences of flavor that you're capable of depend on a complex interplay between taste and smell, as anyone who's ever had a stuffy nose is aware of. When you have a cold, for example, you can still sense the four basic tastes, but that's about it.

Many animals have special glands that emit chemical molecules called pheromones to signal their readiness to mate and arouse sexual interest in potential partners. Humans also emit pheromones—your underarms, for example, contain glands that are especially active in secreting them. Some theorists have proposed that pheromones also stimulate sexual interest, but so far the jury is still out.

All of your senses tend to decline as you age, and smell and taste are no exception. Older people may remark that foods prepared the same way as when they were younger don't taste as good, and they may find themselves using more sugar, salt, or other spices to compensate.

The Skin Senses

The receptors for the skin senses lie just below the surface and come in several varieties. These include receptors that respond to mechanical pressure (touch), temperature, and pain. Signals from these receptors go to the somatosensory areas of the parietal lobes.

However, the experiences of touch, temperature, or pain are not the result of a simple correspondence between the kind of stimulation and the neural impulses sent by the specific receptors. Pain, for example, can result from extreme stimulation of either of the other kinds of receptors, such as when you accidentally hit your thumb with a hammer or burn yourself with a match. Sensitivity to pain also varies considerably from one individual to the next, and people can learn to "control" pain with practice—especially if they have no choice because of bodily damage or disease. The experience of pain is therefore a function of higher thought processes as well as stimulation to the skin.

Kinesthesis and Equilibrium

The receptors for kinesthesis are mostly in muscles, tendons, and joints. They send information to lower areas of the brain about bodily movements such as reaching out and grasping something, walking, or standing, as well as bodily position. The brain then coordinates this information automatically, allowing you, for example, to walk without consciously thinking about specific movements of your legs.

The receptors for your automatic sense of equilibrium or balance are in and around the fluid-filled semicircular canals just above the cochlea of the inner ear. These are bundles of tiny hairs similar to those of the auditory apparatus, but they transmit impulses to lower areas of the brain regarding movement and the positioning of the head and body with respect to gravity. It is through the senses of kinesthesis and equilibrium in interaction that you "know" where you are and what you are doing, even though you aren't aware of how you know it.

> Many people experience a temporary sense of dizziness and loss of balance after they spin around rapidly while standing or being on certain amusement park rides. This is caused by disruption of the functioning of the senses of kinesthesis and equilibrium, which spinning ballet dancers and ice skaters somehow learn to overcome.

Perception

The process of perception involves synthesizing, organizing, and interpreting sensory information in a meaningful way. Researchers often describe perceptual processing as occurring in two basic ways. The first is known as bottom-up processing, and it involves making sense of ambiguous information, kind of like assembling the individual pieces of a puzzle when you don't know what the final image will look like. The second type, top-down processing, involves drawing on your existing knowledge, experiences, and expectations to make sense of the information that you encounter in different situations.

Visual perception begins with specialized neurons in the visual cortex of the occipital lobe. Somehow, these neurons interact to give rise to mental images that include shapes, groupings, location, movement, and color. Perceptual principles that are based on properties of visual stimuli have been around for quite some time and are the focus here.

Gestalt Principles of Perception

The Gestalt psychologists naturally spent much of their time researching how you perceive "wholes" from partial and sometimes fragmentary visual information. One of the clearest illustrations of their idea that the whole is more than the sum of the parts is the principle of *closure*. For example, a line drawing of a familiar object such as a human face can omit many details but still easily be perceived as a face—even if parts of the outline are missing.

Another principle is *proximity*. Here, similar objects that are uniformly spaced tend to be seen as one group. If the objects are spread out in trios, however, the perception will be that there are several groups.

Similarity is the principle that you tend to perceive groups of objects in accord with the extent to which they are alike. A matrix of circles is seen as just that—a bunch of circles. But if you make some of the circles squares instead, the circles and squares are perceived as separate groups.

Finally, *figure-ground* is a basic but somewhat more complicated principle of visual perception in which you attend to part of a visual stimulus as the figure and ignore the rest of the image as the background. The classic "vase and faces" reversible figure provides an example. If you happen to attend first to the light area, you see a vase against a dark background. If you instead attend to the dark area, you see two faces in profile looking at each other.

Perceiving Location

You perceive the location of things and how far away they are in two basic ways. One is binocular vision, which is based on your normally having two eyes that are separated. When you cast your eyes on an object, each eye therefore has a different perspective— that is, the object is seen from two slightly different angles of view. At the same time, the object is projected to slightly different areas of each retina. The visual cortex then integrates the differences in neural impulses from the eyes and determines "where" including "near" or "far."

The other way is monocular cues. With only one functional eye, you can still use certain information to determine location. Or with both eyes, you use these monocular cues in conjunction with your binocular vision to determine location in a two-dimensional scene such as a television picture, a movie, or a cartoon. One such cue is interposition. If one object partially blocks the view of another, you perceive the first object as being closer.

Another is relative size. An object that is larger than another seems closer. Cartoonists in particular make extensive use of height in field. An object that is at the bottom of a cartoon panel appears closer; one toward the top appears farther away.

Among the many other monocular cues is linear perspective. Two lines that begin at the bottom of an illustration and then draw closer near the top appear to be receding into the distance. This perception corresponds to looking down a pair of railroad tracks.

Perceiving Movement and Motion

An obvious way that you perceive movement and motion is that retinal stimuli change as an object crosses our visual field. A less obvious one is that if our eyes move to "track" the object, the muscular changes generate neural impulses that the brain can also use in determining movement. You also perceive yourself as moving by using these cues in addition to bodily ones such as kinesthesis and equilibrium, discussed earlier in this chapter.

> The human ability to detect very small movements in an environment is especially keen, and this may have an evolutionary basis. To our ancient ancestors who lived in the wild, any sort of movement signaled the possibility of danger and being killed and eaten, so those who were less alert to movement were less likely to pass along their genes.

However, cues for movement can be quite misleading. If you're flying in a plane, it may very well seem that the clouds are passing by and the plane is actually standing still. Similarly, while sitting in a car wash with your vision partly obscured by suds and water on the windows, you may get the impression that you and the car are moving and the car-wash machinery is standing still—especially if your car is being rocked a bit by the brushes. These kinds of effects occur because you lack an absolute reference point for what's moving and what isn't.

Optical Illusions

In most cases, perception occurs automatically and unconsciously. You don't have to focus your attention on interpreting your sensory experience of the world—it simply happens with minimal mental effort on your part. Because this process is largely automatic, errors or mistakes in perception can occur. Optical illusions take place when you perceive optical information in a way that is misleading, false, or not in tune with reality.

There are two major types of optical illusions. Physiological illusions are often the result of overstimulation of the visual system. For example, if you stare for a long period of time at a brightly colored object, you might continue to see an "afterimage" of the object even after you look away. Cognitive illusions occur when you make unconscious cognitive assumptions about how things "ought" to be, sometimes making incorrect inferences about how things are in reality. For example, artist M. C. Escher created a famous lithograph print involving a staircase that appeared to both ascend and descend at the same time. The distance, depth, and edge cues used to perceive the direction of the stairs are incompatible, creating a perceptual contradiction.

Why do optical illusions occur? In many cases, the same rules of perceptual organization that allow you to determine size, distance, and location contribute to these errors. For example, the figure-ground principle allows you to determine which objects are closer or further away, but it also creates the well-known "vases or faces" illusion discussed earlier, in which the image can be perceived as either two faces or as a central vase.

Your expectations also play a role in the experience of optical illusions. Researchers refer to these expectations and prior assumptions as a *perceptual set*. Of course, what you expect to see in certain situations depends a great deal on factors such as culture and past experience. For example, if you just accidentally drove through a red stoplight, you would probably be more likely to perceive flashing blue lights in your rearview mirror as a police cruiser rather than a neon sign from a local used-car dealership.

———◆———

ALTERED STATES OF
Consciousness

PSYCHOLOGIST AND PHILOSOPHER William James compared consciousness to a stream—constantly shifting and changing while remaining continuous and unbroken. People have been trying for eons to alter their states of consciousness, whether for enlightenment, relaxation, or escape. As a result, several different ways of accomplishing this have been discovered. This chapter will discuss what consciousness is and the different ways in which consciousness can be altered.

Biological Rhythms

Human and animals all have an internal "clock" that regulates the ebb and flow of consciousness. The most obvious change in consciousness that you experience daily is the cycle from sleeping to waking. In addition, you're probably also very familiar with the daily change in your levels of mental alertness. For most people, peak mental alertness occurs in the morning around 10 A.M. and again in the evening around 8 P.M.

These clocks are known as *circadian rhythms* and represent the psychological and biological fluctuations that occur on a roughly twenty-four-hour timetable. How exactly does the human body "keep time"? A tiny cluster of approximately 20,000 neurons in the hypothalamus known as the *suprachiasmatic nucleus* (SCN) serves as the master control panel for this daily cycle of consciousness. Researchers aren't entirely sure how this process works, but they do know that environmental cues are important.

Sunlight is perhaps the best example of an environmental stimulus that helps regulate the circadian rhythms. When levels of sunlight start to decrease at the end of the day, the visual system transmits this information to the SCN, triggering a message to the pineal gland to increase production of a hormone known as *melatonin*. This hormone causes the body to slow down activity levels and leads to increased sleepiness.

Levels of Consciousness

Before you can begin to understand the different levels of consciousness, you need to have a firm grasp of just what consciousness is. The easiest way to understand consciousness is to think of it as awareness: It is your awareness of your thoughts, memories, feelings sensations, and environment. There are varying degrees of how aware you are of materials and things going on within your body and your environment; these varying degrees determine the levels of consciousness and include conscious, preconscious, unconscious, subconscious, and nonconscious. Let's take a look at each in detail.

Conscious

Conscious is the term used to describe your active awareness. For example, if you stub your toe on your way to answer the door, you are actively aware of the coffee table that you just ran into. You are aware of the pain shooting up from your injured toe. You are aware of the swear word escaping your mouth. You are aware of the sound each time the doorbell rings. You are conscious of all these things.

Preconscious

The preconscious stores memories that you do not have a use for at the present moment but that you can retrieve in the future if needed. You are aware of these memories, but it is not an active awareness until a trigger requires you to retrieve a memory and put it to use, thus becoming conscious of it. For example, you know when your birthday is, but you aren't actively aware of that information until you need to retrieve it. It stays within your preconscious, and then when someone asks you when your birthday is, you activate that memory, bring it to your conscious, and answer the question.

Subconscious

The subconscious handles the information and mental processes needed to perform routine activities that do not require conscious thought. For instance, let's say you are writing a paper for a psychology class. While you are conscious of the words you are typing, your subconscious handles the typing itself. You have already learned how to type and that information was stored in your subconscious, so your fingers can find the appropriate keys in an automatic response to the words you want to type.

Unconscious

The unconscious stores those memories you are unaware of. You may be wondering how the unconscious is even known to exist if the information stored there is unknown to the individual. Often, these memories can be brought to the surface when a person is taken into an altered state of consciousness, such as in hypnosis. During hypnosis, an individual can recall unconscious memories, such as a conversation that the individual heard but was unaware of hearing while under anesthesia in an operating room.

> The unconscious was a subject of primary interest to psychoanalyst Sigmund Freud. He thought that the unconscious stored all memories, thoughts, and emotions that were too troubling to allow into the conscious. He considered it a realm of secrets that held the key to unlocking an individual's true identity, desires, and personality.

Nonconscious

The nonconscious part of your mind stores information that you are not aware of but is necessary for you to live out your daily life. For example, you get up every morning, carry out your daily activities, and sleep at night, and all the while your heart is beating. You are not aware of the information being mentally processed within your body to maintain that heartbeat, but you don't have to be, as your nonconscious handles that.

Sleep

Sleep is a state of consciousness that is essential to your daily mental and physical functions. While no one has been able to determine exactly why people sleep, studies have shown that sleep allows your body to restore itself after a time of wakefulness. During sleep the body has time to repair itself (repair cells, strengthen the immune system, digest, and store the mental processes required in learning) after the damaging effects of everyday activities.

Until the early 1950s when the electroencephalograph (EEG) was invented, sleep was thought to be a time-out period during which the brain shuts down. However, the EEG made it possible to study the brain waves of people sleeping and found that the brain was anything but shut down during sleep. Researchers discovered that there are two basic types of sleep: REM (rapid eye movement) sleep, which is associated with higher levels of body and brain activity, and non-REM sleep, during which body and brain activity slows down. By recording the electrical activity of the brain, researchers were able to determine that the brain goes through four stages of activity during sleep:

- **Stage 1**—During the first stage, you begin to relax and your body prepares for sleep. According to the EEG, your brain first emits alpha waves, which show a slow, regular rhythm. As you drift further into stage 1, the waves become more irregular and slower theta waves begin to emerge. You are in a state of light sleep from which you can easily be awakened.

- **Stage 2**—During the second stage, your brain emits irregular, short bursts of waves that contain peaks, called *sleep spindles*. Slow theta waves are predominant during this stage, but even slower brain waves known as *delta waves* begin to emerge as well. Even though you are asleep at this stage, you may not think you are. Background noise isn't likely to awaken you.

- **Stage 3**—This third stage takes you progressively deeper into true sleep. Delta waves represent approximately 20 percent of the activity during this stage. Your body has relaxed to the point that your pulse rate and breathing slow down. You are more difficult to arouse during this stage.

- **Stage 4**—During the fourth stage, the alpha waves of stage 2 have all but left the scene and the delta waves have taken control. When the level of delta waves reach 50 percent, you are said to have entered stage 4 sleep. You are in a very deep sleep at this point and largely oblivious to outside noises. It will require an outside stimulus such as a loud alarm clock to awaken you.

Once you reach the final stage, you will travel backward through the stages until you reach the first. However, instead of entering the period of semiwakefulness, your body enters REM sleep. REM sleep gets its name from the rapid eye movement that occurs during this stage. The EEG shows that during REM sleep, your brain is just as active as it is when you are wide-awake during the day. During REM, your blood pressure rises, your heartbeat increases, you breathe faster, and you will likely dream.

You will alternate from REM sleep to stages 2, 3, and 4 several times throughout the night. As the hours pass, the time spent in the stages often gets shorter and shorter and time spent in REM gets longer and longer.

Sleep Disorders

Even though sleep is a necessary element for mental and physical well-being, only approximately one-third of Americans get the recommended eight hours of sleep a night. One major national survey of adults in the United States found that more than 50 percent reported experiencing symptoms of insomnia several times a week. While you would probably say that you often feel sleepy at some point during the day (perhaps after a large meal or when facing a project you don't want to start), some people suffer from sleep disorders that inhibit their ability to sleep properly. The American Psychological Association (APA) defines sleep disorders as major disturbances to the regular sleep pattern that result in psychological distress and disrupt normal functioning during the day.

Insomnia

Insomnia is characterized by the inability to fall or stay asleep. It is by far the most common sleep disorder, with nearly 60 percent of American adults suffering from it at least once a week. People who suffer insomnia desire and feel the need for sleep, but for some reason are unable to get the amount of sleep their bodies need. Insomnia can be caused by a variety of things. It can be the result of psychological factors such as anxiety, worry, or depression; biological factors such as the effect of stimulants used before bed, arthritis, or hot flashes during menopause; or environmental factors such as noises emitted from loud neighbors, trains, or traffic.

While insomnia may seem to be just a nuisance, if you are unable to resolve the problem (such as avoiding caffeine or keeping a regular bedtime and rising schedule), see your doctor and discuss the problem. Sleep is vital to your mental and physical health, so take whatever measures you can to ensure proper rest for your body.

Sleep Apnea

Sleep apnea is a sleep disorder in which a person's breathing stops for a moment, causing the person to choke, gasp, and wake up momentarily. Impacting an estimated 20 million Americans, it is the second most common sleep disorder. An individual suffering from sleep apnea will fall back asleep once normal breathing resumes and often doesn't even realize he has woken up. This can happen hundreds of times a night, thus interrupting the stages of sleep and causing exhaustion. Sleep apnea is a serious disorder and is potentially life threatening. It can also cause an irregular heartbeat or high blood pressure.

Narcolepsy

Narcolepsy is a sleep disorder in which a person suffers unpredictable attacks of daytime sleepiness. Onset of this disorder usually occurs during adolescence, and it affects an estimated 250,000 people in the United States. The urge to sleep is irresistible and can last anywhere from five to thirty minutes for each attack. Though this disorder has been the subject matter for several comedy skits, the condition is a serious neurological disorder and can cause the individual harm depending on what the person is doing when the attacks occur. People can fall asleep in the middle of a conversation, or most dangerously perhaps, a narcoleptic person may suffer an attack while driving and cause a serious accident.

Sleepwalking and Night Terrors

While insomnia, sleep apnea, and narcolepsy are most common among adults, sleepwalking and night terrors occur far more commonly among children. Sleepwalking, also known as *somnambulism*, is experienced by about 25 percent of all children at least once in their life. During one of these episodes, the child will leave his bed and walk around in a slow, uncoordinated manner. Night terrors are intense, vivid, and usually brief periods of fear. Symptoms include sweating, restlessness, increased heartbeat, and thrashing. While night terrors are dramatic and frightening, they are generally not viewed as a sleep disorder unless they occur on a regular, frequent basis.

Why Do You Dream?

The answer to this question is debatable, and you will find a wide range of answers, depending on whom you ask. The content and meaning of dreams has been a subject of fascination for poets, artists, and philosophers for thousands of years, but real scientific research on the subject has only emerged over the last hundred years or so. Many scientists will tell you that while dreaming is an altered state of consciousness, the dream itself is a by-product of the brain's electrical discharges and wave patterns—a result of the brain's activities to restore the body during sleep. Neurons are fired during the electrical discharges, and depending on where they end up, differing images within the dream will occur. For instance, if neurons are fired in the part of the brain that maintains your balance, you may dream that you are falling and may even jerk in your sleep to try to keep your balance.

However, not everyone accepts this explanation. Some psychoanalysts believe, as Freud did, that dreams are an outlet for people to live out their desires—desires that may not be socially acceptable—or resolve conflicts. According to this concept, dreams have an underlying meaning that the dreamer is unaware of. Each element of the dream is symbolic of the individual's innermost wishes, conflicts, and/or motives. Though dreams may have a deep-rooted psychological meaning, there isn't a reliable and objective way to interpret one's dreams.

Many cultures believe that dreams are prophetic and/or contain messages from the spirit world. Therefore, dreams are elevated to a high level of importance and are interpreted in all seriousness. In this way, dreams can have a direct impact on the lives of several or all members within the culture.

Still others believe that dreams are a direct result of life experiences and are an unconscious continuation of a person's conscious thoughts and activities during the day. During these dreams a person may express anxiety or worry over a problem that is current in her life. She may also be able to solve that problem or find the root of the problem by interpreting the images, thoughts, and emotions of the dream.

Of course, there are more explanations than those offered here. Individuals, scientists, and cultures are continuously studying and interpreting dreams. However, no one explanation has been substantially proven as the reason why people dream.

Hypnosis and Its Uses

Hypnosis is a procedure in which a hypnotist suggests changes in the feelings, perceptions, thoughts, or behavior of the subject. Many consider a hypnotized person to be experiencing an altered state of consciousness. Those under hypnosis are open to the suggestions of the hypnotist but are not under the hypnotist's control. In other words, hypnosis is not a form of mind control, regardless of what you may have seen in the movies. The subject is nearly always fully aware of what is happening and cannot be forced to do anything against his will.

Hypnotizability

Not all people can be hypnotized. Even the best of hypnotists cannot hypnotize a subject if he doesn't want to be hypnotized. Whether or not a subject enters a hypnotic state is dependent upon the subject more than on the hypnotist. People vary in degrees of hypnotic responsiveness. Those who are able to lose themselves in books and movies, or have active imaginations, are good candidates for hypnosis. Those who are grounded in the real world at all times are not likely to be nearly as responsive to hypnosis. This susceptibility is in no way tied to personality traits such as gullibility or submissiveness.

Uses for Hypnosis

Contrary to popular belief, hypnosis is not a guaranteed way to bring to the surface suppressed memories, not even of alien abductions or childhood abuse. Because the subject is highly responsive to the hypnotist's suggestions, she may be led to answer questions or recall "memories" in a particular way depending on how the suggestion is given. Or perhaps the subject has a vivid imagination and plays out a role from that imagined state. She may believe that the experience is real, when in actuality it is merely a product of her imagination.

> If you ever get the chance, check out a stage hypnotist's show in an entertainment venue. It can be very entertaining. You may even choose to become a participant and experience it for yourself—all in the name of research, of course!

Of course, hypnosis can sometimes successfully stimulate a memory, though the results aren't 100 percent error-proof. For instance, a crime victim may be able to recall the image of the perpetrator's tattoo under hypnosis while in a conscious state she could not. However, if she had an imagined perception of that image, then she may recall it during hypnosis with complete conviction though it may be in error.

Studies have shown, however, that hypnosis can be quite effective in the medical arena. Hypnosis has been used to alleviate chronic pain, stress, and anxiety, to reduce nausea in chemotherapy patients, and to help women manage pain during childbirth. It has even been used to anesthetize patients who are undergoing surgery. Some psychologists are able to use hypnosis to break unwanted habits such as nail biting or to increase self-esteem by boosting a subject's confidence in herself and her abilities.

Meditation

Meditation, a self-induced altered state of consciousness, has been practiced throughout the world in several different cultures. It has recently gained popularity in the United States, perhaps because of its calming effect on the individual in this stress-filled society. Surely you've seen yoga classes and instructional books and videos popping up everywhere. Yoga is a system of exercises designed to bring on a meditative state.

The premise behind meditation is to get your body into a relaxed position and allow yourself to clear your mind of all worries, anxiety, and troublesome thoughts. As your body relaxes and your mind clears, your blood pressure lowers, your mental activity slows down, and your alertness is enhanced. People who have incorporated meditation into their daily or weekly schedules have reported that they are better able to cope with stress, feel more emotionally stable, and even experienced physical health benefits.

Psychoactive Drugs and Their Effects

Psychoactive drugs are those that work on the brain to alter mood, behavior, thinking, and perception. Using these drugs is probably the most common way individuals alter their states of consciousness. There are four major classifications of psychoactive drugs: depressants, hallucinogens, opiates, and stimulants. Let's take a closer look at each of these and their effects on the individual.

Marijuana is typically given its own category. While it does have some hallucinogenic properties, it is also thought to contain a mild stimulant even though the effects mimic those of depressants. The effects of marijuana can vary depending on dosage. Smaller dosages typically create a euphoric feeling, while larger doses can cause hallucinations. It can impair your coordination, create feelings of anxiety, and slow down reaction times.

Depressants

As the name implies, depressants slow down the activity of the central nervous system. The most widely used depressant is alcohol. Other depressants include tranquilizers and barbiturates. Because they slow down mental and physical activity, depressants can make a person feel calm and less stressed. They also relieve anxiety and tension. While this may seem like a bonus, depressants can also impair your judgment and coordination and reduce your inhibitions, causing you to act in a way you normally wouldn't. Large doses of depressants can cause insensitivity to pain, convulsions, blackouts, and irregular heartbeats.

Hallucinogens

Hallucinogens interfere with your normal thought processes, altering your perceptions and affecting your senses. Popular hallucinogens include lysergic acid diethylamide (LSD), psilocybin (mushrooms), and mescaline (peyote). The effects of hallucinogens vary from person to person, and also vary with each use. When a person uses hallucinogens, he is often said to be "tripping." This trip could range anywhere from a pleasant period of enlightenment to the most hellish of nightmares. Hallucinogens can cause sensory hallucinations (hence the name), the most common being visual hallucinations.

Opiates

Opiates impair your ability to respond to and/or feel sensations, most notably pain. As such, you may receive a prescription from your doctor for an opiate to be used as a painkiller. Of course, opiates are also used for recreational purposes, though illegally. The most common opiates include opium, heroin, methadone, and morphine. The effects of opiates vary, but most experience a sudden euphoric feeling, or "rush," at first. This feeling is then often followed by a state of relaxation in which anxiety decreases.

While you may not like to think of yourself as a drug user, if you have that daily cup of coffee or smoke cigarettes, you are in fact using drugs. The caffeine in coffee and the nicotine in cigarettes are both stimulants.

Stimulants

Stimulants are the opposite of depressants. They speed up the activity in the central nervous system. Stimulants include, but are not limited to, cocaine, methamphetamine hydrochloride (speed), and amphetamines (uppers). Because they speed up mental and physical activity, they often create a feeling of excitement, higher energy levels, and confidence. However, large doses can create anxiety and hallucinations, and can even cause convulsions and death.

Drug Abuse and Dependence

Not all drug use is abuse; after all, some drugs are prescribed and used for medicinal purposes. Drug use turns into abuse once it disrupts a person's daily activities or functions and/or interferes with a person's interaction with society or family and friends.

Many drugs are addictive, whether psychologically or physically. As drug use continues, the body can develop a tolerance to it. Once that happens, the drug's effect on the body lessens, and the user will have to take more of the drug to get the same effect. This can continue into a vicious cycle of dependence. It can even reach a point where the user only feels normal when she is using. The hold on the user is so strong that if she were to try to cut back, the body would suffer a withdrawal, which is far from a pleasant experience. Withdrawal symptoms can include abdominal cramps, sweating, nausea, muscle spasms, insomnia, and depression.

> Some people are more at risk of becoming addicted to drugs than others. There are several factors that contribute to your risk of becoming addicted, such as the drug you choose to use, your family history, your genetic makeup, your personality, and your ability to cope with stressors.

Drug abuse and dependency is a problem that unfortunately runs rampant in society today. While the use of psychoactive drugs will alter your state of consciousness, the potentially long-lasting negative effects can far outweigh the pleasant effects you may temporarily experience. If you are looking to alter your state of consciousness to achieve enlightenment, for recreation, or for an escape, there are other better and less harmful ways of accomplishing this.

CONDITIONING
and Learning

TO BETTER UNDERSTAND YOURSELF and others, you need to take a look at how you learn your behaviors and why you do the things you do. This chapter will discuss the various learning processes psychologists study and how they affect your life. You will also learn how cats, rats, and dogs played a part in the existing knowledge of learning behavior. Curious? Read on.

What Is Learning?

Before you delve deeper into the history and research on how people learn, it is important that you first understand exactly what psychologists mean when they talk about "learning." When you talk about learning in everyday life, you're probably referring to the process of acquiring a new skill such as learning to play the violin or learning to speak Spanish. While exact definitions often vary, psychologists use the term in a much broader sense, using it to refer to anything that produces a relatively lasting change in a behavior as result of experience.

Habituation—The Most Basic Form of Learning

To understand how people learn, it is best to take a look at children between the ages of eighteen and twenty-four months. They have a hunger for knowledge that cannot be touched by even the most studious of adults. They are driven to learn by experience and observation. If you have had a child, you are fully aware that he will pick up anything he can get his hands on and possibly even mouth it. While this may be an annoyance to a parent, it is a part of the learning process for a child.

> Through observation, we also know that babies have the ability to remember. When given a choice between two objects, a baby will glance at the object he is already familiar with and then reach for the object he has not seen before. He remembers already learning about the first object.

While a child might not be able to tell you what he is studying and what he wants to learn, through observation you can figure it out rather easily. Pay attention to a child who is surrounded by several objects. You will notice that he will quickly turn his attention to those objects that are new to him. Once he becomes acquainted with one new object, he will discard it and turn his attention to another. This process is called *habituation* and is the most basic form of learning. A child becomes habituated to an item, gets bored with it, and seeks out an unfamiliar object, thus creating a cycle of learning.

Habituation shows that humans have an innate desire to learn about and experience new things. It also shows that people are able to distinguish differences in objects, patterns, colors, and textures and remember those differences. While habituation is the earliest and most basic form of learning, it is not the only process through which people learn.

Conditioning

Behaviorists view learning as a change of or influence on a person's behavior due to experience. In other words, experience is the best teacher. The type of learning behaviorists focus on is conditioning. Conditioning is a learning process in which an environmental stimulus elicits a response, and an individual learns from the association between that stimulus and response. The association is what conditions, or modifies, your behavior and you therefore learn to behave in a certain manner toward the same stimulus in the future. There are two types of conditioning: classical conditioning and operant conditioning. If this seems confusing, don't worry. The following sections will take a closer look at each of these types of conditioning to help you better understand how it works.

Classical Conditioning

Classical conditioning was discovered, rather accidentally, by Ivan Pavlov. As mentioned before, Pavlov was studying the digestive processes in dogs. He inserted a tube into a dog's mouth in order to measure the amount of saliva the dog produced, using food to stimulate the flow of saliva. After visiting the lab several times for this procedure, Pavlov noticed something very interesting. The dog actually began to salivate before the food was in his mouth. The sight or smell of the food or even the sound of footsteps bringing the food stimulated the production of saliva. While Pavlov first considered this to be an obstacle to his experiment, he quickly realized that the dog's salivating was a conditioned response to its anticipation of being fed. As the dog had not done this before, he recognized that the response had been learned through experience. He dropped his study of the digestive system and turned to studying this response.

> Though Pavlov is the one who first identified and studied classical conditioning as a form of learning and was awarded the Nobel Prize for his work in this field, some say that it was actually a student of his who pointed out that the dog was salivating before he had been given the food.

This is essentially the idea behind classical conditioning. By definition classical conditioning is the process by which a normally neutral stimulus becomes a conditioned stimulus, eliciting a response in an individual, or in this case a dog, due to its association with a stimulus that already elicits a similar response. Classical conditioning involves what are known as *reflexive behaviors*. A reflex is an automatic, involuntary response to an external stimulus.

How It Works

There are four components to classical conditioning. Breaking it down, the first two components are an unconditioned stimulus (US) and the unconditioned response (UR). The unconditioned stimulus in Pavlov's study was the dog's food. The food was the stimulus that automatically elicited the unconditioned response, salivation. Remember, these two factors are reflexive. In other words, they were automatic, not conditioned or learned.

The next two components make for an interesting study. In Pavlov's study, he paired the ringing of a bell with the distribution of the food, thus coupling a conditioned stimulus (CS) (bell) with an unconditioned stimulus (food). Eventually, he took away the US and only provided the CS. The CS by itself still produced the unconditioned response, thus making the UR a conditioned response (CR). In other words, the dog salivated when it heard the ringing of the bell even though there wasn't any food present. These two components were conditioned, or learned.

This process of a neutral stimulus becoming a conditioned stimulus is the basis for classical conditioning. Of course, you have to throw experience in there. A dog isn't likely to salivate after the bell is rung when paired with food just one time. The dog must experience this pairing regularly and repeatedly in order to make the association between the two stimuli.

Features of Classical Conditioning

Conditioned responses in classical conditioning aren't necessarily permanent responses. They can be unlearned, or extinguished. For instance, Pavlov's dog could have been reconditioned to have no response to the ringing of the bell. Had someone rung the bell regularly without following it with food over the course of several sessions, the dog would no longer have salivated in response to the ringing of the bell alone, as it did not signal the coming of food—in which case, the conditioned response would have been extinguished.

Classical conditioning can also produce stimulus generalization and stimulus discrimination. Stimulus generalization occurs when an individual has the same conditioned response to a stimulus that is similar though not the same as the conditioned stimulus. For example, if a child is bitten by a rottweiler, he may fear all dogs, not just rottweilers. Though not all dogs are the same, the stimuli are similar enough to elicit the same response. On the other hand, two similar stimuli may produce different responses, which is called *stimulus discrimination*. To use the previous example, another child may be bitten by a rottweiler but is able to distinguish the difference between a rottweiler and a poodle, and will therefore not produce the same response (fear) toward the poodle as she would toward a rottweiler.

Conditioned responses can sometimes reappear suddenly after being extinguished, a phenomenon known as *spontaneous recovery*. In Pavlov's experiment, for example, he found that if a dog was given a few hours of rest after a response was extinguished, the CR would suddenly reappear after the stimulus was presented. This suggests that while a response may disappear, it doesn't mean that it has been "unlearned."

Applications of Classical Conditioning

While people do not behave exactly like Pavlov's dogs, classical conditioning has affected your life, whether you realize it or not. Many of your emotional responses to sights, sounds, objects, or people can be tied to classical conditioning. For instance, let's say a former love interest always wore a particular brand of cologne. Should you smell that particular scent even years later, you may experience a sense of sadness as though you were reliving the loss of that person in your life, because you associated that scent with that person. Perhaps your family bakes a particular dessert on holidays. You may feel a surge of excitement when you catch a whiff of that scent because you associate it with past feelings of excitement.

> Emotions can be a very powerful force. They can cause you to think or act in ways you would never dream of otherwise, sometimes even superseding your rational thought process. Advertisers try to make use of your emotional responses, thus classical conditioning, to get you to buy their products. For instance, think back to all the commercials you saw sporting the American flag following the September 11 attacks. Associating patriotic feelings with a particular product is good business!

Classical conditioning can produce both positive and negative responses, depending on the association made. Take, for instance, a thunderstorm. If a child were to hear the rumbling of thunder and then witness a tree being struck by lightning just a second later, he may fear that rumbling sound during future storms. However, a child who heard that same rumbling of thunder while he was cozily enveloped in his father's arms may later hear the rumbling of thunder and experience pleasant emotions, as the association was one of contentment.

Therapists often use classical conditioning to help people overcome phobias or other anxiety problems. For example, imagine a person has an extreme fear of public speaking. In order to help the individual overcome this terror, a therapist might recommend repeatedly pairing the delivery of a speech with a more pleasant experience. While it may not completely eliminate the public-speaking phobia, the person might feel less anxious when she is confronted with a speech, talk, or presentation.

Operant Conditioning

Another type of learning studied by behaviorists is operant conditioning. Operant conditioning, sometimes referred to as instrumental conditioning, is a process by which a response is followed by a consequence (either positive or negative), and that consequence teaches you to either repeat the response or decrease its occurrence. The main difference between classical conditioning and operant conditioning is that in classical conditioning, the learning process is reflexive and is not dependent upon consequences, whereas in operant conditioning, the learning process is more complex and reliant upon the type of consequences the response elicits. In other words, the learning process results in different types of voluntary behavior. You can't decide whether or not to salivate, but you can decide to go to work if you like getting paid.

Cats and Rats

Edward Thorndike introduced and laid the foundation of operant conditioning in his experiment with cats. He was the first psychologist to systematically study how consequences impacted voluntary behavior in animals. In this experiment, Thorndike constructed cages that he called *puzzle boxes*, in which he placed hungry cats. He then set a bowl of food outside the box where the cat could see it but could not get to it unless the cat was able to escape. The escape route was triggered by a mechanism that the cat had to work. Of course, the cat had no idea it was supposed to trigger this mechanism, so it ran about, bounced off the walls, and cried—in short, it tried everything it knew to try to get to that food. Eventually, the cat accidentally tripped the mechanism, thus escaping and reaching the food. Thorndike placed the cat back in the box several more times, and each time it took the cat less time to find the trigger. After several times in the box, the cat eventually learned to trip the mechanism immediately to escape and get its reward.

Thorndike thus came to the conclusion that the cat's behavior was controlled by the consequences: tripping the mechanism and getting the food, rather than not tripping the mechanism and being stuck in the box.

B.F. Skinner took this idea and elaborated on it. Skinner used rats instead of cats for his experiments. He created a "Skinner box" in which he placed a rat. The box held a device that delivered pellets of food when a bar was pressed. Much like Thorndike's experiment, the rat at first scurried about without any purpose or motive behind its actions. Instead of waiting for the rat to accidentally press the bar and learn on its own, Skinner rewarded the rat with food as it got closer to performing the appropriate response (pressing the bar). Gradually, Skinner was able to shape the rat's behavior and teach it to press the bar. Eventually, the rat was intentionally pressing the bar for food as fast as it could. Skinner said that to understand a person, one must look outside the person, at the consequences of his or her actions, instead of trying to figure out the inside of the person. In other words, the person's experiences of past and current consequences are what shape that person's behavior.

In Thorndike's day, this wasn't known as operant conditioning. Instead, he had termed his theory the law of effect. This theory basically stated that a consequence had an effect on the behavior of an animal or individual and that if the consequence was good, then that particular behavior would be repeated in the future.

How It Works

Operant conditioning is reliant upon the behavior being reinforced, either positively or negatively, which in turn will determine whether the behavior increases or decreases its likelihood of future occurrences. According to Skinner there are three types of consequences to a response: reinforcers, punishment, and neutral consequences. Reinforcers increase the likelihood that the response will occur again. Positive reinforcement is when you add a good thing after the behavior, like a treat. Negative reinforcement is when you take away something bad after the behavior, like the seat-belt buzzer that stops when you put on your seat belt. The important thing to remember is that reinforcements always increase the likelihood of a behavior occurring again, whether they are positive or negative. Punishment decreases the likelihood that the response will occur again. For instance, if you touch a hot burner and your finger gets burned, you are not likely to repeat the behavior. Of course, there are also neutral consequences.

These have no bearing on whether the likelihood of a response will increase or decrease. These are typically ignored and do not affect any of your decisions.

Applications of Operant Conditioning

Examples of operant conditioning surround you in your daily life. Think for a moment about why you do the things you do. Your life is filled with reinforcers and punishers. You go to work because you get paid to do your job. Would you still go to work every day if that reinforcer wasn't in place? Probably not. When you drive to work, you likely stay within a reasonable approximation of the speed limit (at least we hope so) because if you didn't, you could get a speeding ticket, have to pay a fine, and risk having your insurance rates rise or risk getting into an accident. Do you drink coffee in the morning? This too can be a form of operant conditioning. After all, you drink the coffee because the caffeine helps to wake you up, right? Or perhaps you simply like the taste or the warmth it provides. Regardless, the effects of the coffee are reinforcers, increasing the likelihood that you will continue to drink the coffee each morning.

Operant conditioning can lead to bad habits. For instance, smoking is a bad habit and harmful to your health, so the punisher (deterioration of your health) should ideally decrease the likelihood that you will continue smoking, right? Well, unfortunately, many find that the reinforcers of smoking (relaxing feeling, feeding the body's addiction, etc.) outweigh the punishers and therefore continue the habit. Also, the reinforcer is closer in time to the behavior, where the punisher is far away in time—thus not a very effective contingency.

Teaching Behavior to Others

So far, this chapter has discussed how operant conditioning has taught you particular behaviors, but you can also often be on the other side of the fence and teach behaviors to others. Take a parent, for example. If a child throws a tantrum in a store because she wants a particular object and the parent allows the child to have the object in order to stop the tantrum, that child has just learned that a tantrum will be rewarded with what she wants. It's quite likely the child will throw another tantrum the next time she wants something she is not given immediately. Incidentally, the child has just provided negative reinforcement for parental toy-buying behavior, thus increasing the probability that that behavior will occur again. Perhaps you have employees working for you. How you respond to certain behaviors, such as an employee being consistently late, affects how the person responds. If you choose to ignore the situation, the person will continue the behavior because the experience of being late (getting more time in bed, etc.) is reinforcing. However, if you instead use a punisher or reinforcer in response, the behavior is more likely to change. Of course, operant conditioning works on animals as well. If you have ever tried to train your dog to sit or your cat to use the litter box, you understand quite well the effects of reinforcers and punishers.

> Understanding how both classical conditioning and operant conditioning aid in a person's learning process and stimulate certain responses and behaviors will help you better understand both yourself and others.

Effective Reinforcement

When done properly, positive or negative reinforcement is much more effective than punishment in changing behavior, because it increases the desired behavior (remember, reinforcement increases behavior). Punishment stops behavior, but it doesn't teach what to do instead. If you try to change behavior by punishing everything except the correct behavior, whoever you are training will either give up and stop offering any behavior, or will rebel.

Skinner found that different reinforcement schedules produced different rates and patterns of responding. In a continuous reinforcement schedule, behaviors are reinforced each and every time they occur. As you might imagine, this type of schedule is frequently used early in the conditioning process as a new behavior is learned. Once the association has become strong enough, the schedule is usually switched to a partial reinforcement schedule. In a partial schedule, behaviors are reinforced on either a fixed schedule (after a certain number of responses or a specific period of time) or a variable schedule (after a varying number of responses or an intermittent amount of time).

If you want to keep behavior going almost indefinitely, once it is clearly learned, you can put it on an intermittent, random reinforcement schedule. This means that the behavior is reinforced (positive or negative doesn't matter) at intervals that the trainee can't predict. This works especially if the reinforcer is strong. For example, once you know how to buy and play lottery tickets, you will be reinforced at intervals you can't predict—is it the next ticket? If you win $500, how long are you going to keep buying lottery tickets, hoping for another reward? Welcome to gambling addiction.

If you want behavior to go away, and you are very certain what the reinforcers are that are maintaining behavior, you can extinguish the behavior by withholding all reinforcement when it occurs. For instance, if you continued buying lottery tickets and never, ever again won, eventually you would stop buying them. The problem with extinguishing behaviors is that just before the behavior stops, it gets worse. This is called the *extinguishment burst*, and it is deadly for the trainer. So if you're going to withhold all reinforcement from your screaming child who wants a toy—hold the line! Do not buy that toy when the volume increases, or otherwise reinforce the behavior. If you're going to "try to ignore" bad behavior, and end up reinforcing it by providing attention when you can't stand it anymore (because the extinction burst is torturing you), don't do it: this response will make it worse.

Learning Through Observation and Imitation

In both classical conditioning and operant conditioning, experience plays a direct role in learning, either through association, reinforcement, or punishment. Yet another type of learning is learning through observation and imitation, called observational learning. While experience is certainly a great teacher, you needn't experience everything for yourself in order to learn. You can watch the behavior and actions of others and learn from their experiences. In fact, this type of learning is very powerful and prevalent in children, though adults also participate in observational learning.

> Because children are greatly affected by observational learning, telling a child to do as you say, not as you do, is not going to produce the behavior you want. The drive to model a parent's behavior is much stronger than the drive to take verbal orders, even if punishers or reinforcers are involved with the warning.

Observational learning is strongly associated with the psychology behind Albert Bandura and his famous "Bobo doll" experiment that you read about earlier in Chapter 2.

As you may recall, children in the experiment saw adults beating up a Bobo doll in a video. Some of the adults were rewarded, some were punished, and some received no consequence for the behavior. Bandura demonstrated that while the children who saw the adults being rewarded for beating up the doll were more likely to later repeat the behavior, all of the children learned to hit and kick the doll.

Bandura later explained that there are four key cognitive processes at work during observational learning. First, you must be paying attention to the behavior of the person who is modeling the actions. Next, you need to be able to remember the behavior that was demonstrated. Third, you must be able to turn your observations into actions that you are able to repeat. Finally, you need to be motivated to imitate the behavior you observed earlier. So, you are far more likely to perform an action if you saw someone else being rewarded for the same behavior.

Applications of Observational Learning

Watch any child and you will see observational learning taking place. Children begin to learn through observation at a very young age. Infants have been shown to imitate the actions of others as early as twenty-one days after birth! Because they are most often around their parents and siblings, children are most likely going to model those family members' behavior. As they grow older, they will also begin to model the behavior of their peers and even the behavior of characters in movies and on television. They will carefully watch the actions of others and the consequences of those actions. If they like what they see and view a potential reward for a particular behavior, they will likely model that behavior, or one that is very similar. For instance, a child watching his father have fun playing basketball in the driveway will likely try to play basketball, too. Of course, modeling behavior doesn't always produce positive results. A child who watches a classmate bully another child into giving up a toy may mimic that behavior because a toy is the reward.

Adults also learn through observation. A med student learns procedures and bedside manner through observing other doctors on rotation in hospitals. An adult may learn how to climb the corporate ladder by watching and learning from the behavior and consequences of her superior. Think of your daily activities and those people you watch and learn from. You may be surprised to find that you participate in observational learning a lot more often than you may think.

Observational learning has also been utilized on a much larger scale to help promote healthy behaviors and inspire social change. For example, there have been a number of serialized television dramas used in a number of countries including India, Kenya, and China designed to encourage audience members to engage in environmentally friendly behaviors, use safe sex, and encourage financial independence among women.

———◆———

HOW YOU REMEMBER,
Why You Forget

YOUR MEMORIES ARE POWERFUL things. They allow you to store the information you learn and retrieve it at a later date. They are a major component in creating individuality and are essential in carrying out daily activities. But how does memory work and why are people often unable to recall information that they know is stored somewhere in their brain? In this chapter, you'll learn more about some of the basics of how memories are created and stored and well as what happens when this process sometimes goes awry.

Memory—An Overview

Your memory allows you to retrieve a memory. While this may sound simple enough, memory is actually a very tricky and complex thing. Let's first take a look at the basics of how memory works.

Think of memory as a huge, selective storage system that is capable of storing an immeasurable amount of information. Memory is reliant upon three components: encoding, storage, and retrieval. Encoding refers to the intake of information and the brain's conversion of that information into a form it is able to process. Storage refers to the placement of this processed information in the brain. The information may be stored as an image, a concept, or within a mental network. Retrieval, of course, refers to the recovery of that information and putting that information to use.

Filling in the Gaps

Most people would like to think (and may even insist) that they are able to retrieve certain memories with every shining detail in place. For instance, you may swear you remember perfectly well the moment your husband proposed to you, including all details—after all, that was such a special occasion, how could you possibly forget? However, if you were asked to recall the event in detail, you would likely misremember several details and may even make up some others! This is because the retrieval of memories is a reconstructive process in which you retrieve certain flashes of the event but fill in the gaps for those details that the memory didn't store or process properly.

> The memory is selective. It will not store every single event that happens to you or every little detail or bit of information you take in. It has to be selective in order to keep the house clean, so to speak. If it were not, your mind would be cluttered with tons of insignificant and useless information.

Because you are forced to reconstruct the past somewhat when recalling a memory, you often rely on several other sources to fill in the gaps, often without even knowing that you are doing it—which explains why you might insist that you are recalling your memories perfectly. For instance, you may draw conclusions from photos or video of the event in question; stories others have told about the event; anything you may have said, thought, or felt about the event after the fact; or sometimes even wishful thinking (what you wanted the memory to be).

Implicit and Explicit Memory

As you well know, there are some things you work really hard to remember, such as information for an upcoming exam, and other things that you really have no desire to remember, but remember anyway, such as commercial jingles. So what's the difference?

> The retrieval of explicit memory is usually tested in one of two ways: recall or recognition. Recall refers to the ability to actually retrieve that information you stored, such as in fill-in-the-blank or essay questions. Recognition refers to the ability to recognize the information stored, such as in multiple choice or true/false questions.

The information that you intentionally work to remember is stored using explicit memory. Because you have spent energy to deliberately remember this information, it makes sense that the memory would store it. The information that you remember but did not intentionally put away for future use is stored using implicit memory. While it seems that this type of information must have affected you in some way, it is not certain exactly why this information is stored in memory.

Sensory Memory and Incoming Stimulation

The memory's huge storage system is divided into three storage subsystems, the first of which is sensory memory. This is the entranceway through which all incoming stimulation must pass. This subsystem is divided even further into storage areas for each of the senses: hearing, vision, smell, touch, and taste. Information relating to everything you sense is sent directly to one of these memory areas.

The memory of these impressions is stored briefly. Have you ever noticed that after you shut off the radio, you can still hear the sound for a split second? Or perhaps you've looked at the sun (though you know you're not supposed to!) and then shut your eyes: Do you recall the image still being there? These lingering impressions are possible because they are temporarily stored in your sensory memory.

Because you are constantly receiving new information, the sensory memory cannot store impressions for long. For instance, the vision area stores impressions for only a fraction of a second. The hearing area stores impressions for a bit longer, but no more than about two seconds. Amazingly, this is enough time for your brain to decide what to do with this information.

Sensory memory also explains the bird-in-a-cage trick. If you aren't familiar with this "trick," it is where the image of a bird is placed on one side of a card and the image of a cage is placed on the other. When the card is spun rapidly, it appears as if the image you are seeing is the bird inside the cage.

During that short amount of time that the impression is stored, the brain decides whether it is important or insignificant information. If it is deemed important, that impression moves on to the short-term memory. If it is deemed insignificant, the brain discards it and it is lost forever.

Short-Term Memory and Working Memory

When an impression makes it through the sensory memory and then moves on to the short-term memory, it is processed, or encoded, and is turned into a pattern the brain can recognize, such as a word. The information does not stay long in the short-term memory either, only about twenty seconds.

The short-term memory deals with only the present time. It stores everything you are conscious of at the moment: the words you are reading, the food you are eating, the sound of a dog barking outside, the telephone number you just looked up, etc. The brain then decides whether to move this information on to the long-term memory or discard it.

Storage Room

The short-term memory can hold only so much information at any given time. But just how many items can it store? For several years, the magic number was seven, give or take two. This gives a good explanation for the number of digits in zip codes (five digits), phone numbers (seven digits), and social security numbers (nine digits). However, not everyone agrees with this number. Some have placed the number of items to be as few as two, while others place the number of items as high as twenty. Regardless, the short-term memory isn't able to hold very many items at one time.

Luckily, you are able to combine bits of information into large chunks of information, where each chunk counts as one item. Thus you are able to store more information than you think. For instance, most people store the term *DVD* as one item, or chunk, rather than as three separate words (items). Along the same lines, you will often see businesses with phone numbers that can be stored as one chunk, such as 555-PETS, instead of seven individual items.

> The short-term memory can be a source of frustration for many people. Depending on how quickly you are receiving new information to replace the information already there, items may be displaced before you are ready to part with them. However, after you look up a phone number, mentally rehearsing it allows you to keep it in short-term memory until you are able to pick up the phone and dial the number.

The Working Memory

The short-term memory not only stores new incoming information, but it can also hold information that has been retrieved from the long-term memory to be used temporarily. The system within the short-term memory that processes and interprets the incoming information from the long-term memory is referred to as the *working memory*. For instance, if you are thinking of purchasing a sale item with a particular percentage discounted, your working memory handles the numbers you are working with as well as the instructions brought forth from the long-term memory for completing the mathematical equation to find out the price of the item.

Long-Term Memories and How They Are Stored

Your long-term memory is the final destination. Because it is unable to be measured, the long-term memory is thought to have an infinite capacity. You already have a vast amount of information stored there and are continuously storing more every day. For instance, your activities of daily living are reliant upon the memories stored in long-term memory. At some point you learned how to shower, brush your teeth, dress yourself, make coffee, drive the route to work, do your job, make dinner, and set the alarm clock. The memories of how to do all these things are retrieved from the long-term memory, even though you may not be conscious of the retrieval. Of course, this isn't the only type of information stored; past experiences that make up your personal history and give you a sense of identity are stored here as well.

Storing and Organizing Information

While the long-term memory holds a great amount of knowledge, it is not just a jumble of bits of information swimming around in chaos. There is an organizational system present that helps both to store and retrieve memories.

When a memory enters long-term memory, it makes associations with memories already present. For instance, words are stored next to other words in your long-term memory that are similar in meaning, sound, or look. To help break it down even further, your mind creates categories for words, so apple and peach would be stored close to one another since they are both fruits. Chair and table would be stored next to each other since they are both items of furniture. Shirt and skirt would be stored close together because they are both articles of clothing. You get the picture. Items can belong to more than one category—for instance, you might want to remember all the pieces of clothing, jewelry, or shoes that you own that are black, in order to put together an outfit.

As oral storytelling was once the primary way of recording history before the written word, several cultures relied on the long-term memory of their members to recant and pass on these stories. The *Odyssey* and the *Iliad*, for instance, were both originally oral epic poems that didn't get written down until long after they were composed.

The associations made are very important for both storage and retrieval. If your mind is able to associate a new concept or word with a memory already in long-term, then storage is made easy. Retrieval is easier as well, because as you are searching for that concept or word, your mind can look to the associations for help in bringing it to the consciousness.

Categories of Memories

The long-term memory is able to divide types of memories into three basic categories: procedural memories, episodic memories, and semantic memories. Procedural memories are those that provide information on how to do things. For example, riding a bike, brushing your teeth, tying your shoes, and driving are all procedural memories. Typically, this type of memory becomes so ingrained that it requires very little conscious retrieval or thought to carry out the activity. In other words, procedural memories are implicit.

Episodic memories are those that allow you to recall events and situations that you have experienced. Along with the event itself, the circumstances surrounding the event (location, time, etc.) are also stored. Closely related to episodic memory is autobiographical memory—that is, the memory of your own personal life history. This type of memory plays an essential role in your unique sense of self. Semantic memories are basically facts you have learned—the date of your father's birthday, the meanings of words, your address, who invented the cotton gin, and so on. Episodic and semantic memories are both types of explicit memories. They must be consciously retrieved from long-term memory.

Explanations for Forgetting

From forgetting to return an important phone call to not being able to remember where you left your car keys, forgetting is a common complaint that everyone shares. Forgetting is the inability to retrieve information from a memory due to a problem with encoding, storage, or retrieval. Forgetting can be very frustrating, especially since you are usually aware of forgetting when you really need to remember something—such as when taking an exam—or when you should have done something but the moment has passed—such as getting milk from the store before it closed.

> Even though forgetting is natural to most people, if you are fed up with forgetting, there are some techniques you can use to help you remember, such as rehearsal and mnemonics. These techniques will be explained in detail later in this chapter.

Though you don't often think of it as such, forgetting can also be a blessing. For instance, do you really want to remember the pain you experienced in that car accident five years ago? Forgetting allows you to continue your life without giving focus to past painful, embarrassing, stressful, or unhappy experiences. Even so, most people still want to know why they forget. Researchers have come up with various theories to explain this.

Replacement Theory

The replacement theory holds that new information entering the memory replaces old information already stored. Studies that support this theory show that misleading information replaces the original memories of people. For instance, one study showed pictures of a car accident to two groups of people. In one group, the researchers asked leading questions to make the people think they had seen a yield sign, when the picture had actually shown a stop sign. Those in the other group were not asked leading questions and therefore remembered seeing the stop sign. When both groups were later gathered together, they were told the purpose behind the experiment and asked to guess if they thought they had been part of the group that was misled. Nearly everyone in the group that was misled claimed that they had truly seen the yield sign and were not deceived. This led researchers to conclude that the implanted memory replaced the actual one.

Decay Theory

The decay theory holds that some memories will dissipate if not retrieved every once in a while from the long-term memory. According to this theory, the formation of a new memory creates what is known as a *memory trace*, or a change in brain cells. If this memory is not periodically refreshed, the memory trace gradually fades. Why waste space with information you aren't going to use? Fortunately, decay doesn't affect all memories. Many procedural memories will remain in the long-term memory for as long as you live. For instance, even if you haven't ridden a bike in fifteen years, you can still remember how once you get back on. There isn't a specific time limit on when a memory has to be recalled before it decays; some memories will be forgotten the next day, and others may take years to forget.

> Memory loss can also be attributed to brain damage. If you were to suffer a blow to the head, the memories stored in that particular area may be lost. Depending upon the type of damage suffered, the memory loss can be either temporary or permanent.

Cue-Dependent Theory

The cue-dependent theory holds that the retrieval of some memories are dependent upon cues that help to locate that information in the brain; if these cues are missing, then you may not be able to remember. Because the mind organizes information based on associations with other things, if you are able to recall an association, that increases your likelihood of recalling the particular information you are seeking. For instance, if you have forgotten the last name of a classmate, cues for remembering may be her first name, where she sat in class with you, her nickname, or even the circumstances surrounding the situation in which you first met her. Without these cues, you may not be able to recall her last name.

Interference Theory

According to interference theory, information within the memory can interfere with other bits of information during storage or retrieval, thus causing you to forget. This can occur when incoming information is similar to information that is already stored, which can cause confusion when later trying to recall the first-stored information. Or vice versa. The formerly learned information can interfere with the recollection of the recently learned information. For instance, if you've recently met two people with similar names, you might confuse the two names later when meeting one of them again. While this may seem like the replacement theory, it is different in that the new information does not replace the old. Both bits of information are still there; they just become confused.

Psychogenic Amnesia Theory

The psychogenic amnesia theory holds that you forget experiences because of the need to escape the feelings associated with a painful, embarrassing, or otherwise unpleasant experience. In essence, you force the memory to the back of your mind so you do not have to face it. However, this doesn't mean that the memory can never be retrieved. Certain cues can be used to retrieve those memories. This concept began with Freud's theory of repression, which is the involuntary act of moving information that is deemed traumatic or threatening into the unconscious so as to avoid dealing with it. Because the person is unaware of the memory stored in the unconscious, he does not recall the events or feelings associated with the experience. In other words, it is blocked from the conscious memory, so the individual forgets it. The repression theory has become a topic of debate among professionals, as you will soon see.

If you tell someone to "forget it," chances are you have just helped that person to remember. While the information normally may have just resided in short-term memory and then eventually been discarded, your drawing attention to that information may have given it greater meaning and thus helped it to reach the long-term memory.

Imperfect, Distorted, and False Memories

Human memory is a remarkable and complex process, but it can also be surprisingly fallible. As confident as you may be that your memory of a particular event or experience is accurate, research suggests that you may in fact be completely wrong. While people sometimes talk about having a "photographic memory," human memory doesn't function like a camera to record an exact snapshot of a particular moment in time. Instead, your memory is surprisingly apt to change, with details being exaggerated, subtracted, or even added.

False memories have been the focus of considerable debate among researchers, especially within the criminal justice system where there have been numerous cases in which people have been wrongly convicted of crimes based on inaccurate or downright false memories of eyewitnesses.

In one of the most famous false memory experiments, researchers had participants read accounts of four events from their own childhoods. Three of the stories were true accounts provided by family members of the participant, but the fourth was a false story about the participant getting lost in the mall around the age of five or six. After reading the stories, participants were asked to recall as many details about each event as they could. Participants were interviewed again five more times at two-week intervals. By the end of the six interviews, participants were able to describe either partial or full memories of their experience of being lost in the shopping mall. When the participants were finally told that the memory was entirely false, many were shocked because it had become so vivid and deeply entrenched in their memories. Even after learning the true nature of the experiment, some participants were still able to vividly remember very specific details of the fictitious experience.

The Repression Debate

Professionals within the field of psychology have often debated the validity of repressed memories. In the 1980s, some believed that an individual was indeed able involuntarily to push a memory, especially one that was traumatic, to the unconscious, and was thus unaware of its existence. They believed that the individual could retrieve these memories in an altered state of consciousness, such as hypnosis, and recall perfectly the experience or event that took place.

The theory of repressed memories became a hot topic in the 1990s. You've likely heard of at least one case in which an individual was able to recall a repressed memory of sexual abuse years later through psychotherapy and then filed charges against his or her abuser. While some accusations were corroborated with objective evidence, many were not and relied solely on the individual's recall of the repressed memory. Many believed that such recovered memories of abuse should be believed and viewed as accurate.

However, current thinking is that there is no way to know which memories are valid and which are not, other than by outside corroboration, and the client has to learn to live with that reality. The client would never know which recovered memories were real and which were created under hypnosis, and the damage caused by that would be considerable. Because of the way memory works, recovered memories cannot be considered accurate. As stated earlier, memory makes associations, and when recalled, fills in the gaps with information that can come from a variety of sources. As a result, memory is vulnerable to the power of suggestion. Therefore, a therapist who uses leading questions about sexual abuse may cause a patient to "recover" a memory of abuse that he or she had supposedly repressed. Some believe that because objective corroborative evidence rarely accompanies repressed memories, people and the courts should be skeptical of the authenticity of repressed memories.

Techniques for Improving Your Memory

As have seen, your memory isn't always reliable, and often it seems you forget what you need to remember most. So is all hope lost? Is it all just a game of chance? No. There are strategies you can employ to help preserve that information you want to remember and increase the likelihood of its retrieval. You may already have a few tricks of your own, and by all means continue to use them. If you don't have any or would like to learn more, take a look at the following and see if you can use either of these strategies to help you not to forget.

The SQ3R Method

One of the best ways to trap information for future use is to effectively catch it coming in. The way you encode information determines where it is placed in your long-term memory. If information is encoded in a well-organized and efficient manner, the likelihood of its later retrieval increases. The SQ3R method is one of the best encoding strategies.

In 1941, psychologist Francis Robinson came up with a fantastic strategy for studying (and remembering) written materials. His strategy is called the *SQ3R method*—Survey, Question, Read, Recite, and Review. The first step is to survey, or scan, the material you will be reading. Take only a few minutes to do this. Look over the material, taking in the headings, subheadings, and any charts or illustrations. This will give you an idea of what you will be reading and will prepare your brain for how it will be organized.

Francis Robinson's SQ3R method was invented during World War II to help military personnel in the Army Specialized Training Program comprehend the material they were learning in the accelerated college courses they took for those specialized skills they needed to fight the war.

The next step is to create questions that will be answered in your reading. The easiest way to do this is to turn the headings into questions, such as "What is SQ3R?" After you've come up with a list of questions, read through the material and write down the answers to your questions. To help you recall the information in the future, recite the answers and any other key points you encountered in the material. To finish and set the information in your long-term memory, review the material once again, while continuing to recite important points and the answers to your questions.

Mnemonics

Mnemonics are strategies, such as a rhyme or formula, that are used to improve memory and help you retain and retrieve the information by making use of the information already stored in your long-term memory. Most people were taught at least a few mnemonics during our school days. For instance, do you remember the rhymes "In 1492, Columbus sailed the ocean blue" and "Use *i* before *e* except after *c*"? Your teachers used these clever mnemonics to help you store that information for easy retrieval. Word associations, visual images, rhymes, and formulas can all also be used as mnemonics. You can even create a short story including those words or phrases you need to remember.

Another way to boost your memory of facts and information is to teach what you have learned to another person. Study groups can be particularly beneficial to students because each member can take the role of the teacher and relate what he or she has learned to the rest of the group members. As you can see, there are many different techniques that can help boost your ability to store, retain, and recall information. While you should certainly continue to use the strategies that have worked for you in the past, think about incorporating a new method into your normal routine. Researchers have found that adding an element of novelty to your memorization strategy, such as trying a new study technique or varying the location of your study sessions, you can actually boost your long-term recall of the information.

THINKING, LANGUAGE,
and Intelligence

YOU KNOW HOW INFORMATION enters and is stored in the brain, but then how do you use that information and apply it to your daily life? This chapter is going to explore the inner workings of the mind, while focusing on how the units of knowledge in your mind interconnect, your reasoning abilities, and how you solve problems.

The Cognitive Perspective

Cognitive psychology, as mentioned before, focuses on studying the mental processes. In other words, it studies how people think, reason, solve problems, understand language, remember, form beliefs, etc.—all that good stuff that goes on inside your head. The cognitive processes (such as thinking, reasoning, remembering, etc.) are what allow you to understand your environment and how the environment affects you and in turn how you affect the environment.

Studying Thought

You've learned how you learn, remember what you've learned, and where that information is stored. Now, let's look at how you use that information in your mind to interpret and understand the world around you. Think of the world as a mystery you are constantly trying to solve.

Your mind, in turn, is a mystery cognitive psychologists are constantly trying to solve. As you can imagine, studying thoughts isn't an easy thing to do. Unlike observable behaviors, thoughts are not something you can examine and measure directly. Even if you were to split open someone's head and examine the brain, you still wouldn't be able to study his or her thoughts.

One of the first ways researchers tried to study thought was through introspection, in which participants wrote down ideas, images, and feelings as they experienced them. However, this method was far too subjective. How could psychologists possibly know if people's descriptions of their inner thoughts were accurate? Plus, people are too complicated and do not all have the same thoughts and ideas; therefore, introspection did not last long as a cognitive research tool.

Researchers, therefore, have built models that are used to explain the inner workings of the mind, the most popular being the information-processing model. This model is a hypothetical representation, somewhat analogous to a computer, in which the thought process can be broken down into components, or units of knowledge, that work together as though along an assembly line to process information.

The Big Picture

In a moment, you'll learn about those units of knowledge that work together to create thought, but first, let's take a look at the big picture. First of all, an impression enters your brain through your senses. For instance, let's say you are watching a cooking show on television and a chocolate dessert catches your eye. The brain then manipulates the impression to give it meaning and make sense of it. You love chocolate and the dessert looks scrumptious and certainly like something you would enjoy eating. Next your brain runs through possible responses. You try to recall if you have all the ingredients needed and try to figure out how the cook is making the dessert. Finally, you carry out a response and analyze the results. You go to the kitchen, pull out the ingredients, and try to make the dessert. While this may sound simple enough, the brain is processing several bits of information that must work in conjunction to reach this thought process. Now, let's take a look at those units of knowledge.

Units of Knowledge

As mentioned before, there are units of knowledge that make up the components that work together to process information and create a thought. There are three basic units of knowledge: concepts, prototypes, and schemata.

Concepts

The first unit of knowledge is the concept. This is basically a category that groups together items with similar characteristics or properties. These are the building blocks that are used to create the foundation of thought. Concepts can represent objects, abstract ideas, relationships, or activities. For instance, dog is a concept, but so are love, exercise, marriage, and weather. Each concept has a list of characteristics that define it. For example, dog would have a list that included bark, tail, fur, and four legs. A German shepherd, poodle, Chihuahua, mastiff, and rottweiler are all examples of this concept.

> This isn't to say that all examples must have the exact same characteristics. For instance, not all dogs bark and not all birds fly, but those nonbarking dogs are still examples of the dog concept and those nonflying birds are still examples of the bird concept. All examples of the concept will share a "family resemblance."

Prototypes

Taking the idea of a concept one step further, you come to prototypes. A prototype is basically the most recognizable example of a concept and is therefore the representative of that concept. When your mind is trying to decide where to categorize an impression, it compares that impression with the prototype of a concept. If the impression has similar characteristics to that prototype, it will become an example of that particular concept. For example, your prototype of a chair is likely a piece of furniture used for sitting that has four legs, an upright, straight back, and a square or rectangular seat. When you came across a highchair for the first time, your brain processed the impression, comparing it to the prototype of the chair. Once it determined that the highchair had characteristics similar to that prototype, it was filed away as an example of the concept chair.

Schemata

Concepts are building blocks, so your brain uses them to build. Concepts are put together to create propositions, which are units of meaning expressing a single idea. Come up with a sentence, any sentence. This is a proposition. Propositions that are related are linked and create a network of knowledge and information that makes up a schema. A schema is basically a mental model of what you expect from a particular encounter. These schemata are built using your experience and concepts and allow you to have certain expectations when you encounter ideas, beliefs, situations, or people in your environment. You can create schemata about anything from a jog in the park to a particular religion to a race of people.

So what happens when you encounter information that does not conform to your existing schemata? While most people are easily able to absorb and incorporate new information into their existing worldview, conflicting information can cause a few different things to happen. In some cases, a person might simply choose to ignore a piece of new information that disagrees with his or her existing schema. Generally, this happens on an unconscious level and the person is not even aware that the information has been ignored or forgotten. However, when conflicting information simply cannot be ignored, a schema-changing process known as *assimilation* may take place. For example, imagine a child with an existing schema for cats. According to this child's schema, all cats have four legs, a long tail, and fur. So what happens when the child encounters a three-legged, hairless, bob-tailed cat? The child would probably assimilate this new information into the existing schema for cats, but she might even form a new schema for this particular variety of cat.

Heuristics are a type of mental shortcut that people frequently use to reason and solve problems. A heuristic is basically a rule of thumb that is used to guide your actions toward producing the best possible solution, but this does not mean that the best possible solution will be reached; heuristics are just guidelines and cannot guarantee an outcome.

For instance, those who play chess know that a good rule of thumb is to build up a good defense to protect your king. When you take action to utilize this strategy, you are applying a heuristic. Again, winning the game is not guaranteed from using this heuristic, but it certainly increases your chances! Or perhaps you suspect your significant other of being dishonest with you. While you may not have all the premises to work with, you can use a heuristic to help you solve the mystery: trust a man's actions before his words. Can you think of any other heuristics you often use to reach a solution to informal reasoning problems?

Strategies in Problem Solving

Solving problems is integral to learning. You began solving problems at a very young age. Granted, those problems may seem trivial (how to get a toy) now compared to the problems you face as an adult (how to pay the bills), but they certainly didn't seem trivial at the time. Problems are problems, regardless of the importance or severity; they all have a common goal: to reach a solution. So how do you do that? By employing problem-solving strategies. There are numerous problem-solving strategies out there, but let's take a look at some of the most commonly used.

Trial and Error

Trial and error involves trying out all of the possible solutions until one is found that works. It is most effective in situations where there are a limited number of options. As children, the most common problem-solving strategy we employed was likely trial and error. For instance, let's say the problem a child faces is how to retrieve a toy his mother has put up on a shelf. The child may try to stretch his arms to reach the toy. That doesn't work. Next, he tries to climb up on the shelf to reach the toy. He falls; that doesn't work. When he can't get it on his own, he asks his mother for the toy. She says no; that doesn't work. Still undeterred, the child cries a bit for the toy. The mother ignores the cries; that doesn't work. Finally, he throws a full-blown tantrum, complete with screams, kicks, and tears. Exasperated, the mother gives the child the toy to appease him. Bingo—the tantrum worked. What do you think he's going to do the next time he faces the same problem?

Puzzles are a great example of problems solved through trial and error. There are several types of puzzle games out on the market to help children learn, and they learn through trial and error. In order to complete the puzzle, children have to try to fit a puzzle piece in a particular spot. If that doesn't work, they either keep working with that piece until they find its proper location or they move on to another piece and work with the original spot they were trying to fill.

Brainstorming

Brainstorming is a problem-solving strategy in which you come up with as many possible solutions as you can, usually within a certain period of time. You write down everything that comes to mind, regardless of how ridiculous or implausible it may seem. You simply let your mind go. In using this technique, you are often able to come up with some very creative and imaginative ideas. While not all solutions are going to be able to be employed, chances are you are going to come up with a few that just might work. Once you've created a list and the brainstorming session is over, you can then work through each idea and either discard it or set it aside for closer inspection. By narrowing down the list, you are able to focus your attention on those ideas that are most plausible.

> The next time you are facing a comprehensive problem at work, and you just can't seem to come up with a solution, gather a few of your coworkers and suggest a brainstorming session. Brainstorming is even more effective when you are able to tap the minds of more than one person.

Take It Step-by-Step

Probably the best-known (or at least the most-studied) problem-solving technique is the step-by-step method that was introduced by Allen Newell and Herbert Simon (*Human Problem Solving*, 1972). This strategy breaks down the problem into steps that you go through to reach a solution. Here's a look at the basic principle of each step.

The first step is to identify the problem. You must recognize that a problem exists before you can begin to solve it. The second step is to build a representation of the problem, defining it by stating the problem as it was first introduced and the problem's goal. The third step is to create a list of possible strategies and evaluate each. The fourth step is to choose the best strategy out of those possible and to apply that strategy. The final step is to reflect on the effect of that strategy—in other words, see if it worked.

Decision-Making Strategies

If you've ever faced a complicated or major life decision, you've probably found yourself tempted to let the flip of a coin determine your fate. Fortunately, most of the decisions you make on a daily basis are relatively minor—such as whether to have a sandwich or pizza for lunch, or whether to take the bus or ride with a friend to work. For more complex decisions, there are a number of different strategies you can use to arrive at a conclusion that works best for the situation and your unique needs, interests, or desires.

The goal of all decision-making is to choose a particular course of action out of the available opportunities. In some situations, you might base your decision on a single feature of the possible options. Imagine that you are at the grocery store faced with an entire section of kitchen cleansers. Rather than spend a lot of time reviewing the different brands, you simply base your decision on the factor that is most relevant to you—the price. Another common decision-making strategy involves generating a list of features that are most important to you and then rating the relative importance of each factor. In the kitchen cleanser example, you might list qualities such as price, quantity by volume, past experience with a product, and packaging, giving each a score ranging from 5 to 0. If price is the most important factor, you might give a product a 5 for that factor, but you might also rank it low in another area. The product that ends up achieving the top score based on all of your chosen attributes would then be selected as the "best" option.

In the 1970s, a psychologist named Amos Tversky proposed the "elimination by aspects" model of decision-making. According to this theory, you often do not have time to consider and weigh all of the various attributes of each option. In this situation, you would instead start by establishing a minimum criterion that is most important to you. Then, you would systematically go through each option and immediately eliminate it if it does not meet your criteria. For example, if your primary criterion is to find a kitchen cleanser for less than $4, any option that is higher than that price point will be immediately removed as a possible option.

It is important to remember, however, that decision-making is a very complex process that becomes even more complicated based on the distinctive qualities of each situation and individuals involved. In reality, you are likely to use a wide range of strategies on a daily basis and you probably even utilize aspects of different techniques when making a single decision.

The Characteristics of Language

One of the most amazing aspects of human cognitive abilities is the capacity to understand, learn, and produce language. Language can be defined as a systematic way to convey meaning using symbols and sounds. Communication and language are integral to the study of human psychology. Although there are more than 3,000 languages, spoken and signed, in the world today, all human languages share the same basic characteristics, which will be examined in this chapter. You'll also see whether language is a uniquely human characteristic.

In order to scientifically approach the study of language, you must dispense with some false but widely held linguistic beliefs. First, many people believe that there are languages with no grammar. All human languages have a grammar. Second, many people believe that some languages or dialects are inferior to others. This is often a point of contention with people who worry about "substandard" dialects of their language. In fact, every person speaks a dialect. "Standard" usage is usually determined by the class of speakers with the most social power. There is nothing inherently superior about one dialect versus another. This also holds for different languages. There is simply no such thing as a primitive language. All languages are complex and creative systems used with full efficiency among their speakers.

American Sign Language meets all of the criteria for a language, including generativity and syntax. Researchers have used brain-imaging scans to demonstrate that the same areas of the brain that are activated in people who hear spoken language are also activated in deaf individuals when they use sign language.

While some words correspond to the sounds that they represent, such as *buzz, hiss*, and *bang* in the English language, the connection between the symbol and the meaning is most often completely arbitrary. Language is incredibly flexible for this reason, allowing new words to be created as well as permitting the meaning of existing words to evolve or even change entirely over time. All languages undergo change. For instance, if you read Shakespeare, you will see the drastic changes in the English language that have taken place in just a few centuries.

Each language also has its own rules of syntax and grammar. These rules determine how and when certain words should be combined and in what order they should be presented in order to communicate meaning. In addition to these basic rules, however, it is important to realize that language is infinitely generative, allowing speakers to combine words to produce an endless array of sentences, phrases, and paragraphs. For example, consider the book *Pride and Prejudice* by Jane Austen. While the book does not contain any words that are new to the language, Austen presents these words in a way that is entirely unique and conveys an entirely distinctive story.

Gestures and Other Nonverbal Communication

The human communication system is not limited to language alone. Nonverbal communication is a very important part of human interaction that is so natural it is often overlooked altogether when discussing communication. Facial expressions and hand gestures are a couple of the more obvious forms of nonverbal communication, but posture, stance, eye contact, and even use of space are often used to convey messages. Experts suggest that nonverbal signals make up a huge portion of human communication. Some nonverbal signals can convey meaning on their own, such as a nod of the head to indicate a "yes" response. Other signals—such a smile, wink, or hand movement—can help emphasize spoken words.

Nonverbal communication adds a flavor to everyday communication that just can't be matched in any other way. Consider facial expressions. If you were to approach someone who is smiling broadly as she says hello, you would interpret this as a sign that you are a welcome sight to the person. However, if you were to approach someone and he said hello but had a let-down or annoyed look on his face, you would interpret this as a sign that you are not a person he is particularly happy to see, even though he welcomed you with "hello."

While you may think that the gestures you use are universal, many aren't, so be cautious when using gestures in foreign countries. For example, former president George Bush flashed what he considered to be the peace sign in Britain, though there the gesture was an obscene one, akin to the "middle finger" here in the States.

You use nonverbal communication every day. You nod your head to convey to another that you understand or the answer is yes. You allow others their personal space to convey that you are not a threat. You make eye contact with a speaker to show that you are listening to what is being said. You wave hello and goodbye. The list could go on and on.

Pay attention to your use of nonverbal communication and gestures for just one day and you will soon understand how important it is to human interaction and the conveying of messages. If you want to improve your own ability to understand nonverbal behaviors, start by looking carefully at the signals presented by the people you encounter every day. Watch for gestures that don't seem to match up with what a person is saying, such as a friend with slumped shoulders and a somber expression saying that he is having a great day. However, always remember that nonverbal signals can sometimes be misread and don't be afraid to ask questions if you're not quite sure what type of message someone is trying to send out.

Can Other Animals Learn Human Language?

The short answer to this question is no, animals cannot learn human language. In order to answer this question, one must distinguish between human language and other forms of communication. Language is a creative and infinite system. Many other animals have complex systems of communication. Some bees, for example, can communicate information about their food: where it is and how far, and its quantity. Several species of birds and monkeys are known to have complex signaling systems. These forms of communication are different from language in that they are very limited. Humans can talk about the past, future, or fictional events. They utter sentences that they have never seen or heard before. They have the ability to use language to alter the thoughts and ideas of other humans.

There have been many attempts to teach animals language. Usually the pupil is a primate, being a human's closest relative. One such attempt involved a chimpanzee called Nim Chimpsky after the famous linguist Noam Chomsky. While Nim was quite successful compared to many other subjects, his linguistic abilities never even reached a level comparable to the level of a four-year-old human child. He could not master syntax and his vocabulary was quite small. Many scientists theorize that the primates are not actually mastering symbolic language but rather are learning behavioral responses to their human trainers. Language is uniquely human. This is not denigrating to animals. Each species has its own communication system.

The Clever Hans controversy involved a horse that appeared to be able to do math and communicate messages by tapping his hoof. It turned out that Clever Hans could not do this when he could not see his trainer. His was a feat of perception only.

One of the most interesting examples of research on animal cognition was with an African Grey parrot named Alex (an acronym for Avian Language EXperiment). Psychologist Irene Pepperberg trained Alex for two decades and he was able to acquire a vocabulary of approximately 100 words for objects, colors, shapes, and numbers in addition to some simple phrases. When asked a question, such as what color a particular object was or how many of a certain item were presented, Alex could accurately answer the question. This research provides a fascinating look at what animals might be capable of in terms of communication and language, but conclusions whether animals can actually "think" are far from confirmed.

Measuring Intelligence

So far, you've learned about some of the major cognitive abilities studied by psychologists including problem solving, decision-making, and language. All of these abilities can be considered part of what psychologists commonly refer to as intelligence, a subject that has served as a major point of interest and controversy in psychology. While few psychologists agree on a single definition of intelligence, for its purposes this book will refer to it as the ability to mentally comprehend information, which involves the capacity to reason, think abstractly, plan, learn, utilize language, and solve problems.

The earliest attempts to measure intelligence began early in the twentieth century when the French government asked psychologist Alfred Binet (1857–1911) to devise a method to identify children who might need specialized assistance in school. Binet devised a series of questions focused on things such as problem solving, memory, and attention. After observing that some children answered questions that were typically known by children of either a lower or higher age group, Binet introduced a concept referred to as mental age, a measurement of intelligence that is based on the average abilities of a given age group.

Does a high IQ predict success in life?
In one longitudinal study of 1,500 California children, researchers found that having a high IQ as a child was no guarantee for later life success. Other factors such as motivation, social support, and hard work also play a major role in life success.

The intelligence scale that Binet developed became the basis for the modern intelligence tests that are still being used today. One widely used assessment tool is the Stanford-Binet, which presents a measurement of intelligence in a single number known as an *intelligence quotient* (IQ). The average intelligence score is 100, and two-thirds of all IQ scores range between 85 and 115.

Theories of Intelligence

As you learned earlier, intelligence is one of the most talked about topics in psychology, but there are a wide variety of definitions of what exactly constitutes intelligence. Some researchers believe that intelligence is a single, general ability; others feel that there are actually many different kinds of intelligence. British psychologist Charles Spearman (1863–1945) suggested something he referred to as general intelligence, or the "g" factor, was responsible for a person's overall performance on a wide variety of tests and was the driving force behind a number of different mental abilities. On the other hand, psychologist Louis L. Thurstone (1887–1955) disagreed with Spearman's theory and instead suggested that intelligence was actually made up of seven different primary mental abilities that included reasoning, perceptual speed, numerical ability, and word fluency. He believed that each person has a different pattern of abilities.

In recent years, a man named Howard Gardner (1943–) has expanded Thurstone's original concept of primary mental abilities to create a much broader interpretation of intelligence. Gardner suggests that numerical test scores cannot fully or accurately represent the full range of human intelligence, and instead proposes a theory of multiple intelligences. His theory focuses on eight distinctive intelligences, such as linguistic intelligence, musical intelligence, and mathematical intelligence, which are valued in different cultures. While Gardner's theory has become quite popular among educators, many critics have suggested that the "intelligences" he describes are simply specialized talents. Another prominent researcher named Robert Sternberg (1949–) has proposed a triarchic theory of intelligence, which suggests that intelligence is made up of three different mental abilities. Analytic intelligence involves problem-solving abilities, practical intelligence involves the ability to adapt to changes in the environment, and creative intelligence involves the ability to use prior knowledge and existing skills to deal with new situations and experiences.

The exact nature of intelligence and how to best measure it are bound to be a hot topic in psychology for years to come. As you have learned, people draw on a wide range of cognitive abilities to solve problems, make decisions, and communicate with others.

MOTIVES—

Why You Do the Things You Do

THINK FOR A MOMENT about what inspired you to pick up this book. The "thing" that led you to begin reading this text is what researchers refer to as motivation, which includes the biological, social, emotional, and cognitive forces that instigate and guide your behavior. This chapter will distinguish between the different types of motives people respond to; how to recognize them cognitively, physiologically and emotionally; the dangers of misinterpreting their signals; and their role in sexual behavior.

Varieties of Motives

Motives that have not been learned, such as the need to acquire physical things, are called basic motives, distinguishable in that humans share them with other animals. They can be broken down into three classes: survival (hunger and thirst), social (sex and maternal expression), and curiosity (conscious investigation).

Since survival motives are directly dependent on a healthy physical state, homeostatic systems are crucial in picking up on body signals that warn of an imbalance and disruption of the internal mechanisms. The ability of the body to adapt to constant change allows it to recognize, for example, when blood sugar levels reach a point below what is healthy. Once this recognition occurs, a cry for help is put out (need) and the appropriate drive is stimulated, causing the organism to perform the actions that are necessary (obtaining food high in sugar) in returning blood sugar levels back to normal.

> Diabetes is a lifelong disease that occurs when there are high levels of sugar in the blood. It can be caused by too little insulin (type 1), resistance to it (type 2), or both. Type 2 diabetes is usually developed during adulthood. Currently, there is no cure for diabetes.

The Brain's Role in Motivation

Regulation of body temperature, specific metabolic processes, and other autonomic activities all take place in the brain's hypothalamus region, which also determines blood temperature by way of sensors. These sensors are additionally present inside the mouth, skin, spinal cord, and brain, allowing you to differentiate between hot and cold.

Setting the Thermostat

The anterior, or frontal, portion of the brain is responsible for making sure body temperature remains consistently normal by following a process similar to that of a thermostat. Existing temperature is "read" by sensors and compared to what the normal temperature should be. If the readout turns up an irregularity, specific physiological adjustments will attempt to correct the problem by producing sweat when hot and shivers when cold. In addition, external behavioral adjustments may be prompted, for example, covering up with a blanket when you're cold and tossing the blanket to the side when you're warm.

Although both physiological and behavioral adjustments occur in the hypothalamus, the differences between them are as follows:

Behavioral

- Willful acts of selfishness

- Drive elicits the response

- External conditions are influenced

- Housed in the lateral area of the hypothalamus

Physiological

- Uncontrollable physical acts

- Need elicits the response

- Internal conditions are influenced

- Housed in the preoptic area of the hypothalamus

Behavioral and physiological adjustments, as different as they are, work together toward the shared goal of regulating the body's temperature, a process necessary to survival. Temperatures too high above or too far below the norm of 98.6° Fahrenheit (F) must be treated immediately, otherwise organs may become permanently damaged or death may result.

> Hypothermia (body temperature below the norm) must be treated when temperature drops below 95°F, and becomes fatal when it drops below 90°F. Fever is when body temperature rises above normal, but doesn't become much of a concern until it reaches at least 100°F.

Severe weather conditions when not guarded against can cause the body to go into shock. For example, Alaska's lowest average temperature during winter (between December and February) is –15.7°F. A person simply cannot walk outside with only one layer of clothing and a heavy jacket without experiencing instant frostbite and symptoms of hypothermic shock.

In contrast, Arizona's climate can reach temperatures as high as 120°F, so if a person takes a day trip to the middle of the desert with only a short supply of water, the body's ability to keep cool is dominated by extreme external temperatures that cause it to "over-heat" and suffer from heat stroke. Drastic irregularities in body temperature result in various degrees of physical decline.

When the body reaches certain degrees of temperature, specific reactions are experienced as shown here:

- 82.7°F = muscle failure

- 91.4°F = unconsciousness

- 107.6°F = breakdown of central nervous system

- 111.2°F = death

Theories of Motivation

- A number of broad theories have been proposed to explain motivation. As you read through these theories, it may immediately become clear that each theory is useful for explaining certain aspects of motivation, but no single theory can fully illuminate all of the many reasons why people do the things they do. In order to gain a full and complete understanding of human motivation, it is essential to understand the basic concepts behind each theory.

- Instinct theories suggest that motivation arises from evolutionary programming. For example, certain types of animals are motivated to migrate seasonally due to instinctual patterns that are inborn in their species.

- Drive theories propose that behavior is motivated by homeostasis. Unmet biological needs, such as hunger and thirst, motivate humans and animals to perform actions that will fulfill those needs and reduce internal tension.

- Incentive theories suggest that behavior is motivated by external rewards. For example, you are motivated to work by the potential rewards of money, security, and recognition.

- Arousal theories are centered around the idea that people are motivated to maintain optimal arousal levels. When arousal levels are too low, you might seek out arousing activities such as exercise or watching horror films. If arousal levels become too high, you might look for relaxing activities such as meditation, yoga, or a hot bath.

■ Humanistic theories emphasize the role of self-concept and the need to achieve your full potential to explain human motivation. One of the most famous humanistic motivation theories was proposed by psychologist Abraham Maslow, who suggested that the ultimate human motivator is the desire for self-actualization, or to achieve your fullest individual potential.

The Physiology of Motivation

Your survival is directly dependent on two fundamental operations: body temperature and sufficient water supply. Homeostatic processes ensure these operations run smoothly and when necessary activate emergency systems in an effort to restore balance to the body. When these systems fail—temperatures are too high or too low for too long, or dehydration is present for several days—death is inevitable.

Blood Temperature

Since protein is one of the major components that propel a cell's activity, when it becomes dormant in temperatures above 113°F, cells cannot perform their responsibilities. Similarly, when water inside cells freezes, ice crystals develop and ultimately shut them down.

When temperature is not at the desired level, physiological adjustments in addition to possible behavioral adjustments are automatically induced in a variety of ways, including sweating, panting, and shivering. The skin's capillaries expand and contract to control blood by either producing excessive amounts of it beneath the surface of the skin (expansion) or reserving the depleting supply of it for organs (contraction). Excessive heat is then released through sweat glands located on the body in the form of sweating, as seen in humans, horses, and cows, or through sweat glands located on the tongue in the form of panting, as seen in dogs, cats, and rats. The act of shivering resolves heat shortages by creating warmth.

Internal Water Supply

Water is essential to human existence because it transports nutrients and oxygen to tissues and helps purge wastes from the body. If you become dehydrated, your basic thirst motivation is triggered and replenishing liquids in your body becomes a primary goal. Because constant water loss is a natural function of the body, it is kept in check by maintaining intracellular and extracellular fluid.

Depletion of intracellular fluid occurs when water outside a cell contains higher quantities of sodium than water inside a cell. The cell then becomes dehydrated and shrinks, sending the message that an adjustment needs to be made.

> Kidneys play an important role in this adjustment. Before water is released through urination, the antidiuretic hormone (ADH) is unleashed, allowing water instead to be retrieved and directed to the bloodstream.

Extracellular fluid loss is caused by excessive amounts of blood loss as well as loss of sodium through sweating. The kidneys become key players in regulating fluids by restoring blood volume to normal levels. They do this by constricting blood vessels, which allow blood loss to take place, through the release of an enzyme into the bloodstream.

Since it is impossible to decide when these fluids are fully restored without being monitored by machines, satiety sensors (found in the intestines) do all the work by telling the body it has enough water to regulate dehydrated cells.

The Hunger Motive

When you're hungry, you eat. It seems like a simple and straightforward process, but the reality is that the hunger motive is influenced by biological, psychological, cultural, and social factors. One element alone doesn't make you hungry; rather several occurrences working together to provide the body with energy trigger the motive to eat. Homeostasis contributes by regulating metabolism and digestion via monitoring supplies needed to produce nutrients, while satiety sensors (as first encountered in relation to the thirst motive) serve as lookout stations set up to detect when supplies are on the way. On a more abstract level, external influence and culture-specific rituals can sometimes stimulate your desire to eat by recalling memories of how certain foods or celebrations made you feel euphoric.

Homeostasis Gets the Ball Rolling

One of the main reasons you experience hunger is that your body tells you it is so. Much like a new mother learns to distinguish between her baby's cries for hunger, cries for discomfort, and cries for sickness, a person who is "in tune" with his body learns to differentiate between hunger pangs and nervous rumblings. If you listen to your body, the hunger subsides; however, if you ignore the signals your body gives off, more signals will be given—physical weakness and lethargy, for example.

While all this action takes place externally, a different kind of internal action is responsible for what eventually produces the hunger pangs you experience. In order for your cells to function properly, nutrients must be made available. This is the primary goal of digestion. Food goes in, breaks down into simpler compounds, and gets recycled into concentrated forms of energy. Glucose, or the primary sugar found in blood, is a major source of energy for the brain and can be regulated either by obtaining it from the liver's storage supply or by eating food.

Sensors Make Sense

Now that you know you're hungry, how do you know when you're full? In other words, how is the body informed that nutrients will eventually be present if digestion itself takes four hours to complete? The decreased desire to eat is known as *satiation,* and the body sends off a number of satiation signals to let you know when to stop eating. Sensors located in the stomach and liver let the body know that nutrients will be coming shortly. Stretch receptors in the stomach send sensory information to the brain stem, alerting your body that the stomach is full. Psychological factors play an important role as well. After polishing off a big plate of spaghetti, eating more spaghetti seems very unappealing.

Abstract Motivation

The desire to eat food that you know tastes good is often mistaken for the need to eat it. After consuming a satisfying, seven-course meal that made you feel "stuffed," why would you continue to eat when dessert is brought to the table? You already fulfilled your body's request for food, so it certainly has nothing to do with your need for it.

An abstract idea concerning eating habits involves "the holidays," a three-month period in which massive quantities of food are readily available at almost any given time at any given place. Why do we continue to prepare and eat so much food year after year during the holidays when we know it is not necessary to our physical well-being? Because these rituals are part of the customs that define our culture and society, and since we are members of that society, our participation in the rituals is an expression of celebration.

Memory can provide a possible explanation. Remembering how you felt the last time you ate dessert might trigger your desire to feel that way again if the reaction was favorable. And, considering the amount of sugar most desserts are made with; the "rush" one feels after eating dessert is similar to the feeling of euphoria.

Eating Disorders

The physical need for food is a normal function of the body to remain in healthy, working condition, and more important, to stay alive. Although the physical need for food is the primary motivator that directs humans to consume food, emotions, behaviors and attitudes are also important contributors. Eating disorders involve serious disturbances in eating behavior and attitudes toward food. These disorders can involve drastic reductions in food consumption, eating excessive amounts of food, and distorted thinking about weight and body image. Anorexia, bulimia, and binge eating are all examples of eating disorders; however, the most prevalent eating disorder in our society is obesity.

Genetically Inherited Obesity

Body fat is stored in fat cells, and genetic inheritance is one of the factors that dictates the number of fat cells an organism has. Members of an obese family are more likely to produce additional obese members, thus perpetuating the cycle. Research shows that in addition to the number of fat cells you have, the size of the fat cells can cause you to become obese. Overeating during the stages of infancy can contribute to the size of fat cells, but overeating, at this stage, is controlled by guardians who most likely inherited nursing practices from one of their own family members. According to the National Center for Health Statistics, more than 64 percent of U.S. adults (approximately 115 million people) are overweight or obese.

Memory can provide a possible explanation. Remembering how you felt the last time you ate dessert might trigger your desire to feel that way again if the reaction was favorable. And, considering the amount of sugar most desserts are made with; the "rush" one feels after eating dessert is similar to the feeling of euphoria.

Emotion as a Motive

When hunger is confused with other feelings, emotional eating ensues. One hypothesis suggests that this mix-up established its roots in infancy when our caregivers interpreted most of our cries as cries for hunger, thereby frequently mistaking anxiety for hunger. Another hypothesis suggests that because caregivers regularly comforted the infant with food, obese adults innately mimic that behavioral response because it seems to calm them down. As mentioned earlier, when you associate euphoric feelings with eating, the act of eating becomes something desirable rather than something needed. For example, someone going through a very stressful period of time might overeat as a way to lower anxiety and induce pleasant feelings.

Metabolism and Exercise

The lower the metabolism, the fewer the calories spent and, incidentally, the higher the body weight. Dieting slows metabolism as well, which helps explain the "breaking even" point during dieting that may halt weight loss.

Exercise helps maintain a regular metabolism, and when it is absent from an obese person's life, it may cause a domino effect of repeated inactivity. Four out of ten adults in the United States report that they never exercise or engage in physically demanding activities. Excessive body weight makes it difficult and uncomfortable to exercise, so the opportunity to burn a substantial amount of calories is lost. Fat tissue then replaces lean tissue, causing a reduction in the person's basic metabolic rate. This combination of unspent calories and reduced metabolism makes for rapid weight gain that can become dangerously out of control if not addressed right away.

The Motive for Sex

Whereas survival motives such as thirst and hunger occur in relation to the self, social motives like sex mostly involve another person. The obvious difference between sex and other motives is that sex is not necessary for your individual survival. While it is certainly necessary for the continuation of the species, you won't die if you don't have sex. Social motives do not need to be regulated in order for survival to continue; their influences are hormonal and environmental.

Hermaphrodites are individuals who are born with both male and female genital tissues—ovaries and a penis, for example. An imbalance in prenatal hormones is responsible for this abnormal development and occurs when there is an excess of the genital development hormone androgen in the female fetus or not enough of it in the male fetus.

Hormonal Changes

Puberty occurs somewhere between ages eleven and fourteen and causes people to think in depth about their sexuality for the first time. Hormones in females (estrogen) produce breasts, "shapely curves," and genital advancement, while hormones in males (testosterone) produce development of facial and underarm hair, voice changes, muscle definition, and genital growth.

These natural changes prepare the body for sexual interaction by displaying obvious external developments that tell the world (potential mates) it's ready to reproduce. While teenagers may become physically mature, all too often their response to their own sexuality involves choices that have not been analyzed with maturity, and all too often result in circumstances they are not yet prepared for.

Environmental Influences

Different cultures have different levels of tolerance for the same behaviors, such as premarital sex, masturbation, or homosexuality. The same behavior, such as intercourse with a girl who hasn't reached puberty, may be punishable by death in some cultures, while it is more acceptable in others.

Even further, specific attitudes differ significantly between men and women and involve emotion, self-worth, desire, and frustration. The following sexual attitude differences between men and women was developed after asking college students to list their concerns with all aspects of sexuality and was taken from Carol Tavris and Carole Offir's *The Longest War: Sex Differences in Perspective* (1977). Women listed such things as fear of pregnancy, fear of being raped, and fear of being rejected if they said no to sex. Men listed such things as not being able to have sex when they wanted to, being expected to know everything about sex, and the inability to communicate feelings and needs during sex.

Sexual Orientation

In the past, homosexuality was considered to be either a mental illness or a sexual abnormality related to hormonal imbalance. Multiple studies have shown that homosexuals can be as well adjusted as heterosexuals, and experiments involving hormonal manipulation by injection seemed to affect only the person's sex drive and not his or her sexual preference.

The cause for homosexuality still remains to be discovered; however, new theories are constantly being developed and tested. Considering that biological factors play a strong role in motivating sexual behavior, it is only natural that there has been considerable interest in the possible biological causes of sexual orientation. The results of twin studies suggest that there is a genetic component involved in determining sexual orientation. Among brothers, for example, the closer the genetic similarity the more likely it is that both siblings will be either homosexual or heterosexual. If one brother is homosexual, just over 50 percent of identical siblings will share this same-sex orientation, while the number drops to just over 20 percent among fraternal twins. The brain structures of heterosexuals and homosexuals have also been studied, and researchers suggest that differences in a small cluster of neurons in the hypothalamus may be involved in determining sexual orientation. At any rate, homosexuality has become more accepted; same-sex marriage in some parts of the world is legal. While the exact cause of homosexuality is unknown, researchers have found that two of the most commonly repeated myths about sexual orientation—that homosexuality is caused by childhood sexual molestation or by an abnormal relationship with a parental figure— are both false.

—◆—

EMOTIONS—
Feeling Up, Feeling Down

THE GAMUT OF EMOTION one human being is capable of experiencing can certainly make a person feel like he's on a roller coaster—going up, coming down; becoming excited, then fearful; anxious and tense, then joyful and relieved. This chapter looks at the attempt to define what an emotion is by exploring both the physical and nonphysical factors that contribute to its genesis.

Emotions Versus Motives

In order to understand the similarities and differences between emotions and motives, it's important to establish a guideline for what an emotion is. Possible definitions combine mental and biological aspects of emotion and spotlight the physiological, subjective, cognitive, and reactive elements that make up an emotion. Each of these elements will be discussed in more detail later on in this chapter.

Like motives, emotions can set behavior into action and direct its course to achieve a goal. Some can also be directly associated with motives—the same activity fulfills a need as well as provokes an emotional response. Eating, for example, is the result of a motive to satisfy hunger, as well as a possible means to experience joy. But as similar as emotions and motives may be, it's important to recognize their differences in order to understand their effects on your life.

Initiating a Response

One of the major differences between emotion and motive is how the response is triggered. External occurrences cause emotions to surface internally as a reaction to the situation, whereas internal occurrences such as thirst elicit direct activity toward an external objective such as water. Where emotion is a psychic and physical reaction that is subjectively experienced, motive is a need or desire that propels a person to act.

> Results from surveys conducted by the Centers for Disease Control concluded that during a period of almost ten years the proportion of the population with obesity increased 61 percent. Emotional eating is a major contributor to these statistics because both overweight and obese individuals have reported that their food intake is more extensive during intensely emotional situations.

However, this observation is not set in stone. Have you ever flipped through a magazine and, after coming across a photograph of, for example, a delectable, honey-glazed baked ham with all the trimmings, suddenly realized that you were hungry? Looking at food, whether in a magazine or on the shelf at the grocery store, can trigger what you think is hunger. But is it truly hunger if you weren't hungry before you picked up the magazine? As you learned in Chapter 10, hunger is a basic need of survival, but when it becomes confused with emotion, the need to survive is replaced with the need to feel good, and the mental and physical aspects of hunger can become indiscernible.

Looking at the photograph of the ham may bring back memories of how delicious it tasted the last time you ate it, so your initial response is emotional—tasty food is enjoyable—but in order to justify your need for eating the ham, you have to assume that you were hungry.

Activating the Autonomic Nervous System

Another difference between emotions and motives is that emotions may indirectly stimulate the autonomic nervous system, in which dramatic physical changes progress rapidly, such as increased heart rate, muscle tension, dry mouth, or "butterflies" in the stomach, while motives may not. The sympathetic division of the autonomic nervous system controls these symptoms and is responsible for the following internal changes as well:

- Individual breaths become shorter and occur faster.

- The pupils become dilated.

- Levels of perspiration rise, while saliva and mucous dispersion decreases.

- Energy is produced due to an increase in blood sugar levels.

- Accelerated blood clotting occurs to prepare for wounds.

- Skin hairs rise, producing "goose bumps."

These homeostatic imbalances occur especially when fear or anger is experienced at extreme levels. When anger is expressed, the sensation of rising body temperature feels as if the blood is "boiling" and the face becomes so red it seems as though you might "blow your top." In fact, this type of anger causes one literally and physically to "lose his cool," causing the body to begin restoring itself to its normal state by bringing down its temperature via perspiration.

Arrectores pilorum, or hair erector muscles, contract when stimuli such as cold or fear create a nerve discharge. As a result of the tiny contracting muscles, hair follicles rise above the skin, developing what we call goose bumps.

Just as emotional reactions can result in physical responses, physical feelings can also lead to emotional responses. When a person is suffering from the physical torments of relentless hunger and the motivation to obtain food cannot be satisfied, emotions such as depression and sadness can ensue.

The Physiology of Emotion

Internal, physical reactions to emotion occur when your autonomic nervous system is called into action. Depending on the emotion and its intensity, the body's energy distribution either increases or decreases. When anger or fear is experienced, the pulse quickens and shortness of breath and trembling may take place, while emotions such as heartache, grief, and regret may cause bodily functions to slow down significantly. When this takes place, you fall into a depression, resulting in excessive sleeping and physical weakness.

The James-Lange Theory of Emotions

How you are able to differentiate emotions is the subject of much debate. William James and Carl Lange (1834–1900) theorized that it is the physical actions and reactions that determine the subjective experience of an emotion. Common sense tells you that you run from danger because you're afraid. In complete opposition, James's idea focused on the physiological aspect of emotion, holding the position that you are afraid because you run and you are excited because you shout. Lange's ideas were similar, only he took it further and included autonomic responses as well. He suggested that not only are you afraid because you run, you are afraid because your heart is beating rapidly. So, for example, imagine that you are walking through the woods and you come upon a mountain lion. Your heartbeat races, your breathing quickens, and you start to tremble. Based on James's and Lange's ideas, your brain looks at these physical reactions and concludes that you are frightened, leading to your emotion of fear. Arriving at these conclusions at about the same time, the two positions were combined and the James-Lange theory was born.

Arguments Against the James-Lange Theory

Walter Cannon (1871–1945) strongly disagreed with the James-Lange theory for several reasons. First, he argued that due to the body's lack of nerve-sensitive organs, visceral changes are too slow to take place and therefore are not contributing factors in felt emotions. Second, emotions that are experienced after epinephrine injections are not true emotions as much as they are physical affectations (accelerated pulsations, sweaty palms). Cannon's final argument acknowledged that the autonomic patterns of emotions are often too similar to be a source of distinction—for example, fear, anger and love all incite a faster heartbeat. This suggests that other factors are at work in differentiating emotions.

The Brain's Role in Emotion

Although technological advancements have been able to detect internal differences from one emotion to the next, it doesn't hold true for all emotions. Fear is the emotion most studied by psychologists, perhaps because it's effects are among the most pronounced out of all emotional responses. Brain research has found that the amygdala, a tiny structure in the limbic system, plays a critical role in emotion. Brain imaging scans have shown that this tiny cluster of neurons becomes activated when people view pictures of threatening faces. Researchers have found that damage to the amygdala causes people to lose their ability to distinguish between friendly and threatening facial expressions. Additional factors play a major role in emotional responses, and one of those factors is how the brain expresses and recognizes facial expressions.

Emotions that are universal, such as happiness or anger, utilize distinctive muscles to express those emotions. This implies that the neurological system that makes this possible was part of human evolution, allowing nonverbal communication through facial signals and recognition of those signals to be valuable to hunting and survival techniques.

Located in the right cerebral hemisphere, this neurological system is not your only aid in the process of enabling you to express emotion. Variations in voice projection (pitch, tone, and stress), which are also controlled by a specific neurological system housed in the right cerebral hemisphere, make it possible for you to scream or laugh.

Varieties of Emotions

Emotions vary in intensity, and your interpretation of day-to-day situations through cognitive appraisal dictates the quality and type of emotion you experience. In S. Schachter and J. Singer's study published in *Psychological Review* (1962), they detail an experiment conducted to determine if cognitive appraisal indeed would create a subjective response regardless of autonomic behavior.

What is cognitive appraisal?
It's an individual's personal estimation of events or situations in relation to her or his goals and beliefs. It also affects the significance and level of intensity at which the emotion is experienced as well as the seriousness of the threat.

Preconditioned Appraisals

Subjects were injected with epinephrine and given specific information regarding the effect the drug would have on them. Some of them were told the drug would make them euphoric while others were told it would make them feel angry. In actuality, all subjects experienced the same physical reactions to the drug, including increased heart rate, trembling, and rapid breathing. Each subject was then directed to a waiting room where he or she encountered a person posing as another subject who had also been injected with the drug. If the real subject had been told he or she would experience euphoria, then the confederate would act out that emotion by amusing himself with paper airplanes, wastebasket basketball, etc. In the rooms where subjects were told they would feel angry, the accomplice would display that behavior by complaining or storming out of the room.

In addition to stimulating autonomic nerve action, epinephrine is used to reverse the advanced stages of anaphylaxis, a potentially life-threatening allergic reaction that severely attacks the body by affecting the skin, the respiratory system, gastrointestinal tracts, and the cardiovascular system.

Since the autonomic responses of both anger and euphoria are similar (increased heart rate, fidgety behavior, and breathing patterns), the injection worked in conjunction with the preconditioned mindset (anger or euphoria) to elicit a total emotional experience. Those who encountered the euphoric confederate generally recorded their feelings as happy, while the subjects who came in contact with the angry confederate recorded negative feelings.

Assessing the Situation

Rather than subscribing to the theory that emotion is rooted solely in physical reactions, the previously outlined experiment suggests that both autonomic arousal and the interpretation of the situation that causes the arousal are key factors in producing an emotional response. In fact, your perception of life experiences becomes even more important in determining the emotion and, in turn, the physiological repercussions of that emotion.

A single occurrence, then, can provoke a full range of emotions depending on the person experiencing the event. For example, if a young woman marries a very attractive young man with a severe drinking problem, her feelings may be primarily joyous. At the same time, her rival might experience sadness, her parents' anxiety, and his parents' relief. Each person's assessment of the same experience triggered a completely different emotion, although all parties involved most likely had a shared anatomic response: tears.

Aggressive Behavior

Innovative technological advancements result in many positive improvements to our society as a whole as well as in relation to other societies, but they consequently lead to inevitable negative aspects such as weapons of mass destruction. In return, the presence of aggressive behavior in our society continues to rise in part because of our continual exposure to it via the media, movies, and video games, and also in part because of our innate, primitive drive toward instinctive aggression.

Behind the Wheel of Aggression

Freud's psychoanalytical theory that almost all of humankind's actions can be traced to sexual instinct is formulated around the idea that unfulfilled sexual desire leads to frustration, which is expressed by aggression. In *Frustration and Aggression* by John Dollard, et al. (1939), Freud's theory is further developed with the frustration-aggression hypothesis, which proposes that whenever something prevents a person from achieving a goal, it's perceived as an obstruction, whether animate or inanimate, and needs to be injured, hence the aggressive drive.

Steering the Wheel of Aggression

Almost all reported instances of violence, whether in newspapers or on the local news network, fail to give the complete history of the aggressor. More often than not, the chain of events that led up to the eventual crime is pertinent information in attempting to trace the nature of aggressive behavior. The snowball effect, which begins with repressed frustration and leads to a buildup of destructive behavior patterns that manifest themselves in a variety of hostile ways, comes to an end with an ultimate, barbaric act. If the root of this eventual act is not discovered, understood, and treated, the cycle may be triggered and the sequence will begin all over again.

From a biological standpoint, arousing specific regions of the brain causes equally specific aggressive reactions. Stimulating different regions of a cat's hypothalamus causes the cat to react either in a wild display of aggression by hissing and striking out or in a sophisticated form of premeditated hunting that results in the prey's death. Monkeys, on the other hand, follow a hierarchy of dominance and act accordingly based on recollections of past experiences.

> Since parents possess the most influential power over their children by constantly being observed by their children in natural settings, the way they treat violence and the frequency with which they resort to aggressive behavior is likely to be imitated by their children.

In Chapter 2 you learned about one famous experiment in which children observed an adult beating up and abusing an inflatable doll. When children were later placed in a room with the same doll, many of them imitated the aggressive behavior they observed previously. The children were even more likely to mimic the angry actions if they had observed the adults being rewarded for this type of behavior.

The Effect of Television and Video Game Violence on Children

As seen in the experiment with the Bobo doll, young children often imitate viewed aggression because they associate people on television with being role models for adulthood. Children believe the action is justified because a "grownup" did it, and therefore understand it to be a part of "growing up" in today's society. Television violence's effect on children results in aggressive behavior for a number of other reasons, including the following:

Elevated levels of arousal—D. K. Osborn and R. C. Endsley's study published in the journal *Child Development* (1971) shows how children are more apt to become emotionally aroused while viewing violent programs by measuring the increase in their galvanic skin responses. The increase is notably higher when viewing violent behavior.

Excessive exposure leads to desensitizing people to violence—The shock of violent behavior subsides after repeated incidents of violence are experienced, thus stunting our ability to react appropriately and effectively to real-life situations and provide help when needed.

Mixed messages on settling conflicts—Children don't often recognize whether a situation is fictional or based in reality, so when they see the timeless struggle of good versus evil played out on television by their favorite cartoon characters, they also develop a positive image of how good triumphs over evil through violent means.

The potential impact of video game violence has become a hot topic among psychologists, educators and, parents. In one study by Craig Anderson and Karen Dill (2000), researchers found that participants who played a violent video game scored higher on a measurement of aggression than those who had played a nonviolent video game. Some psychologists suggest that the influence of violent video games may even be more pronounced than television and movies since children are actually taking on the role of the aggressor during game play. In a 2005 report, the American Psychological Association concluded that, based upon their research, exposure to violent video games increases aggressive feelings, thoughts, and behaviors.

Do We All Have the Same Emotions?

Some emotions are indeed universal in scope. Happiness, anger, fear, and sadness produce similar facial expressions, which are recognizable in cultures outside of Western civilization. This shared reaction illustrates Darwin's belief that emotions are instinctive responses that evolved from a crucial need to develop multiple survival techniques.

Although certain emotions are shared, individual expression of that emotion is what makes it appear to be different. Each person's reaction to a situation is subjective, and how that situation is interpreted is based on personal beliefs, past experiences, and physical capabilities. The level of intensity at which the emotion is felt and the individual's dramatic expression of it are what make our communication of emotions different.

HUMAN DEVELOPMENT—

Conception, Infancy, and Childhood

DEVELOPMENTAL PSYCHOLOGY CAN help you understand the physical, cognitive, and social changes that occur in a human life. Beginning with the union of two cells and ending in a full-grown human being, the development of a person is incredibly complex. This chapter will start with the biological development of the human and advance into the psychological development of a baby and continue to follow this developmental journey up to infancy.

Genes, Gametes, and Conception

The conception process is very complex and important to understanding human development. Conception begins with the fusion of an egg cell and a sperm cell, or gametes. At birth, a female has all the immature eggs that she will use throughout the course of her life. A male human being starts producing sperm when he reaches puberty (around 1,000 sperm in a second, but this rate slows as the male ages).

> Though a female is born with all her eggs, not all these eggs will reach maturity. Approximately only 1 in 5,000 of a female's eggs reach maturity. When an egg reaches maturity, that egg is then able to produce offspring.

From 200 to 600 million sperm are released in the average ejaculation but a rare few make it to the actual egg, and only one sperm is needed to form a zygote (or a fertilized single-celled egg, the earliest form of human beings). As soon as that one lucky sperm begins to penetrate the jellylike outer coating of the egg cell, the egg becomes defensive and the surface of the egg cell hardens to block out any other sperm cell from penetration. The sperm uses digestive enzymes to work its way through the egg's surface.

Cell Division

Once the zygote is formed, the cell goes into the division process. The first division is called *mitosis*. In mitosis, the zygote divides to form two identical daughter cells. Later, the cell begins another form of division called *meiosis*. Meiosis produces four daughter cells, each daughter cell containing half the chromosomes of each original parent cell. Meiosis is necessary to keep the chromosome number constant from generation to generation. The divisions will continue, until a human being is formed. The cells move, or migrate, in relation to other cells, forming the first shape of the embryo; this migration is called *morphogenesis*.

Gene Codes

Each gamete (egg and sperm) has twenty-three chromosomes, and when the human is completely developed, she will have forty-six chromosomes. Your genes are located on your chromosomes. A gene is a small piece of one chromosome; it is a code for a specific sequence of amino acids in a protein. Each code is different and very complex, which brings about many different traits.

Most people are familiar with genes as a transportation of hereditary traits. Genes can affect whether or not you will be born with attached earlobes, freckles, or a widow's peak. Genes are the hereditary codes that are passed on to an off-spring. Traits, which are caused by your genotype (or genes for a particular trait), can be dominant or recessive. Dependent upon the alleles carried on the chromosomes you received from your parents, your appearance will develop accordingly.

Prenatal Development and Birth

Over a relatively brief nine-month period, a single-celled zygote transforms into a fully formed fetus made up of around 1 trillion cells. This period of astonishing growth consists of three distinct phases: the germinal stage, the embryonic stage, and the fetal stage.

The Germinal Stage

The germinal stage is sometimes referred to as the *zygotic period* and represents the first two weeks of development from the time of conception through the development of the cluster of cells known as the *embryo*. First, the zygote begins to divide and become a blastocyst, which will attach itself to the uterine wall during a process known as *implantation*.

The Embryonic Period

The embryonic period lasts from fertilization to the beginning of the third month. The human being begins to develop very distinctly after morphogenesis. Cells begin to take on specific functions and structures in a process called *differentiation*. For the first time, the actual size of the daughter cells begins to grow. Up until this point the cells that were divided were no larger than the parent cells, causing no growth in size.

The cells begin to develop into layers. The upper layer is the ectoderm, which later becomes the skin and nervous system; the middle layer is the mesoderm, which becomes the muscles, circulatory system, and connective tissue; and the lower is the endoderm, which becomes the linings of the digestive and respiratory tracts.

The effect of the embryonic period on the mother is significant. This is the period when the mother may experience "morning sickness" symptoms such as nausea, fatigue, and loss of appetite. The uterus at this time develops from the size of a hen's egg to bigger than an orange and can be felt above the pubic bone.

At this point the fetus also has developed a circulatory system; however, it is slightly different from adults in that it shunts blood away from its unused lungs. Organs like the spinal cord and heart have developed.

The Fetal Period

The fetal period lasts from the third to the ninth month of pregnancy. The fetus is now looking more humanlike and grows to resemble a baby more every day. The growth of the body begins to speed up to catch up with the large size of the already developed head (from the embryonic period). The epidermis (outer layer of skin) begins to be polished, developing eyelashes, eyebrows, head hair, and fingernails.

Month-by-Month Breakdown

During the third month of pregnancy, the difference between sexes is visible. By the fourth month, the fetus begins to look much more human. Beginning at the fifth month, the mother is able to feel the movements of the fetus. By the end of the seventh month, the fetus weighs about three pounds and its eyes open. Toward the end of the fetal period, the fetus usually begins to shift in position, with its head nearing the cervix of the mother. Fat accumulation beneath the skin causes weight gain in the fetus; it should weigh around seven pounds by the end of the ninth month.

Maternal Health and Nutrition

An expectant mother has many things to worry about while her child is solely dependent on her. A fetus has no other way of maintaining its health than by the attentive care of its mother. Poor maternal health and nutrition are associated with a range of complications, including low birth weight and nutritional deficiencies.

When people think of a pregnant woman, one of the first things to come to mind is the outrageous cravings they've all heard tell of. While these cravings may seem bizarre, such as a craving for pickles and ice cream, they may reflect the nutritional needs of the pregnant mother. While supporting herself and her baby, an expectant mother has to balance the nutritional needs of both. A mother who has a bad diet will develop a placenta that is not up to par. An undernourished placenta cannot perform its transportation of nutrients as well as a well-nourished one, thereby leaving the fetus of an undernourished woman in want of nutrients and oxygen.

Weight Gain

A pregnant woman should not be scared of gaining weight while carrying. The average and expected weight gain for an expecting mother of a normal weight is from twenty-five to thirty pounds. Research suggests that obese women need to gain between fifteen and twenty-five pounds, while underweight women may need to gain thirty-five pounds or more depending upon how underweight they are. Although this seems like a lot of weight, keep in mind that the increase in weight includes not only the baby but also the increase in breast size, the placenta, amniotic fluid, enlarged uterus, increased blood volume, stored fats, and water retention.

Maternal Diseases and Drug Use

The placenta carries the nutrients and wastes to and from the body of the baby and the mother. Any harmful things that the mother ingests are transported into the baby through the blood. Although the placenta has the ability to screen and block certain harmful substances from entering the unborn baby's blood, it allows some harmful substances to slip by unnoticed.

Teratogens are harmful agents, particularly drugs and viruses, that the placenta allows to pass through. Many people know that an expectant mother with the AIDS virus can pass the virus on to her unborn child during pregnancy, labor, and delivery, or through breastfeeding. The risk of transmission can be reduced significantly if the mother is given antiretroviral (ARV) drugs and if the baby is fed formula rather than breast milk.

> Women smokers also have a great impact on their baby's health. The baby receives the nicotine that the mother brings into her system. This substance causes the baby to be unable to receive as many nutrients and thereby causes unhealthy weight loss. Very heavy smoking may also cause brain defects in the fetus.

The use of psychoactive drugs has also been linked to a number of birth complication, including low birth weight, premature labor, and long-term brain deficits in children. If the mother happens to be addicted to heroin, the baby will also receive her frequent heroin doses during gestation, and in turn, be born a heroin addict.

Fetal Alcohol Syndrome

One of the most common and notorious problems caused by a mother's insufficient monitoring of what enters her body is fetal alcohol syndrome (FAS). While some people have suggested that small amounts of alcohol will not harm the fetus, no amount of alcohol during pregnancy has been proven safe. Even moderate drinking can affect a fetal brain. When alcohol enters the bloodstream of the expectant mother, it depresses both the mother's and the child's central nervous system. Fetal alcohol syndrome causes physical and cognitive abnormalities in children. Some of the more serious results of fetal alcohol syndrome in babies include the formation of small and disproportional heads and brain abnormalities. Fetal alcohol syndrome is the leading cause of mental retardation in children.

Physical Growth

During infancy and childhood, the human goes through many changes physically. Researchers used to believe that people are born with all the brain cells they'll ever have, but recent findings indicate that new brain cells continue to emerge after birth and even into adulthood. When a child is born, he is without a mature nervous system. As an infant grows, he develops complicated nervous structures, enabling him to perform functions as he grows, such as walking and talking.

Maturation

Infants go through a process called *maturation*, in which the biological growth processes enable changes in behavior in an orderly fashion. A simple example of maturation is that all humans perform certain actions in a particular order, such as standing before walking.

Memory

Most children are unable to place things in their long-term memory before the age of three, which is why most people do not have memories from before that age. The human infant lacks the neural connections to keep the memory of experiences for a long period of time.

Studies have shown that babies can remember things for short periods of time, however. In different studies testing their ability to remember actions that have been performed in front of them, infants have been found capable of remembering certain things (such as recognizing pictures they had been shown at a previous time) from one day up to three months later.

All the time parents spend taking care of their babies (i.e., changing diapers, feeding, and doctors visits) is not likely to be remembered by their children. Older children will accept the stories of their parents staying up with them all night without sleep, but will not remember a moment of it. This lack of memory does not, however, affect the attachment a child feels to the nurturers surrounding her when she is a baby.

Development of Motor Skills

After birth, a human's body begins to develop a more mature nervous system. With this more complicated nervous system come more complicated actions. The development of motor skills causes much grief among mothers. Many mothers will worry if their child is not sitting up or walking when his peers are; however, children in general, unless they have been abused or have some kind of inhibiting disability, tend to develop at nearly the same rate as far as motor skills are concerned.

There are two different kinds of motor skills: fine motor skills and gross motor skills. Fine (or small) motor skills use small muscles such as the eyes and the fingers, and also use more than one part of the body at the same time. Gross (or large) motor skills involve, obviously, the larger muscles like the arms and legs, and also include balance and coordination.

Developing at Different Rates

It is important to understand that a child's brain develops in sections, and that development of different capabilities may happen at different rates. If a child is speaking and reacting to speech better than his peers but still lacks the motor development of his peers, there is no problem with the child in question. Children develop motor skills later on, so a child could be talking quite effectively and not yet walking.

Children in different cultures tend to develop at slightly different rates as well. For example, 90 percent of babies in the United States will walk by the age of fifteen months, but most babies will be able to walk by the age of ten months in Uganda. But even blind children will begin to walk at nearly the same time as their peers in their culture because of the maturation process.

A human being is born with the ability to suck, swallow, spit up, eliminate, and breathe, but other functions develop as the baby's nervous system further develops. The human body matures from the top to the bottom. First an infant will move her head, neck, and shoulders, then her arms and trunk, and eventually her legs. An infant should be able to turn her head at two weeks, sit on her own at eight to nine months, and skip by age five—but as mentioned earlier, that is just a generalized outline of development.

> Don't try to force your child to develop skills before he is ready. Biologically speaking, the cerebellum develops very rapidly at this time, giving children the ability to learn to walk at nearly the same age. Genes also affect the maturation process of children's motor skills, causing slight differences in timing, but on the whole these differences usually even out within a short period of time.

Increasing Development of Motor Skills

Some doctors suggest things, which most people take for granted as just being part of child's play, to increase the development of motor skills. For example, playing with stackable toys, turning pages in books, and scribbling all help to develop a child's motor skills. Preschoolers who cut paper with scissors, finger-paint, and play with Play-Doh are helping along their motor skill development. These activities will eventually develop into tying shoes, buttoning clothes, and later on to playing tag and skipping.

Cognitive Development—How Infants and Children Think

As you know, cognition refers to all the mental processes associated with thinking. This section will rely heavily on the research of Jean Piaget (1896–1980) on the development of children's cognitive abilities. While previous theories often suggested that children passively absorb information around them, Piaget was the first to suggest that children actively work to make sense of the world around them. Although some of his findings have been proved different by later research, his theories about the basic process of development are still useful.

Schemata

Piaget's work used the concept of schemata to understand the cognitive processes of children. Basically, Piaget suggested that children make a mold for an experience and will put everything similar to that experience in the same mold. For example, a child will be familiar with the family dog and the proper word for it, but when she sees a dingo on television, she still calls the dingo a dog, assimilating it into her schema for dogs. Later on in the cognitive development of the child, she will understand that there are different kinds of dogs, and even later that a dingo is not a dog and accommodate for this change.

Stages of Cognitive Development

Piaget categorized the cognitive development into four stages: the sensorimotor stage, the preoperational stage, the concrete operational stage, and the formal operational stage. The transitions between these stages do not occur abruptly, but rather, are gradual.

The first stage, the sensorimotor stage, begins at birth and lasts until the child is about two years old. In this stage, a child experiences the world solely through his five senses. The second stage, the preoperational stage, lasts from around two years old to six years old. This stage is the stage in which a child learns to use language but doesn't yet understand concrete logic, even though children in this stage do possess the ability for symbolic thought. Egocentrism is introduced in this stage as well. Piaget did not mean that children were egocentric in that they were selfish, but that they did not yet have the mental ability to take the perspectives of other people.

For example, if a child draws a picture and shows it to his mother, he will expect her to know exactly what is drawn on the page, because in his eyes, the picture is as plain as day. Egocentrism also explains why a child who hides her eyes thinks her mother cannot see her—which leads to countless rousing games of "peekaboo!"

The next stage, the concrete operational stage, lasts from when a child is about six years old to around eleven years old. In this stage, children are able to use the mental operations needed to think logically about concrete events. In the concrete operational stage, children begin to grasp the concept of jokes and arithmetic problems. As the name implies, children at this stage tend to think in very concrete terms and often struggle with hypothetical or abstract situations.

The final stage, the formal operational stage, begins around age twelve. This stage is when children are able to think logically about abstract concepts. Although there are certain pieces of Piaget's theory that are being challenged, the general cognitive development of human beings seems to follow the basic outline of his model.

Language Development—Part Prewired, Part Learned

Language may not seem like an important part of psychology, but some psychologists see language as what sets humans apart from the rest of the animal kingdom. Language is also something that psychologists continue to learn more and more about.

A behavioral psychologist, like B. F. Skinner, would say that language is learned because children get positive reinforcement for speaking the correct words. Parents will hug, kiss, and smile when a child says "mommy" or "daddy" for the first time, prompting the child to do so again.

> Children will rarely make huge grammatical errors such as saying "ball my" instead of "my ball" even though they have not yet learned the proper subject, verb, and object rules. This knowledge suggests that Chomsky is right in thinking humans are predisposed to language.

Psychologist and linguist Noam Chomsky looked at language from a biological standpoint. His claim is that humans are biologically born to speak, prewired for language. Chomsky noticed that all languages share common characteristics (such as the fact that the most commonly used words are generally the shortest) and said that languages developed this way because humans are predisposed to these characteristics.

Development of Language

Children from different cultures seem to follow, in general, the same development of language. At around four months, children will look in the same direction as parents when parents begin to point and label things. At around age one, children usually start to speak, saying variations of words like *mom* or *dad*." It is at this stage in their development that children make the mistake of overextension. An example of overextension is when a child refers to all males as "dad." A child also uses holophrastic speech around the twelve-month mark. Holophrastic speech is the use of a single word to express a complete idea. For example, a one-year-old may say "car" when she really wants to go for a ride.

> **What is overregularization?**
> Overregularization is when a child overapplies the rules of grammar. For example, a child might say, "I holded the puppy" and find nothing grammatically incorrect in that statement because the child is overapplying the rules of past tense that he has learned.

At eighteen to twenty-four months, children develop telegraphic, or two-word, speech. In this stage, children delete the nonessential words, speaking in a very Tarzan-like way. For example a child wanting to say "Hand me the cup" would merely say, "Give cup." After twenty-four months, a child's language develops rapidly. Once a child learns grammatical rules, however, it is common for her to make the mistake of overregularization. As children enter the preschool years, what is commonly referred to as a *language explosion* occurs. During this time, children suddenly begin learning and producing an astonishing vocabulary of words and sentences.

Developing a Sense of Self

Self-concept is a sense of an individual's identity and personal worth. Self-concept develops by around age twelve. Developmental psychologists are not able to determine an infant's self-concept since that question is too difficult for someone barely speaking to understand. However, psychologists use the behavior of infants and children to hypothesize about their sense of self.

By around fifteen to eighteen months, a child begins to recognize himself in a mirror. When children begin to attend school, they describe themselves according to comparisons with their peers. And finally, around age eight or ten years, stable self-images are fully developed, for better or for worse.

Types of Parenting

A child's self-image is influenced by his or her caretakers' parenting style. Psychologists have identified three different types of parenting styles: authoritarian parents, permissive parents, and authoritative parents. Authoritarian parents are those who develop rules and lay down the law, so to speak. If the rules are not followed, the parent punishes the child. The permissive parent does what the child wants and rarely punishes her for doing wrong. The authoritative parent follows a comfortable in-between style. The parent sets and enforces rules to exert appropriate control but also explains the reasons for the rules. The parent is open to (and in fact encourages) discussion and will consider a compromise or exception when making rules.

Many studies have shown that authoritative parents have children who are well adapted and happy. Children with authoritative parents have the highest self-esteem, self-reliance, and social competence. Those with a somewhat controlled upbringing are more motivated and self-confident. Children of overly permissive parents are often found to be more helpless and incompetent, with difficulties in dealing with frustration or limits.

Social and Emotional Development

It is not a secret that infants develop a strong emotional attachment to the people who provide them with a caring and nurturing relationship. Infants are familiar with the faces of family members and react positively to seeing their faces and being held by them. However, the situation is very different when the infant comes in contact with Great Aunt Irma, whom the baby has never seen before. When the baby is passed from its familiar mother to caring but unfamiliar Great Aunt Irma, the baby will most likely not react in the same manner as she did with her mother. Instead the infant will cry and reach for the more familiar mom. This fear is called stranger anxiety, and it occurs in babies between six months and two years old.

Attachment

Attachment is an emotional tie with another person. In young children attachment is shown by their desire to be held by their parents or other familiar caregivers and by their becoming upset or distressed when separated. Attachment has a strong evolutionary component, since it aids in survival. Just as you would see cubs following the mother lion around in Africa, a baby stays close to its mother for protection.

Attachment comes from three key components in relationship between the child and caregiver: body contact, familiarity, and responsive parenting. An infant seeks body contact with the mother or main caregiver. This soft, warm body gives the infant a safe haven from which to explore his or her surroundings and also a place to go to when upset. A mother's or caregiver's body is very important in attachment with the infant because it allows a sense of security.

Although it is thought to be the mother's job to provide the most nurturing for her children, the father's presence is important to the development of his child. Studies show that children who grow up without a father can be at an increased risk for various psychological and social pathologies. Of course, single parents of either sex are often exposed to poverty, increased stress, and more limited resources, which impact what they can offer their children.

Familiarity is based on the critical period of infants, which is that period of time shortly after birth in which the infant is exposed to stimuli that will produce proper development. Attachments based on familiarity must happen during the critical period. It is not necessary for a child to be in contact with her main caregivers right at birth to develop an attachment to them, as is seen in adopted children, but human attachment develops very slowly and is helped along when an infant is in contact with her main caregiver from the beginning.

Forms of Attachment

Attachment comes in two basic forms: secure attachment and insecure attachment. Secure attachment is shown when a baby can happily play in and explore a new environment in his mother's presence. An insecurely attached baby will not be eager to explore the surroundings, but rather will stick to his mother. One explanation for the secure and insecurely attached babies is the mother's actions.

Responsive mothers who act with sensitivity and attentiveness toward their children most likely have securely attached infants. Mothers who are insensitive toward their children and ignore them will most likely have babies with insecure attachments. A child's temperament may also influence the parent's behavior. For instance, a child who is generally more anxious, less cuddly, and more easily upset will elicit different parenting behavior than a cheerful, calm, relaxed child. It goes both ways.

Researchers have also described three major variations of insecure attachment: ambivalent, avoidant, and disorganized. A child displaying signs of ambivalent-insecure attachment will become very distressed when the caretaker leaves the room, but does not seem to be particularly comforted when he or she returns. Those with an avoidant-insecure style show little preference between a parent and stranger and generally don't seek comfort from caregivers when they are distressed. Disorganized attachment is marked by a pronounced mix of behavior, where children may avoid or even resist attention from caregivers. Researchers believe that this attachment style is linked to inconsistent parenting behavior. Sometimes the parents may be a source of comfort, but at other times they might be a source of neglect or even fear.

Much of this chapter has discussed the child's attachment to the mother. Though the mother's attachment seems to be a very important role in the development of a child, the father's presence also makes a big difference. However, it need not be a biological mother or father to satisfy the child's need for attachment. The presence of safe, caring, responsible adults in a child's life is what seems to be important in nurturing healthy development.

HUMAN DEVELOPMENT—

Adolescence

FOR MANY AMERICANS the word adolescence brings forth memories of the teenage years: fights with their parents, trying to establish themselves as individuals, and contradicting this newfound individuality by acting in a herd animal–like fashion, sporting the trendiest of clothing worn by their peers. This turbulent period will be explored in this chapter.

Physical and Sexual Development

Adolescence is the period of time between late childhood and adulthood. It is a time of important physical development as well as social, emotional, and psychological growth. The most obvious signs of adolescence emerge at around age eleven or twelve as puberty and sexual maturation begin. Other changes such as cognitive development and the emergence of a self-identity are more difficult to see but are just as important.

Human adolescence officially begins with the onset of puberty. What is puberty exactly? It is the point at which a person becomes physically able to reproduce. A huge rush of hormones begins puberty and a two-year period of rapid physical development ensues. Puberty usually begins in a girl around age eleven and around age thirteen in boys, though the age of onset can vary.

The physical changes associated with puberty fall into two different categories. The development of primary sex characteristics involves the rapid growth of the reproductive organs and external genitalia. The development of secondary sex characteristics includes the development of traits such as breasts and wider hips in girls and deep voices and facial hair in boys.

Factors That Influence the Timing of Puberty

As you probably noticed during your own adolescence, not all children enter puberty at the same age. While people think of puberty as something controlled purely by biology, research has found that both genetics and environmental factors play a role as well. For example, girls typically begin to menstruate around the same age that their mothers did, suggesting that heredity plays an important part. Environmental factors such as nutrition and overall health also determine when puberty begins. Girls who are well nourished typically begin menstruating at an earlier age, while those who are malnourished or suffer from health problems during childhood tend to reach menarche much later.

The Impact of Early and Late Maturation

Adolescents are generally very aware of the physical changes associated with puberty and frequently compare their own rate of development with that of their peer group. While most adolescents reach specific milestones at about the same time as most of their friends, some children develop earlier or later. Studies have found that boys who develop more quickly than their peers are found to be more popular and independent, as their muscular development prompts them to be proud. However, girls who develop earlier than their peers are more likely to experience negative psychological and health outcomes. Girls who develop earlier than their peers are more prone to teasing than a boy who is developing faster than other boys. Early maturing girls are more at risk for having poor body image, more likely to experience symptoms of depression and have higher rates of teen pregnancy than late maturing girls.

Cognitive Development—How Adolescents Think

Adolescence seems to be a very troublesome stage, especially for parents. After reaching puberty and becoming more aware of their surroundings, adolescents will begin trying to break away from their parents' influence and begin developing into their own person.

Adolescents begin to develop abstract reasoning skills. It is during this part of life that humans, as teenagers, are capable of exploring abstract thoughts. Along with trying to figure out who and what they are, adolescents begin to criticize others as well as themselves. They begin to spot hypocrisy in other people, especially their parents, leading to many typical fights between parents and adolescents.

In the past, the stunning shifts in moods displayed by most teens were often attributed simply to "raging hormones." Recently, researchers have utilized brain scan technology to demonstrate that these shifting emotions have little or nothing to do with hormones and everything to do with changes in the brain itself. During adolescence, the brain goes through a period of neural growth and pruning. Some connections are strengthened and reinforced, while others are pruned. The last areas of the brain to undergo these changes are the parts associated with cognitive functioning, such as a person's ability to reason, solve problems, and make decisions. Experts believe that this process is not complete until people reach their mid-twenties. Is it any wonder, then, that teens and young adults are so prone to poor judgment when the part of their brains associated with this ability is still maturing?

Preconventional Morality

Adolescents also start developing a sense of morality, learning to distinguish right from wrong, and developing their character around their choices. Psychologist Lawrence Kohlberg (1927–1987) examined the moral development of children and adolescents and placed them in three general categories. The first stage, he suggests, is the preconventional morality. In this first stage, children, or adolescents even, will only obey the rules and choose to do right to either avoid punishment or gain a reward for acting "good." This stage mostly applies to children under nine years of age.

Conventional Morality

The second stage, the conventional morality stage, is the stage in which adolescents will begin to uphold laws because they understand the concept of rules and that they should be obeyed. This is also the stage in which adolescents start doing good out of caring for others. In this stage, acceptance in the social order by doing good is key. If an adolescent chooses to do wrong, he will not be accepted by the social order as a positive influence and therefore will either be punished accordingly or pushed to the outside of the group.

> Adolescence is a period in which, although much of your moral thinking is developed, you may not choose to follow the voice in your head solely due to the decisions being made around you by your peers. Studies have shown that although teenagers have a set of standards, they may cross these in order to fit into the crowd.

Postconventional Morality

The third and final stage of moral thought processes is postconventional morality. This is an advanced stage (most likely not reached by very early adolescence) in which an adolescent will act according to her own basic ethical principles. This stage is fully separated from parents, friends, and authoritative figures, although these people may have had an influence on the child's development. This is the stage where adolescents make decisions based solely on their ideals in their own mind. However, many psychologists have debated over the postconventional level, saying this level is only blatant in adolescents raised in Western countries that promote individualism.

Differences in Moral Development

There are differences in moral development between boys and girls. Some interesting research by Carol Gilligan (1936–) suggests that, in general, girls develop a different kind of morality than boys do. In Kohlberg's research, he utilized a scenario known as the "Heinz dilemma," in which a man must decide whether to steal medicine to save his dying wife. In this scenario, girls tended to move toward an ethic of caring—what is "right" means what is good for people and relationships, even if it stretches the law. Boys at an equivalent stage believe that "right" means how closely behavior adheres to the law, or rules that govern society. While Kohlberg identifies decisions based on caring as an inferior stage of development, Gilligan argues that girls and boys are equally developed in their moral understanding, but because women in our culture are generally responsible for caretaking and men for defending life and property, they develop along parallel but different tracks. Of course, this is an overgeneralization in both cases, but it bears thinking about.

Developing a Sense of Identity

Adolescence is a very important part of human development. It is at this point that people will summarize their entire life and decide who they want to be. Teenagers will test different roles until deciding which identity they fit most comfortably in. Teenagers may try on different roles with different people, behaving in different ways around their school friends and their sports friends.

When psychologists talk about identity, they are referring to the beliefs and values that guide a person's behavior and actions throughout life. Your sense of identity gives you a sense of who you are as a person. While the formation of identity is an important part of adolescence, it is a process that will continue throughout your entire life. While attempting to develop a set identity, teenagers also develop the capacity to experience intimacy with others.

Developing an identity is also very taxing on relationships with parents. Adolescents tend to break from their strong childhood connections with parents in order to find their appropriate identity. Peer influence begins to replace parental influence. Teenagers seem to lean toward friends for advice in matters while breaking the bonds with their parents.

> This change in behavior could be explained through a biological stance. A human at this point is looking for courtship or possibly more than that, and in doing so, will display the appropriate biologically important aspects in order to gain a mate: men as protective creatures and women as nurturers.

A psychologist names Erik Erikson (1902–1994) was very interested in the formation of identity. Erikson believed that during adolescence teens experience a conflict that he referred to as "identity versus role confusion." In order to form an identity successfully, teens experiment with different roles until they develop an integrated self-definition, incorporating the many dimensions of their personalities with the role they hope to someday take up within society as a whole. In a 1980 article published in the *Handbook of Adolescent Psychology*, researcher James Marcia suggests that the key to finding a balance between identity and role confusion hinges on whether a person makes a commitment to this identity. Some individuals reach what is known as *identity achievement*, in which they have gone through a period of exploration and have made a commitment to an identity. These individuals are typically happier and healthier than people who are still struggling to carve out a unique identity.

HUMAN DEVELOPMENT—

Adulthood and Aging

WHILE THE DRAMATIC CHANGE and growth from infancy to adolescence helps establish the basis for the rest of human development, the story certainly doesn't end once you reach adulthood. This chapter will explore the changes that occur during adult life. While many people look on aging with a sense of fear, this chapter will show that the elderly are quite capable of enjoying fulfilling, healthy, and active lives.

Physical Health

When people think of aging, most tend to think first of the changes in physical health. Many associate aging with numerous medications, disease, inability to function on one's own, and a body waiting to die. This is certainly an outdated way of looked at the aging process, especially in today's society in which people are living longer, healthier, and more productive lives.

There are three stages of adulthood: young adulthood (twenties and thirties), middle adulthood (forties and fifties) and later adulthood (sixty and older). In none of these stages is it inevitable that all people will suffer the aforementioned afflictions associated with aging. There are physical changes that take place with aging, but even these do not necessarily have to lead to a sedentary and unhealthy lifestyle in later years. A major factor in how well your body functions in later years is how well you treat it in the younger years.

Be Healthy Now; Be Healthy Later

Studies have shown that many diseases resulting in death or debilitation in later years begin during young adulthood. How you treat your body during those early adult years will have a direct impact on how well your body functions in later years.

As you know, nutrition is very important for your physical health, young or old. By developing healthful eating habits now, you will not only be more likely to maintain those habits in later years, but you also may stave off diseases that could very well affect your well-being later in life. Whether you are an adolescent or already into later adulthood, it is never too late to adopt a healthful lifestyle. Not only will it make your quality of life better, but it can also prolong your life.

Be Energetic Now; Be Energetic Later

If you are a young adult, you are living in the prime of your life, at least as far as physical fitness, health, strength, and stamina go. Even though this may be the prime, it doesn't mean that you cannot maintain energy levels into middle and later adulthood. Studies have shown that people who are active in early adulthood are able to establish healthful habits that persist into old age. Of course, there are external factors that can impact your activity levels such as diseases like osteoporosis, arthritis, and various diseases of the organs. But even so, regular exercise increases one's chances of living a long, healthy, and disease-free life.

Living a sedentary lifestyle in your younger years is likely to carry over to your later years. Because later adults do suffer some deterioration in physical ability, such as strength and flexibility, it is of the utmost importance that they do not aid that deterioration by living a sedentary lifestyle.

If you are able to incorporate a regular exercise routine, whether it be walking or spending an hour at the gym regularly, in your younger years, your body comes to expect that exertion and you will feel like you are in a slump if you slack off. By building this into your routine now, the likelihood that you will continue exercise patterns into your later years increases. There is nothing out there that says elderly people cannot exercise. In fact, it is highly recommended, as those who do get regular exercise find that they are able to live more active and enjoyable lifestyles than others who do not exercise. While later adults may not have the heightened energy levels, strength, and stamina of young adults, physical exercise can keep these qualities up to par for the activities you wish to participate in.

Changes During Middle Adulthood

People within the years of middle adulthood are going through several changes that can drastically affect their ways of life. While most people typically think of this time period as being the most stressful and unpleasant of all, if you ask those who are living it, you may receive a different answer.

This is the period of time in which children often leave the home and parents face a new phase of life that does not involve rearing young children. Some parents go through the empty-nest syndrome in which they have difficulty adjusting to life without their children, but this is usually temporary and many adults begin to enjoy the new freedoms that come with middle age.

Many use this time to re-evaluate their lives (which may be where the misconception of midlife crises comes into play, though this will be discussed later) and take stock of what they have accomplished and what they yet want to accomplish. This is often a period of new adventures, hobbies, and sometimes more community involvement.

Menopause

Menopause is a time of great physical change in which menstruation ceases and the ovaries stop producing estrogen. While you will often hear horror stories of menopause, most women typically view it indifferently or positively. Most women are relieved not to have to worry about pregnancy and deal with monthly cycles. Granted, there are some physical symptoms that accompany menopause as the body adjusts to the decrease of estrogen. The most common symptom is hot flashes. Regardless of what you may have heard, menopause does not typically throw a woman into depression, make her irritable, or cause irrational behavior. Some women do experience severe physical symptoms, but the percentage is very low.

Midlife Crises

A popular misconception is that men often experience midlife crises during middle adulthood, in which their personalities seem to change overnight and they may suddenly regress to their earlier years. There is absolutely no foundation for this belief. Men do not suffer any type of crisis pertinent to a particular age period, other than the re-evaluation of priorities and goals that normally happens during these years.

> The aging process does not bring about a midlife crisis. Those things that may bring about a "midlife crisis" are drastic and sudden life-altering events such as the death of a loved one or the loss of employment.

While men may have the time, money, and inclination to delve into new hobbies or purchase expensive toys during this time, this is in no way associated with a crisis. Instead, it is considered a productive period of mental well-being. Men are no more susceptible to a midlife crisis than women.

Changes in Sexuality

Many people are under the assumption that once you reach a certain age, sex is no longer an important part of your life, if it is a part of your life at all. This is simply not true. Granted, elderly people may not be as rambunctious as young adults when it comes to sexual exploits, but they do still have the desire to have sex, even into their late eighties. Sex is an important part of any relationship and does not exclude itself from the relationships of older people. However, men and women do undergo changes in their sexuality as they age.

Changes in Men

One of the main concerns of men as they age is that their ability to achieve erection is affected. In some men, it may take longer and require more stimulation to achieve erection, and even then it may not be as firm as it was in their young adult years. Some men are unable to achieve erection at all. This is referred to as *impotence*. Impotence doesn't only affect elderly men; younger men will also likely suffer this at least once in their lives.

> If you are experiencing erectile dysfunction, you may want to look into the possibility of Viagra. This medication has proved to be quite effective in cases of impotence. It also has very few side effects, but possible side effects include headaches and stomach queasiness. Men who have heart conditions cannot take it. Because impotence may be related to other medications, it's important to discuss it with your doctor.

Impotence can result from psychological or emotional issues, including excessive stress, worry, fatigue, anger, or depression. Impotence is also linked to certain physical causes or disease including reduced testosterone levels, heart disease, diabetes, drug use, or as a side effect of taking certain medications. An inability to perform is rather embarrassing and frightening for a man. As he feels more and more pressure to perform or feels anxiety about the changes in his body, a man may psyche himself up so much that he is unable to achieve erection. While impotence is usually only temporary, some men may become so frustrated with it that they begin to fear sexual experiences and thus feed the pressure to perform, in turn causing erectile dysfunction.

Changes in Women

Menopause is probably the greatest change a woman will undergo during middle adulthood. Menopause is the most common cause for sexual changes in women as they age. Following menopause, a woman's vaginal canal may be shortened and thinned and sometimes even becomes smaller all around. Many women also experience a decrease in lubrication. The combination of a smaller vagina and less lubrication can make sex uncomfortable. Both men and women experiencing sexual changes due to aging should discuss these issues with their partner. By maintaining open communication, romantic partners can take steps to deal with potential problems that may arise.

Cognitive Growth and Decline

Unfortunately, certain mental functioning aspects do decline with age, such as memory, reasoning, and complex problem solving. This isn't to say that these abilities necessarily disappear; they sometimes just take a little longer to process. For instance, you may notice that it takes elderly people longer to think of names or other information than it does for younger people. The information may still be there, but the speed of cognitive processing has slowed, making it difficult at times to retrieve that information. The ability to utilize deductive reasoning and/or to use new information in problem solving also declines with age. While it may seem as if a large portion of your mental processes is vulnerable to deterioration, it really isn't as bad as it sounds. It may be annoying, but this doesn't mean that an elderly person becomes incapable of taking care of herself.

> Many people assume that to get older means to get depressed and lack interest in activities that used to be stimulating. This is simply not true. While depression can certainly affect the elderly, the two do not go hand in hand. There are many elderly people living their lives the happiest they've ever been.

Not all aspects of mental functioning decline with age. Some skills that you have consistently used throughout the course of your lifetime, such as the ability to define words or solve mathematical equations, tends to remain stable and retrievable throughout the later years. The best part is that it is even possible that these skills will improve! Of course, this depends on the education you've received and the amount of experience you've had with the particular skill.

Treatable Cognitive Conditions

Thankfully, researchers have been able to dispel some of the preconceived notions of senility and other conditions formerly associated with old age. Not only are some of these conditions not brought on by the aging process, but they are also treatable, ultimately improving the quality of life for the elderly.

For instance, senility was once thought to be just an accepted by-product of old age. However, recent studies have shown that many cases of senility aren't senility at all, but rather side effects of certain types of medication or combinations of medications. As you learned earlier, exercise and proper diet can do a lot for a person's energy levels, strength, and stamina. Therefore, whereas frailty was once considered an inevitable effect of aging, it is now known that frailty and weakness do not have to be accepted. Doctors can help set their patients on exercise and diet regimens that will help them to live more active lives.

Alzheimer's Disease

Alzheimer's disease often crosses the minds of those who worry about aging, and with good reason. Alzheimer's disease is a degenerative disease that results in the loss of brain cells. Those with Alzheimer's suffer a variety of symptoms, including memory loss, disorientation, problems with reasoning, personality changes, agitation, anxiety, delusions, hallucinations, and an inability to perform routine tasks. Such a disease is incredibly frightening both for the sufferer and for his family.

The duration of the disease can last anywhere from three to twenty years. While there is no cure as of yet, there are several drugs being employed to slow down the degenerative process, thus adding several years of independence to the patient's life. Eventually, however, the disease progresses to the point where the patient will require twenty-four-hour care and could even possibly lead to death due to the loss of brain function.

According to the Alzheimer's Association, approximately 10 percent of people over the age of sixty-five have developed Alzheimer's disease. Approximately 50 percent of people over the age of eighty-five have the disease. Obviously, age does play a role in a person's risk of developing the disease.

No one knows exactly what causes Alzheimer's disease; however, it is pretty commonly known that age plays a role in its development. This isn't to say that everyone who reaches age sixty-five and beyond will develop the disease. Of course, some people are more susceptible than others, especially those with a family history of the disease.

Retirement

Retiring from full-time employment is considered one of the major events in an individual's life. As much as people may complain about their jobs, they are an important part of life, for social, economic, and personal identity purposes. After having worked forty-plus years, an individual may feel a significant loss once she retires. All of a sudden the individual is left with lots of time on her hands, less money in her pocket, and sometimes even a feeling of worthlessness.

Of course, how individuals cope with retirement depends on numerous factors, including family life, how prepared they are for retirement, how active they are socially, and their physical health. Those who have supportive families, have saved up enough money as to not have to worry about financial hardship, have social structures outside the workplace, and are in good physical condition are more likely to deal well with retirement and view it as a freedom that can be enjoyed. However, those without families, with limited funds, with no social groups outside the workplace, and in poor health are more likely to view retirement as a loss that cannot possibly be replaced. These individuals may experience symptoms of depression and have a more difficult time making the switch from employment to retirement.

> If you find yourself facing retirement, take a few moments to write down a list of activities you enjoy, projects you would like to complete, or new hobbies you would like to try out. Those who are able to find productive ways to employ their time after retirement are more likely to make a smooth and positive transition.

Stress accompanies any type of life-altering event and making the transition from employment to retirement may be a struggle for many. However, you can help combat this struggle and any psychological disturbances you may face by being as prepared as you can be for the event. Understanding the loss and having a plan of action in place will ease your mind a bit when the time comes. Of course, you will have to go through an adjustment period, but if you are able to look at the event in a positive light, your years spent in retirement will likely be more enjoyable and productive.

Death—The Final Stage in Development

Death, of course, is the inevitable final stage of human development. While death may occur at any age, those who are in later adulthood focus more on death than do most others. They know that they cannot live forever and often begin making plans for their death.

While the thought of planning for death might seem rather morbid to some, it can actually create peace of mind in some of the elderly. If they are in later adulthood, it is likely that they have experienced the death of a loved one at one time or another during their lives. They understand the effect it can have on those family and friends left behind. By preparing for their death, they are able to rest assured knowing they have done what they can to make the process of burial, funeral arrangements, and divvying up the assets as smooth as possible. Some may even go to the extent of detailing the plans down to the songs they want sung or verses read so as to spare loved ones the burden of making decisions under bereavement.

This isn't to say that all are ready to accept the fact that they will die. Some fear death and will never be prepared to go. However, studies have shown that those who believe in some form of afterlife are more accepting and at peace during their later years than those who believe in the finality of death. Regardless of your beliefs, death is inevitable, so for the sake of your mental health, do all that you can do to make your last years of life the most enjoyable they can be.

PERSONALITY AND
Personality Tests

THE STUDY OF PERSONALITY has been a major topic within psychology since its earliest beginning, and whether you realize it or not, you probably make assessments of other people's personality on a daily basis. When describing a friendly coworker, you might tell people that she has a "kind personality." When describing your cranky next-door neighbor, you might complain that he has an "abrasive personality." This chapter explains why and how personality not only affects the decisions you make, but also defines who you are.

What Is Personality?

How you perceive and react to your environment on a day-to-day basis can be measured by your behavior, thoughts, and emotions. You're an "individual" because a unique combination of these characteristics provides the basic foundation of who you are and makes up the personality that your friends and family have come to like (and dislike!).

Personality is something that arises from within and remains quite consistent throughout life, but the environment and the situation play an important role in determining how different aspects of your personality are expressed. There are four fundamental characteristics of personality. First, it is constant and people tend to behave in the same way when they encounter similar situations. Second, personality not only influences actions, but it also actually causes people to behave in specific ways. Third, personality is influenced by both psychological and biological factors. Finally, personality is expressed not only in behaviors, but through emotions, thoughts, social behavior, and close relationships.

Types of Behavior

Behavior is how you react to social and physical aspects of your environment based on your personality. Where one person may never show emotions of anger, joy, grief, or anxiety, another person's responses may be dramatically colored with facial expressions, voice inflections, and hand gestures. Behavior is examined in two ways: internally controlled and externally controlled. Internal theorists believe the individual characteristics of a person dictate the behavioral pattern, while external advocates hold that the behavior is a result of the situation at hand.

Public and Private Personalities

How the world perceives you is a direct reflection of and reaction to how you present yourself to them. Race, age, and gender are qualities you have no control over, but certainly contribute to your personality because of how the world perceives you based on these features. A person who continuously experiences racial discrimination may guard himself against it by at first seeming cold and unfriendly. But once he opens up, you may discover someone completely different inside.

Physical attributes, which you develop over time, also contribute to your personality, and include mannerisms (soft speakers are dubbed "shy" whereas loud speakers are labeled "obnoxious"), gait (purposeful, long strides, bouncy sauntering, etc.), eye contact, and facial expressions. How you want the world to perceive you influences how you present yourself to others. Characteristics such as attitude (friendly, outgoing, standoffish, introverted, etc.), response (polite, thoughtful, rude, arrogant, etc.), and general mindset (are you usually upbeat or moody?) create the surface of your one-of-a-kind personality.

> If you're like many people, the aspects of your personality you choose to display might depend the people you encounter. For instance, the personality you exhibit around your boss or psychology professor is probably a lot different from the personality you reveal to your closest friends.

Dig a little deeper, and the private aspect of your being appears: dreams too bizarre to discuss; experiences too sentimental to reveal; fantasies that may seem childish to others; goals, standards, and morals you aspire to; daily internal dialogue, thoughts, and ideas—all of these elements make up the "you" that only you truly know. And only you can decide when to share these parts of your personality with others. For example, you might be outgoing, courageous, intelligent, and have a lovely voice, but when you step up to the podium to deliver a speech in front of twenty people, you suddenly become anxious, fearful, and at a loss for words.

Heredity, Environment, and Personality

Since the moment you were born, biology has influenced your behavior in ways that may have seemed insignificant then, but are more relevant now. For instance, active babies frequently look around the room and at the people in it, whereas a quieter baby tends to hold a steady gaze in one direction, focusing on a single activity. Granted, these babies may grow up to develop adult personalities that are quite different from their newborn personalities, but studies have shown that these characteristics are often a good indicator of who the child will grow to be. In addition to biological factors, both common and unique life experiences help shape your personality.

Biological Factors

Determining the amount of genetic influence that contributes to the makeup of personality has proved to be a difficult task. However, in studying both fraternal and identical twins, we're able to gain some insight into this mystery. After a series of tests, studies have shown that identical adult twins were more likely to answer questions in the same way than fraternal twins were. In subsequent studies, identical twins who were separated for long periods of time compared to those who weren't separated continued to exhibit the same level of personality traits.

Physiological Differences

Monoamine oxidase (MAO) is an enzyme that functions in the nervous system by breaking down the neurotransmitters said to be a key factor in emotional and motivated behavior. It's an important element to consider, because the levels of MAO in a person's body change due to age and sex hormones. Also, since MAO is an inherited, physiological trait, adventurous parents, for instance, pass that trait along to their offspring and are more likely to have children who are just as adventurous as they are than parents who are not adventurous at all.

Shared Versus Solitary Experiences

Your surroundings and the common belief systems that are established and shared within those surroundings are major contributing factors in the development of your personality. Culture, religion, education, custom, and family tradition all have something to say about how you should act. Even the most extroverted person would behave in a subdued manner at a funeral, while a normally shy person may try to be more outgoing when hosting a bridal shower. One instance of how adults conform to the general standards of society takes place in the business world. You wouldn't walk into a board meeting of executives wearing jeans and a T-shirt; rather, you'd wear a professional suit or jacket and skirt. Similarly, you're not going to walk into church wearing a bikini top, sarong, and flip-flops, and you probably won't attend a barbecue wearing a prom dress.

Biological and social differences aren't the only factors influencing your personality. Individual experiences make their marks in your life especially because of the personal nature in which they are dealt with. For example, if the last jar of honey in the house contains only one drop, Winnie the Pooh views it as a positive experience because there's still one drop left; Piglet is anxious because he's afraid the honey will attract bees; and Eeyore thinks they're all doomed because the food supply has dwindled down to only one drop of honey. How can three individuals be in the same situation yet view it differently?

Past experiences affect attitudes and sway reactions. Pooh realizes there is more honey in the forest, Piglet recalls how much it hurt the last time he was stung by a bee, and Eeyore thinks there won't be any more honey left in the forest because he is used to never getting what he wants. Surely it will be gone before they get to it! This scenario illustrates how a delicate blend of common and unique experiences, external influences, and inherited characteristics are the makings of a full-bodied personality, unique in its own right, despite the situation. Personality development operates on multiple levels and can be examined by breaking it down into four different perspectives: traits, psychodynamic, psychoanalytic, or humanistic (phenomenological).

Traits

The trait theory, introduced by Gordon Allport (1897–1967), is the belief that the individual qualities of a person are what determine her behavior. The theory also holds that these traits can be measured on dimensions, or scales, each one measuring a characteristic, or trait, of that person. Some examples include rating a person's scale of aggressiveness and emotionality. Is that person quick to get angry? Does she cry easily? How trusting is she? But with all the different types of personality traits available to describe, how do you arrive at determining what traits are most important?

Factor Analysis

Factor analysis is the statistical method used to help interpret the scores of multiple personality tests by computing the minimum number of characteristics needed to discover the truest assessment of that personality. For example, when measuring the trait dimension of cheerfulness, you would fall somewhere between serious and enthusiastic, the former having the lowest rating of 1 point and the latter having the highest rating of 10 points. Raymond Cattell (1905–1998), after extensive research, testing, and data collecting, concluded that sixteen factors make up the basic elements of personality. Following is a list of these factors:

Warm	Cheerful
Suspicious	Experimenting
Conscientious	Intelligent
Self-sufficient	Imaginative
Bold	Emotionally stable
Self-disciplined	Shrewd
Sensitive	Dominant
Tense	Guilt prone

A trait is considered to be a relatively stable characteristic of your personality. Though your personality certainly changes somewhat due to the environment you are in, traits, such as race or age, are supposedly those that are always underlying and never affected by changing situations.

Each trait is rated on a scale of 1 to 10 points in which each level is assigned an adjective, as seen in the previous example with cheerfulness. Cattell also developed a questionnaire of over 100 yes-or-no questions to measure the level at which each person possesses the traits listed and to be able to create as accurate a personality profile as possible for each individual based on his answers to the questions.

Problems with the Trait Theory

Although the trait approach succeeds at determining the character of a person based on her tendency to lean one way or another regarding certain traits, it doesn't really paint a complete picture. Introversion-extroversion and stability-instability levels prove that behavior can sometimes depend on the situation at hand. Someone who is shy and quiet around acquaintances at the office may let loose and be outgoing on the weekends around her friends. Similarly, a twelve-year-old boy may be nervous and well behaved around his strict parents, but his aggressiveness increases when he's around his friends in the schoolyard. Psychologists have found that developing tests to measure personality is not an easy task, especially since individual experiences and interactions in social situations pave erratic paths that are difficult to follow.

Differing Views of Personality

The main target of trait theorists is the behavior of the individual, whereas social-learning theorists believe external elements, such as the environment, hold the key to understanding what causes particular types of behavior. They also believe that both individual and environmental aspects work together by ultimately contributing to each situation indirectly. Understanding how a person handles certain situations based on his personal traits is the first step toward pinpointing behavior patterns.

Aiding and Abetting Behavior

Rewards and punishments—reinforcements—influence your behavior in many ways and are encountered by direct, vicarious, and self-administered learning. Instances of direct reinforcements include concrete rewards of money, plaques, and trophies, as well as punishments that include being yelled at, denounced, or taking something important to the person away from her. Through vicarious learning, you think twice about doing something because you remember observing a similar situation with someone else, or you recall a story a friend or coworker told you that involved the same variables. Your behavior is then affected by your thoughts and conclusions about whether or not the observed behavior was favorable.

> If you've been feeling a little blue lately or even if you're just having a bad day, look at yourself in the mirror and (out loud) tell yourself how great you are. It may seem silly and will probably make you laugh (is that such a bad thing?), but it will also likely improve your mood somewhat.

Finally, reinforcements that are self-administered may arguably be the most powerful contribution to your overall demeanor. Statements you administer to yourself like "I can do it," "Hang in there," "I look good," "I look bad," "I'm too tall," or "This is my color" shape your personality in that they can either build or crush self-esteem and in return, project a positive or negative image of who you are to the world.

Reacting to Situations

Personality is determined by many factors and functions on many levels. Thus, social-learning theorists contend that your behavior and reactions to situations are the combination of the specifics of the situation at hand, how you see those situations, and what you learned from observing similar situations in the past. Distinctive personal differences come to the forefront of your thoughts when you're preparing to react to a given situation. The following list is a compilation of some of those differences that social-learning theorists think are important:

Proficiency—intellectual, physical, and social skills

Point of view—interpretation of situations and opinions

Estimation—determining whether results of behavior will be favorable or rejected

Level of importance—behavior in one situation may be more important than behavior in other situations (for example, performing acts to impress coworkers and performing acts to impress the boss)

Personal goals—the ability to set realistic goals and act accordingly in order to achieve them

The relationship between the previous behavioral differences and the situations you encounter on a daily basis follows a give-and-take model. What you contribute is what you get back. Acting disinterested toward people who approach you causes them to stop approaching you, leaving you in a self-created world of solitude. Being friendly and responsive to people will make them feel warm and encourages them to approach you.

Psychoanalytic Approach

In stark contrast to the previous theories, which focused on the public personality and behavioral patterns, psychoanalytic theory turns inward to your private personality where unconscious motives are responsible for the behavior you exhibit.

Free Association

In Sigmund Freud's *Outline of Psychoanalysis* (1940), he compared the human mind to an iceberg in order to describe the structure of personality. The small portion of the iceberg that lies above the water represents the conscious mind, or all of the thoughts, feelings, and desires that you are fully aware of. The massive chunk below the surface represents your unconscious mind where all of the dreams, impulses, and repressed memories that are outside of your conscious awareness are housed. In order to begin to understand these unconscious mysteries, Freud used free association tactics to get a glimpse at what lay beneath. This exercise required the patient to talk about whatever came to mind no matter how relevant, nonsensical, or foreign the thoughts sounded. This technique, along with dream analysis and childhood memory evaluation, attempted to help patients understand themselves and their actions.

> Stream of consciousness is a term applied to a writing exercise utilized by James Joyce, Virginia Woolf, and Beat writer Jack Kerouac, to name a few, as a means of recording the conscious experience of a continuous flow of ideas, feelings, and images running through the mind at the exact moment they occur.

In addition to free association, Freud's idea that personality is constructed of three components (the id, ego, and superego) is one of the most widely recognized theories in psychology, and is often the subject of cartoons and comics.

Id

The id is the aspect of personality that wants immediate gratification of physical distress such as hunger, thirst, and sexual tension. These biological instincts dictate the id's loyalty to the pleasure principle in that it wants to get rid of pain and discomfort in order to experience satisfaction and relief. The id says, "I seek pleasure."

Ego

Of course, if you acted on the desires of the id you might find yourself acting in some very socially inappropriate ways. Left to its own devices, the id might drive you to snatch food right out of other people's hands or simply take the things that you desire from stores. The ego is the part of personality that mediates between the desires of the id and the demands of reality. Although the ego still seeks to gain pleasure, it operates on the reality principle where impulses are controlled when situations aren't favorable for meeting its demands. For example, finding a restroom, rather than using the sidewalk in the middle of a busy city to urinate on, is a decision made by the ego. It says, "I seek pleasure when it's appropriate."

Superego

The superego is best described as the little angel that sits on your right shoulder whispering morals into your ear. The superego censors and restrains the ego, makes value judgments, sets standards, and weighs consequences. It is the part of the personality where all of the moral standards and values that you have learned from your parents and society are internalized. It says, "I seek pleasure only if I don't have to do something unpleasurable to receive it."

All three parts of Freud's personality model seem as though they're vying for the spotlight, but usually they share the stage in order to approach a situation with as complete an understanding of it as possible. When they are struggling with each other, feelings of anxiety may become repressed only to show up at a later time, or they may be expressed in other forms such as rigorous exercise or extreme competition. These reactions are called *defense mechanisms* and are put into place to avoid feeling the conflict that goes on among the three impulses.

Defense Mechanisms

According to Anna Freud, daughter of the famous Sigmund, you employ several types of defense mechanisms in order to get yourself through tough times until you are capable of handling the situation from a more realistic approach. Repression, rationalization, reaction formation, projection, intellectualization, denial, and displacement are all ways in which you engage in some form of artifice. Let's take a closer look at these.

Repression is the most basic and most important mechanism in which painful and frightful memories that incite guilt, shame, or self-worthlessness are kept out of your conscious reach and stored in the unconscious region of the mind. Rationalization is best illustrated by Aesop's fable where the fox decides the grapes are sour only after he can't reach them. You follow the reasoning that sounds good at the time, rather than the reasoning that best reflects the situation, taking on an "I didn't really want it anyway" attitude.

Reaction formation is hiding a motive from yourself by performing acts that display the extreme opposite of that motive. For example, you may hate your mother-in-law, but are ashamed that you feel that way, so you go out of your way to be extra nice to her. Projection is when you assign your own offensive traits to other people in an attempt to avoid disliking yourself. Intellectualization is coping with stressful situations in purely abstract and intellectual terms. People who work in a field where suffering and death are constant must attempt to detach themselves emotionally in order to perform the job successfully (doctors, police officers, firefighters, etc.).

Denial occurs when the reality of the situation is too hard to accept, and therefore you refuse to acknowledge it. Displacement is the defense mechanism in which motives that cannot be fulfilled in the intended way are expressed in other ways such as art, music or poetry.

Humanistic Views

The humanistic approach is often discussed in relation to an individual's phenomenology, the study in which only a human's conscious interpretations and subjective experience of objects and events are relevant to their personality traits. This belief is in direct opposition to the previous theory, because it rejects motivational and subconscious drives. Carl Rogers pioneered this way of thinking and, like Freud, created his beliefs based on his experiences in working with emotionally afflicted people.

Rogers encouraged a positive, optimistic outlook, believing a person has the ability to change for the better. He practiced person-centered therapy that included sessions in which the client would discuss the problems she was having and what she would like to do about them. As a therapist, Rogers developed the concept of "unconditional positive regard." This means that although Rogers would respond genuinely to patients' behavior even if it angered or irritated him, his essential care and respect for the client was not damaged by negative things the client brought up in a session. Centered on a patient's ideal self, thoughts, feelings, and solutions emerged in order to help the person assess the problem, find a solution, and develop a set of goals and plans that would help her become who she would like to be.

In analyzing one's own characteristics and abilities, self-conscious thought patterns develop and the person begins to ask herself a series of questions. Placing the responsibility of personality traits in the hands of consciousness allows the person to direct her own fate, live up to her real potential, and ultimately feel happy and satisfied with the results.

Popular Personality Tests

Psychological tests are often used to assess different aspects of an individual's personality, and can range from formal tests administered by psychologists to informal assessments that you perform on an almost daily basis. First impressions are often the most judgmental exchanges humans can have with each other. Stereotypes can be placed upon people based on the kind of clothes they wear, the people they are with, or even the type of food they eat. For instance, upon meeting someone for the first time, you notice his nose is pierced. In just an instant, you conjure up images of punk rockers, motorcycle gangs, and other rebels of society. Sleeves of tattoos must surely be hidden under that long sleeved sweater! By solely focusing on his pierced nose, you've given it such a high level of importance that all your judgments of him were based on that one aspect of his personality. However, more substantial methods have been developed to assess personality. These include observational methods, personality inventories, and projective techniques.

> If you are interested in taking a personality test in your spare time, you can find several on the Internet. However, as many of these are not proved to be accurate, don't put too much faith in the results. Regardless, they can be a fun way to pass time and perhaps learn a bit more about yourself.

Observational Methods

People can be observed by watching them in their natural settings, placing them in difficult situations to see how well they perform, and by conducting an interview.

The interview can be unstructured (the majority of the information revealed is decided by the interviewee) or structured (the interviewer covers predetermined topics in order to compare and contrast, for example, multiple job applicants). Rating scales are also popular when conducting job interviews. An example of what might be rated includes but is not limited to self-confidence, poise, emotional stability, interaction with others, personal relationships, and initiative.

Personal Inventories

Self-observations are measured by an individual's personal inventories in which a questionnaire, much like Cattell's factor analysis and yes-or-no test, is presented to the person so their feelings, thoughts, and reactions to situations can be recorded and analyzed. Both the Minnesota Multiphasic Personality Inventory (MMPI) and the California Psychological Inventory (CPI) feature statements that measure personality traits.

The MMPI was initially geared toward people with personality disorders or serious mental illness, but it has also been used extensively in examining typical personality traits. The MMPI does not encompass a broad enough range to measure "normal" personalities; therefore, others have been developed that better address that. The CPI, for one, includes a measure of academic capabilities.

Projective Techniques

The most recognizable example of projective techniques is the famous inkblot series that comprise the Rorschach test. Developed by Hermann Rorschach (1884–1922) in the 1920s, the test is conducted by presenting a person with an inkblot. The person is asked to look at it and describe everything he thinks the inkblot looks like. The idea is to get the person's initial response (open-minded, agitated, insightful, disagreeable) so a personality evaluation can be determined. Extensive training, more than that of any other test, is required in order to make professional assessments.

Rorschach came up with the idea for the inkblot test after observing a game of "Blotto" that children were playing in a psychiatric hospital. He happened to notice the differences in answers given and how these answers could provide insight into the children's minds; thus the Rorschach test was born.

A similar test called the Thematic Apperception Test (TAT), created by Henry Murray (1893–1988) in the 1920s, presents up to twenty photographs of ambiguous subjects to individuals who, in turn, create their own stories about what is taking place or what is about to take place in the illustration. As the story is being told, the psychologist picks up on the underlying messages by looking for clues to the person's motives, emotions, and characteristics.

Both tests are used as a starting point in predicting behavior and are considered in conjunction with further investigation such as the person's observed attitudes, or life history.

SOCIAL COGNITION—
Thinking About Yourself and Others

SOCIAL PSYCHOLOGY IS THE STUDY of how you interact with people, what you think of them, and how you act when you're around them. Beliefs and attitudes mold your perceptions, distort them, and often bias your thought processes. They come into play when you decide who you like or dislike and to what extent you allow society to influence your behavior and perceptions.

Humans as Social Beings

As a human, you perform certain thought processes that help shape your perceptions of people and social situations. First, you observe or collect data (what is the information?); second, you detect covariation (how is the information relative to other information?); and third, you infer cause and effect (what causes the information?). Though you operate on this intuitive level of scientific reasoning, your attitudes and beliefs influence your decisions, as you'll see later in this chapter. Observing data and detecting covariation are explained here, while inferring cause and effect will be explained later when discussing interpreting behavior.

Observing and Collecting Data

Out of all the many different types of information you collect on a daily basis, the kind of information that seems to stand out the most in your mind is vivid information. Studies have shown that humans are more reactive to graphic, dramatic information than they are to less dynamic information. Even if it is the same information, when it is presented in a way that stands out more clearly in your mind, you will most likely be influenced by that information.

Mass media plays a major role in this kind of data collection, and in some cases can be one of the most influential in our decision-making. If a news station dryly reports the results of an abortion survey by simply stating there are more people that believe a woman has the right to choose, you are more likely to remember the vivid, two-second photo spot portraying an antiabortion march than you are the results of the survey. Thus, you might inaccurately conclude that there are more antiabortionists than there are people who are pro-choice.

> Those warnings against allowing your children too much time in front of the television certainly do have some bearing. If a child grows up watching too much television, she might develop her social reality based on what she is seeing on television.

Another way you collect information is by developing theories of your own, especially concerning subjects such as capital punishment, abortion, and racism. Your theories often distort how you interpret the data you receive, for example, from television or the newspaper. Two people on opposite sides of the capital punishment debate can read the same article that analyzes both the pros and cons of the issue, yet still feel their argument was either strongly supported or strongly biased against. This illustration of how people filter information can also be seen in schemata and scripts, which will be discussed later in the chapter.

Detecting Covariation

When two elements vary in their relationship to each other, such as height and weight, they are said to have a correlation. Part of how you interact socially involves your ability to understand or misread these correlations. For example, you might believe that people who are antiabortionists tend to be against capital punishment as well. A lot of times these correlations are assumed and turn out not to be correct. Thus, a platform for stereotyping and prejudiced judgment evolves.

Beliefs and Attitudes

You tend to make assumptions about a person's attitudes and beliefs based on a known belief. For example, if you know your coworker is against abortion, you might conclude that she believes in gun control, is against capital punishment, and believes marijuana use should be severely penalized. This way of thinking is based on cognitive consistency—the theory that all people try to be consistent in their beliefs and attitudes as reflected by the consistency of their behavior.

Consistency Between Beliefs and Attitudes

One way to look at the consistency between beliefs and attitudes is to examine how people rationalize things. If you believe that a particular television produces the best picture, color, and sound, you start to persuade yourself that they are the most desirable qualities. On the opposite scale, wishful thinking is when you believe that the television is acceptable; therefore, you persuade yourself that it has the qualities you're looking for and is indeed acceptable. Both rationalization and wishful thinking show how one can affect the other, and in turn, account for how you perceive things on a somewhat unrealistic basis.

Consistency Between Attitudes and Behavior

Attitudes are a combination of beliefs and feelings and can be affected when confronted with social pressures. An example of inconsistency between attitudes and behavior can be seen in a study conducted by R. LaPiere during the 1930s and published in the journal

Social Forces. A white professor traveled the United States with a young Chinese couple. At the time, prejudice against Asians was strong and there was no law against denying guests accommodations based on race. The three commuters stopped at over 200 hotels, motels, and restaurants and were served at all the restaurants and all but one hotel without any hassles. Later, a letter was sent to all the businesses that they visited asking them if they would be willing to provide services to a Chinese couple. Of the 128 replies received, 92 percent said they wouldn't. In conclusion, the business owners displayed behavior that was far different from their actual beliefs.

> When confronted with a situation, people often do things they don't like. Their behavior is affected then, not only by our beliefs and attitudes, but by social pressures as well.

Similarly, peer pressure can induce actions that aren't consistent with what you believe, but are consistent with your attitudes toward social situations and what others think of you. Teenagers often drink alcohol to "fit in" and may put their beliefs aside in order to conform to the social pressure. Although attitudes don't always predict your behavior, attitudes based on direct experience can influence it. For instance, a person whose mother died in a drunk-driving accident may advocate harsher penalties for drunk drivers and take part in the annual drunk-driving awareness campaign.

Cognitive Dissonance Theory

As attitudes can affect behavior, behavior can affect attitudes. Leon Festinger's (1919–1989) theory of cognitive dissonance holds that when your beliefs and attitudes oppose each other or your behavior, you are motivated to reduce the dissonance through changes in behavior or cognition. The theory itself has been influential in predicting behavior that reflects an inconsistency in attitudes. Behaving in ways that conflict with one's attitudes causes pressure to change the attitudes in order to be consistent with the behavior.

Social Schemata and Scripts

Schemata and scripts are a way of collecting data in order to develop your own conclusions and theories about everyday social situations and interactions. Those conclusions and theories can change, however, when new information is introduced.

Schemata

Schemata refer to cognitive structures stored in memory that are abstract representations of events, objects, and relationships in the real world. It is a key ingredient of cognitive theories of psychological phenomena. Schematic processing is the process of retrieving the schema from your memory that is most consistent with the information being received.

Since you already have pre-existing notions and ideas about what a situation or a person should be all about, any new information you receive on the subject is compared with what you already have. Schemata and schematic processing allows you to store and organize the most relevant and striking information, which will surface when the need arises. For example, when you're told you're about to meet someone who is an extrovert, you automatically think of that person as energetic, friendly, warm, loud, and sociable. You then prepare yourself for the meeting based on these schemata that you've collected.

> While schemata help you to understand information easily and quickly, they can have a drawback. When you already have information for a particular schema in place, you may have a tendency to pay attention only to new information that fits in with the old information and ignore new information that contradicts or doesn't fit with the old information.

Scripts

Scripts are schemata or abstract cognitive representations of events and social interactions. When you greet someone with "How are you?" the script calls for the person to respond, "I'm fine, thank you." Whereas schemata are the data you've collected for forming impressions of people, scripts represent the data you have for social events and interactions. A greeting script like the previous one can sometimes be misinterpreted and one person might go on and on about how his life is not going well while the person who initially asked the question waits for a chance to escape! The birthday script tells you that you should dress a certain way, act a certain way, bring a gift, and expect certain situations like a birthday cake and the blowing out of candles. Scripts break the ice, making it easier to start conversations with people whom you don't know.

Forming Impressions

People often use mental shortcuts to form impressions of other people. For example, social categorization involves sorting people into different groups based on common characteristics. While this is a natural process that allows you to make decisions and judgments quickly, it can lead to very inaccurate impressions of those around you.

While first impressions are indeed important, additional information that you receive after the initial impression can change what you think about and how you behave around a particular person. Using the primacy effect, you can determine how much of an impact first impressions have on you and how much they influence any new information you might receive. Primacy effect is the tendency for initial information to carry more weight than information received later (also, in memory experiments, the tendency for initial words in a list to be recalled more readily than later words).

As seen in A. S. Luchins's *The Order of Presentation in Persuasion* (1957), the following paragraph was used in an experiment to determine if the primacy effect was apparent in people's assessment of what kind of person "Jim" was:

> *Jim left the house to get some stationery. He walked out into the sun-filled street with two of his friends, basking in the sun as he walked. Jim entered the stationery store, which was full of people. Jim talked with an acquaintance while he waited to catch the clerk's eye. On his way out, he stopped to chat with a school friend who was just coming into the store. Leaving the store, he walked toward the school. On his way he met the girl to whom he had been introduced the night before. They talked for a short while, and then Jim left for school. After school, Jim left the classroom alone. Leaving the school, he started on his long walk home. The street was brilliantly filled with sunshine. Jim walked down the street on the shady side. Coming down the street toward him, he saw the pretty girl whom he had met on the previous evening. Jim crossed the street and entered a candy store. The store was crowded with students, and he noticed a few familiar faces. Jim waited quietly until he caught the counterman's eye and then gave his order. Taking his drink, he sat down at a side table. When he had finished with his drink he went home.*

The description, when split in half, describes Jim in two different ways. Up until the sentence that begins "After school, Jim left . . . ," Jim is friendly and outgoing. After that point, he's described as a shy, introverted, and unfriendly person. Of the people who read only the first half of the description, 95 percent thought him to be friendly, whereas of the people who read only the last half of the description, 3 percent thought him to be friendly. What's interesting is that of the people who read the entire description with the "unfriendly Jim" description first, only 18 percent thought him to be friendly. This shows that our initial impression of a person has the most significance in our general opinion of a person.

Interpreting Others' Behavior—And Your Own

As mentioned earlier in the chapter, inferring the cause and effect of behavior helps you understand not only the behavior of others, but your own as well. An attribution problem is the attempt to infer the cause of a particular behavior. Distinctiveness, consistency, and consensus are all criteria you use when determining the cause and effect of behavior.

Distinctiveness

One morning you wake up with a runny nose. You look out your window and notice your flowers are blooming, so you assume they are causing the sniffles. You test this hypothesis by leaving the area where the flowers are to see if you still have the symptoms. If the symptoms are still there, you decide that there is nothing distinctive about the flowers and decide they are not the cause. You have just used the criteria involved with distinctiveness to determine the cause of the problem.

Consistency and Consensus

If the symptoms occurred around the same time every year for the past few years, you might be convinced that the flowers are definitely to blame. If it's the first time it's occurred, then the consistency isn't relevant because it never happened before. You then call the doctor and he explains that a lot of people have called to complain about the same symptoms, which is always the case at that particular time of year when flowers are in bloom. Since you're not alone in the situation (others are reacting to the same stimulus), this is the consensus.

The attribution theory is challenged when one takes into consideration the biases that lead us to explain behavior. For instance, many will base our ideas of an individual's personality according to his behavior without taking into consideration environmental factors. That particular behavior may not reflect that individual's personality on an everyday basis; rather, it is reflecting the situational factors at hand.

You use the same criteria when trying to determine and understand the behavior of other people. When a friend tells you that the food was great at the Chinese restaurant she just went to, you have to determine if your friend said it was great because the food was really great, if it was because your friend is biased toward Chinese food, or if it was because of the social situation—for instance, it was her birthday, everyone was in a great mood, and everything was great. Thus, in an effort to interpret others' behavior, you examine why something occurred and what caused it to occur.

Self-Perception

The theory of self-perception concludes that you make the same judgments about yourself, use the same processes, and make the same errors as you do when making judgments about others. When an athlete endorses a product, you may wonder if he really uses that product and believes in its consumer benefits, or if the athlete is just using it as a means to gain wealth and publicity. You often take a look at your own beliefs and attitudes in the same manner. Did you buy the shirt because it was on sale or because you actually liked it?

An induced-compliance experiment was conducted to illustrate how people go about understanding their own behavior. College students were offered money to go into a room, one at a time, and perform repetitive, dull tasks for one hour. After finishing the tasks, some students were given $1 to tell the next student that the tasks were fun and interesting, while other students were given $20 to say the same thing. Subjects who were paid only $1 said they actually enjoyed the tasks, but students who were paid $20 didn't find it any more enjoyable than the control subjects who were given money to say something to the next student.

According to the self-perception theory, the students had to ask themselves why they were saying the tasks were fun and interesting. The student who was next in line observed the previous student getting paid $20 and then saying it was fun, thus he assumed anyone would say the tasks were fun for that amount of money. On the other hand, students who observed the previous student getting paid $1 assumed that he must have really enjoyed the tasks if he only received a dollar for performing them.

Stereotyping and Prejudice

As seen previously in this chapter, first impressions often invoke stereotypical judgments about a particular person. This is based on your beliefs and attitudes and even on your own behavior. Gender, race, political stance, and personality contribute to the stereotypes we place on others.

One kind of stereotype is self-fulfilling stereotypes. When schematic processing causes you to create stereotypes of a person, it's not always with bad intent. Lack of experiences, both socially and casually, often result in a lack of information—information you need to process in order to form your impressions of a person.

When you interact with the very person or group you're stereotyping, you may be doing so in order to self-perpetuate and self-fulfill these stereotypes. For example, after the terrorist attacks on September 11, 2001, some people developed the stereotype that all Muslims were violent and aggressive toward non-Muslims. As a result, people holding this stereotype may feel uncomfortable around people with a Middle East background, mistakenly believing that these individuals have hostility and anger toward people outside of their religion. As a result, the person who associates with a Muslim individual will justify his own discomfort by hiding behind a stereotype that is neither true nor accurate, but may seem amplified because of his preconceived ideas about Muslims.

> Stereotypes are also called implicit personality theories because, in essence, stereotypes are small-scale theories of covariation, in which one set of traits or behaviors go with another set of traits or behaviors. For example, homosexual males are often assumed to be effeminate, even though that is only true of some homosexual men and is also true of some heterosexual men.

Studies show that you may also act differently with attractive people than you do with people you find unattractive. If the stereotype of an attractive person leads one to believe that the person they just met is sociable, trustworthy, friendly, kind, and fun, then the reaction to that person will lean in a positive direction. But, because of your prejudiced attitude toward attractive people, you may be blinded to the fact that the attractive person you just met is actually obnoxious, arrogant, selfish, and rude.

SOCIAL INTERACTIONS
and Interpersonal Behavior

NOW THAT YOU UNDERSTAND something about your own emotions, motives, behaviors, and thought processes, this chapter will look into how you take all of that and relate it to other people—such as in forging friendships, building relationships, and being in love. In addition, you'll explore how your behavior differs within society as opposed to social functions.

The Person and the Situation

One way to gain insight into how and why you relate to others is to look at how the people around you and the society you live in influence your behavior. For example, when you're having a terrible day and you're in a nasty mood, how is it that you can find it in yourself to be extremely courteous, pleasant, and kind to your boss, the store clerk, or your coworker? For one, it depends on how much you want them to like you and how much you want to be accepted by them.

The boss provides an obvious reason to be wary—he's not the guy you want giving you the evil eye all day because you were rude to him in the hallway! But, you might be aware that the store clerk and your coworker had nothing to do with your bad mood, so you treat them as you would want to be treated. Others in this situation don't care if their bad mood is misplaced as they take it out on the wrong person; they're not thinking about how much a person likes them at that particular moment. As you'll see, it only takes one person to distract you from your task, interrupt your train of thought, and cause you to behave in ways that don't represent your true form.

The Presence of Another

In 1897, to study how a person works in the presence of another person, psychologist Norman Triplett conducted an experiment to test coaction by monitoring how fast children turned a fishing wheel while they were alone in a room and when another person was present. (*Coaction* is the term used to describe how individuals interact together. In this experiment, it describes the act of two children performing the same task.)

In this study, Triplett placed two children in the same room and gave them both the task of turning a fishing wheel. He monitored how fast the children worked. He compared these results with how quickly the children worked when alone in the room and given the same task. Triplett's findings showed that children worked faster in coaction than when working alone. Psychologists then followed in Triplett's footsteps and conducted similar experiments that tested how well an individual performed in front of a group of people, or an audience. The same outcomes were witnessed, and together, the ramifications of coaction and audience influence were termed *social facilitation.*

Additional studies related to social facilitation have been generated in other animals. In the scientific journal *Physiological Zoology* (1937), S. C. Chen details how ants will dig at a faster rate when they're working in groups than they will when they're working alone.

Monkey See; Monkey Do

While you're affected by the pressure of being driven to work harder and strive for more when another person is performing the same task as you, you're also pushed outward, prompted to help others in need when you see that the help is coming from someone else.

How you interpret situations is the key element in whether or not you're going to contribute your services. For example, it's become so common to see people sleeping on sidewalks and park benches that you just assume the person is homeless and catching a nap wherever and whenever he can. It's a rare occasion when someone stops to see if the person is really sleeping, if he's extremely ill and in need of care, or if he's dead.

Bystander apathy is common within social situations. Remarkably, the size of the group can affect whether a person will take action, often moreso than the typical attitudes or behavior of the person herself. The larger the group, the less likely someone will contribute, because she assumes there are enough people around that surely someone else will act.

But is it "okay" simply to walk by and ignore someone who appears to be sleeping in a public area? The term *pluralistic ignorance* may help in answering the question. Pluralistic ignorance describes a state of thinking in which individuals in a group take their cues from other individuals in a group. For example, if everyone else is being calm about the person sleeping on the sidewalk, and no one is offering assistance, then the situation must not be an emergency and therefore doesn't require my help.

Diffusion of Responsibility

Since most people tend to look to others as models for how they should behave, diffusion of responsibility may take place. Diffusion of responsibility takes place when a group of people witnesses the same emergency, yet certain people do not offer assistance because other people are present, therefore diffusing their need to act—"someone else will offer help, so I don't need to."

One of the most frequently cited examples of this diffusion of responsibility was the 1964 murder of a young woman named Kitty Genovese. As she returned home from work late one evening, she was brutally attacked and repeatedly stabbed outside of her apartment entrance. Genovese cried out that she had been stabbed and screamed for help. One neighbor yelled out his window to tell the attacker to leave the woman alone, none of the neighbors contacted policed until approximately 30 minutes after the attack began. While the initial report that appeared in the *New York Times* sensationalized the case, later investigations have revealed that there were other factors about the situation that contributed to the failure of the witnesses to call for help. A 2007 article by Manning, Levine, and Collins that appeared in *American Psychologist* suggests that many of the witnesses did not realize that Genovese had been stabbed and that the layout of the apartment complex made it difficult for the neighbors to clearly see what was actually happening.

While the Genovese case has often been misrepresented in popular psychology literature, the incident did inspire a wealth of social psychology research on group behavior in crisis situations. Unlike pluralistic ignorance where one observed behavior affects another's behavior, diffusion of responsibility took place because the neighbors were unable to see the reactions of others; however, no one took action because they thought, "Someone else will take care of it." The need to behave in a socially acceptable manner also plays a role in the failure of witnesses to take action in such situations. In the Genovese incident, many of the witnesses believed that they were simply hearing a domestic dispute and had no idea that the young woman was actually being murdered. When the situation is unclear and the behavior of those involved seems ambiguous, it becomes even less likely that witness will take action.

Compliance

Yielding to another person's wishes without changing your true beliefs puts you in a situation of compliance. You believe Granny Smith apples make a better apple pie, but your mother-in-law thinks Red Delicious makes the better pie. You agree to make the pie with Red Delicious apples, but you still believe Granny Smith apples are tastier. Though you've submitted to your mother-in-law's request, you haven't given up your own opinion on the subject.

Rebellion often develops when none of the choices presented to an individual are favorable. For example, if the choice is either to conform to the decision at hand or obey the main influencer, a person might choose neither as a complete act of rebellion against the situation as a whole.

Johnny has the choice of either going to school and having to listen to the teacher and actually participate in class discussions, or stay at home with his alcoholic father who will continue to yell at him all day. Not liking either of the choices, Johnny decides to rebel against both of them by neither going to school nor staying at home. Instead, he spends his day hanging out by the river with some of his neighborhood friends.

> There are two types of compliance—conformity and obedience—both of which will be discussed later in this chapter. Both instances involve a main influencer in which a positive (reward) or negative (denunciation) response is elicited from the influencer in reaction to the person's compliant or noncompliant behavior.

Conformity and Peer Pressure

One type of compliance is conformity. Conformity is best explained in relation to peer pressure, especially when large groups of people hold the same opinions and beliefs. It's not uncommon to feel uncomfortable in a situation where your opinions and beliefs are not the same as others in the group. As a child, you know smoking is bad for your health, and if your parents caught you, you'd be in trouble, but when you're standing in that circle with all of your friends and everyone is taking a drag to see what it's like, it's all too tempting to give in to the pressure. You may argue that smoking causes all kinds of diseases, but your friends will argue back that one little drag won't do anything. Do you conform, or do you hold your own? Everyone else thinks its okay, so it must be. Besides, if you don't conform, your friends might think you're a coward, right?

One of the best-known experiments on the powerful effects of conformity was conducted in the 1950s by a social psychologist named Solomon Asch (1907–1996). Participants were shown a line and then asked to select the line that was the same length out of three other lines. When they were in a group where the other "participants" (who were actually in on the true nature of the experiment) claimed that an obviously longer line was the correct match to the original line, nearly 75 percent of participants agreed with the rest of the group.

The next time you are faced with a situation in which you are feeling peer pressure, think first of your own responsibility for your actions. If you get it out of your head that you can blame peer pressure for bad behavior and there's no one to blame but yourself, you are more likely not to fall prey to peer pressure.

This way of thinking can be applied to almost any group situation—even as adults. Consider the group of jurors who are given the difficult task of deciding someone's fate—innocent or guilty. If eleven jurors decide on a guilty verdict and the twelfth juror disagrees, how long before he conforms to their verdict, if he ever does? It's possible that he might conform simply because he doesn't think they'll ever see his point since the odds are so stacked against him.

In both the smoking and the jury example, the individual has to re-evaluate information he's already formed an opinion about. Part of growing up is learning how to distinguish between what you believe, what others want you to believe, and how willing you are to understand another point of view. But it doesn't get any easier as adults. With all the information available to you at any given moment, by way of the media and the Internet, you're forced to constantly reassess copious amounts of information in order to form strong, well-rounded choices, beliefs, and opinions. And while "majority rules" in most instances, it's a tough road to follow when you find yourself disagreeing with popular opinion.

Obedience

Being submissive to authority is an everyday reality that all people share. Paying taxes, working to earn money, obtaining a driver's license, obeying rules of conduct in public places and so on are just a few examples of how you obey a higher source. Just as it's important for children to obey their teachers, it's important that teachers follow the principal's rules about curriculum, which in turn follows the standards set by the local school district. There are four elements—social norms, surveillance, buffers, and justifying principles—that help determine what causes you to be (or not to be) obedient:

> **Social norms**—These are rules that have been established and are delegated by the community, government, or other empowered group for individual associates and constituents to follow on a regular basis.

Surveillance—When the delegators of the established rules and regulations are not around to administer them, they aren't always followed. However, when they are present, obedience levels increase as every effort is made to display how the rules are being followed.

Buffers—A buffer is a device or situation that permits obedience or disobedience to occur more easily. For example, the guard hitting the switch on the electric chair may find it easier to obey his superior's orders because he doesn't have any real contact with the ill-fated convict.

Justifying principles—The guard may not believe it's right to kill another human being, but his duty is justified by the ideals of his superior: the person performed inhumane crimes and therefore must be punished, and the guard believes in following the orders of a superior without question.

In many ways, obedience can be a good thing. It causes children to do as their parents and teachers ask and helps maintain an ordered, lawful society. But what happens when people obey orders that are unjust, immoral, or downright evil? Social psychologist Stanley Milgram (1933–1984) conducted one of the best-known experiments on obedience, demonstrating the dramatic affect that authority has on how far a person will go to obey. In his experiment, people were asked to take the role of a "teacher" and deliver an electric shock to a "learner" if questions were answered incorrectly. The learner was actually an accomplice in the experiment, who was simply pretending to be shocked. After each error, the "teacher" was instructed by the experimenter to proceed to a progressively stronger shock. Eventually, the "learner" began begging to be released, even screaming in agony, while the experimenter continued to insist that the experiment must continue. Shockingly, more than 65 percent of participants continued participating and delivered the maximum shocks. Milgram's experiments, while obviously unethical by today's standards, demonstrated that obedience can be a dangerous thing and that the situation can play an important role in how far people will go in order to obey an authority figure.

Friendships and Romantic Relationships

You are attracted to others in a variety of ways and on a variety of levels: acquaintances, friendships, intimate relationships, and family bonds. While you cannot choose your family, you can choose your friends and life partners. How you choose them and why is what the next sections will explore.

Physical Attraction

First impressions, stereotypes, and behavior are all affected by a person's physical appearance. Whether you like to believe it or not, a person's looks count—at first. Once you go beyond the surface and delve into the greater mysteries that define an individual, the importance of appearance seems to fade away. But why do attractive people seem to get more attention than those who are less attractive?

Perhaps one explanation can be found in the following experiment conducted by Kenrick and Gutierrez in 1980. In the study published in the *Journal of Applied Social Psychology*, male college students were shown a television program that featured several young, striking women. Similarly, a separate group of men and women were shown a picture of a beautiful woman with very attractive features. After watching the television show, and after being shown the photo of the attractive female, both the male college students and the group of men and women were shown a picture of an average-looking woman. Both groups gave the woman a low rating on the level of attractiveness.

The results of this experiment point to the notion that standards for beauty may be so elevated that recognizing and admiring ordinary beauty can be difficult. Had the groups been shown the photograph of the average-looking woman before they saw the images of the extremely beautiful women, they might have given her a higher rating. Thus, the "picture" of beauty in your mind is of the women you see on television, and that is what you're comparing the rest of the world to. This may cause you to treat attractive people better because they represent your ideal of beauty and because you assume they have all the internal qualities you admire.

Likeness

Finding something in common with a coworker, neighbor, or classmate is one of the easiest ways of building relationships. Making friends that like to do the same things you do makes life more fun and interesting and provides a gateway for you to appreciate their differences as well.

Love

Once you start building friendships, it's only a matter of time before a serious, loving relationship can start to evolve. According to social psychologist Zick Rubin, romantic love is comprised of three key elements: caring, attachment, and intimacy. Intimacy is shared at a greater level when experiences are exchanged in more depth. Stronger feelings emerge and more is at stake. While everyone has her own idea of what love is and what makes her fall in love with one person and not another, the right blend of physical attractiveness, likeness, and intimacy usually does the trick.

It appears that both men and women hold the same opinion concerning romantic love. In a study conducted by Campbell and Berscheid in 1976, 86 percent of men and 80 percent of women said that marriage was out of the question if they didn't feel they were in love with their partner.

Altruism and Prosocial Behavior

Altruism is often perceived as random acts of kindness in which the giver is willing to make a selfless and sometimes life-threatening act on the behalf of someone else, even someone unknown to the giver. The founder of sociobiology, Edward Wilson (1929–), holds the belief that altruism in human beings is similar to that seen in other animals in which mothers will risk their own lives in order to save the lives of their offspring and ultimately their genes. Humans are loyal to their kin and many heroic acts can be found in soldiers who risk their lives every day in numerous ways to protect the survival of their country's communities. On the other hand, critics of this type of heroism believe they defend their cultural and religious beliefs, as well as their honor.

> Critics argue that there are no selfless acts and therefore altruism in its purest form does not exist. They state that the giver derives pleasure in one form or another from the "selfless act," and thus the giver is rewarded and the act is no longer selfless.

So how is altruism defined? There are two working definitions. Biological altruism is making a selfless act on the behalf of another in order to attempt to save that person's life, even though your own life may be at risk—for instance, jumping into a rushing river to try to save someone caught in a current. Psychological altruism is making a selfless act to the benefit of another though it does not reward you in any way—for instance, giving up your seat on the subway for someone else to sit down though you know you will be uncomfortable standing in the crowded train. Regardless of how you choose to define altruism, it is a phenomenon that is as of yet inexplicable to social psychologists.

There are a number of different factors that influence how likely you are to either help or not help another person. Some variables that increase the chance of helping behavior include the desire to feel good about being of assistance, having some type of personalized relationship with the other person, and actually knowing how to provide assistance. For example, if you see the woman who usually makes you your coffee each morning get struck by a car as she is going to lunch, you will be more likely to rush to her aid because you have a desire to help her, you know who she is, and you know how to provide basic first aid. Factors that decrease the likelihood of helping another person include being in a large group of people and not being sure if the person really needs assistance. For example, if you are in a crowded subway station and you see a man doubled over grabbing his throat, you might think that he is choking However, you might be less likely to help because you assume that someone else will do something and you might not be sure if the man is actually choking or if he just coughing because of a bad cold.

Aggression and Its Causes

Aggression is something that is seen in all walks of life. In fact, it's one of the defining characteristics humans have in common with other species within the animal kingdom. Not to be confused with how a bird might kill a rat for its food source, aggression is an act of hostility that one animal displays in front of another animal when it feels threatened, challenged, or an immediacy to protect its territory.

While the cause of aggression in animals is mainly about food supply, land territory, and dominance, human beings can show aggressive behavior for a number of different reasons. Aggressiveness can also take a number of different forms, such as verbal, mental, or physical behavior. How aggression is displayed can also vary depending upon whether you're a man or woman. Men are much more likely to display aggression through physical violence, while women usually display aggression through nonphysical or indirect methods.

One common reason why people display aggression is in order to defend their personal space. Think of the brother and sister who are constantly at each other's throats because the younger sibling won't leave the teenage sibling alone and he certainly can't seem to stay out of her room. Or recall a situation where an acquaintance physically got too close to you during a conversation, in which you felt so crowded you had to take a few steps back.

Certainly human beings act aggressively toward anyone or anything that jeopardizes the well-being of their children, but when finances are compromised because of a mix-up at the bank or when a newly purchased, expensive appliance fails to operate properly after just a few days, things can get pretty heated between the parties involved. So humans not only have a need to protect their personal space and the safety of their children, but humans are very touchy when it comes to their hard-earned financial abundance (or lack thereof) as well.

The Mentality of Groups

Identifying with a group is the process of adopting its beliefs, attitudes, and standards, as well as complying with its rules and regulations in an effort to gain closeness to other human beings and feel part of something larger than an individual's personal life. In other words, it makes you feel like you belong. You belong to a country, a state, a city, a county, a community, a parish, a family, a credit union, a gym, an art club, etc. Each group helps define who you are and exploits your talents and morals, and in turn you help define the group itself. This symbiotic relationship nourishes your spirit and gives you a sense of society.

> The groups you identify with are also called reference groups, because you refer to them when you need to understand your own opinions and analyze your behavior or reactions to situations.

The importance of groups starts at a young age. Children form groups in their classrooms as well as in their neighborhoods, and groups like the Girl Scouts, Boy Scouts, and the Boys and Girls Club of America help children develop strong personalities, learn skills that boost their confidence, and meet friends who could possibly last a lifetime.

Everyone wants to feel like they belong somewhere. That is why groups are so important to social lives. When you can relate to others, you are able to justify your beliefs and actions even though that justification isn't necessarily needed. Even so, you often feel more secure in your beliefs if you have a support group. Humans rely on the social interactions with others both to learn about their environments and to grow as individuals.

CHAPTER 18

STRESS,
Coping, and Health

REGARDLESS OF HOW SUCCESSFUL, healthy, proficient, or happy you are, stress is an unavoidable factor in life. Stress is such a common part of daily life that people often forget that there are actually many different sources of stress, ranging from personal issues to large-scale disasters. How often you experience it and how capable you are of handling it can be examined by exploring some of its main causes, different reactions you have toward it, and the physical dangers you face in coping with it.

Stressors and Stress

Stress refers to the response you have to extreme pressure, hardship, or pain that either occurs suddenly or builds up over time. It can be an emotional struggle; a physical obstacle that must be overcome; the result of being pulled in many different directions by demands from family, friends, and work; a response to an unpredicted emergency such as a natural disaster or loss of a loved one; and many other factors that cause unpleasant restlessness, which will be explored later in this chapter. While there are conflicting ideas as to what stress is—a response to stimulus, the stimulus itself, or the relationship to the stimulus—there are several main categories of stress: conflict, readjustment, daily inconveniences, and individual influences.

Conflict

One of the most common causes of stress is conflict, or being pulled between opposing goals, wishes, or motives. When you can't have the best of both worlds, such as needing money to buy a car and needing a car to get to the job that will supply the money, a conflict of motives occurs. Finding a working solution to this conflict produces a lot of stress, especially when you don't have social support from close friends and family. In addition to this common conflict, the following are the most common conflict-causing, motivational struggles that people experience, and therefore are the most problematic:

Independence/dependence—Turning to family and friends who have the resources to help is not always an easy thing to do because you may want to show them that you are mature enough, intelligent enough, and strong enough to make it in this world on your own.

Intimacy/isolation—While you have a strong desire to share love and intimacy with another person, the fear of being disliked or hurt presents a powerful opposing force. Relinquishing control and independence to another person is another troubling conflict that may get in your way of forming close relationships with other people.

Collaboration/competition—It is often emphasized that working together as a team produces the most rewarding results; however, putting your best foot forward in order to be respected and accepted by society entails showing off your own individual talents and making your abilities known.

Impulse/morals—When you set personal standards, you're able to exercise self-control, restraint, and etiquette as you take your environment into consideration. Conflict emerges when acting impulsively for selfish reasons, as in sexual or aggressive situations, produces guilt and regret.

Operating in intense opposition, these motives induce stressful situations that require extremely difficult choices to be made, usually decided upon after a lot of back-and-forth internal dialogue.

Readjustment

Major life changes involve both positive and negative readjustments. Being offered your dream job in an area that requires you to move 3,000 miles away from home can raise both emotional and physical stress levels. The Holmes-Rahe Social Readjustment Scale rates events that cause the most stress because of the pressures of time and the level of importance they carry. In 1968 while studying the relationship between stress and physical illness, Holmes and Rahe looked at the medical records of more than 5,000 individuals. These patients were asked to select the events that occurred in their lives during a one-year period. Score totals were then used to predict the odds in which a person would show signs of illness throughout the following year. Scores below 200 resulted in a 30 percent chance for illness; more than 50 percent of people with scores between 200 and 300 had health problems; and approximately 80 percent of the people whose scores totaled more than 300 got ill.

Although these conclusions remain the subject of skepticism, the scale continues to be a model for the development of new scales, as well as for new ways to measure how important a role stress plays in physical illness.

Life's Little Challenges

Daily inconveniences like the alarm not going off in the morning, losing your car keys, contending with traffic, spilling coffee on yourself, bills, and too little time to spend with loved ones may seem small enough on their own; but when encountered repetitively, they can cause enormous distress. Psychologists often refer to these types of stressors as "daily hassles." While these things often feel like small annoyances, they can add up to a major source of life stress. According to research by Burke and Martin (1985), the number of daily hassles you experience is a better predictor of physical illness than that of major life events such as changing jobs, moving, and divorce. Why? Because these small stressors have cumulative effects by adding up to take a toll of your psychical and psychological health.

The loss of a spouse, while hard enough to deal with on an emotional level, can effect stress in your daily routine because you find yourself having to take care of tasks you're not normally used to taking care of, like maintaining upkeep on your car, tracking finances, etc. These changes can be physically exhausting and learning how to handle them efficiently can produce an extreme amount of stress.

> There are several ways in which you can work to de-stress yourself. For instance, you can use relaxation techniques such as yoga, find ways to make yourself laugh such as watching a funny movie or going to a comedy club, and of course, exercise is always a great stress reliever.

A person's general outlook on life can also affect how he responds to small nuisances. A person brimming with optimism might handle being stuck in a traffic jam calmly by realizing "it is what it is" and there's nothing he can do to change it. So instead of becoming frustrated, he tries to come up with alternative methods to pass the time, such as reading. In contrast, the person in the next car might have had an awful day and proceeds to shout, bang his steering wheel, and beep his horn. Why people react differently to the same stressful experience is discussed in the next category of stress.

Individual Influences

While a person's individual assessment of a situation may contribute to her or his reaction to it, the distinctive elements of the stress itself are an important factor in determining the level at which the person experiences the stress. Predictability and controllability affect how this level is felt and dealt with.

Predictability is important because it gives you time to prepare a course of action as well as mentally ready yourself for the stress that's forthcoming. The results of experiments done with rats, in which signals were used to warn the rats a shock treatment was about to occur, proved that animals preferred to know when a stressful situation was about to happen. By pressing a metal bar, the rats received an audible signal preparing them for the shock; if they didn't press the bar, no warning was received. All the rats learned to press the bar, meaning all the rats preferred anticipating the displeasure rather than experiencing the uncertainty of when it would take place.

If you have a tendency to procrastinate, you'll likely need to keep an eye on your stress levels. Procrastination and stress feed off each other: you put off doing a task because the thought of doing it stresses you; you become stressed because the project is not completed.

Similar studies with humans yielded the same results. Women whose husbands were declared missing in action in Vietnam had more physical and emotional health problems than wives whose husbands were killed or taken as prisoners. Unable to experience "closure," these women lived life wondering about the state of their husbands, waiting for answers from the government, and struggling with when they should make the decision to let go and move on.

Controllability is another element that helps reduce stress. If you know you have the ability to stop the stressful situation, the stress itself won't be as severe. For example, the stress of holiday shopping can be dealt with more easily if you resolve you can always leave the store when it gets too exhausting.

How Stress Affects Physical Health

Headaches, heart attacks, and weakened immunity are just a few of the potentially dangerous physical effects of stress. These symptoms can become even more pronounced and potentially deadly when it involves long-term, chronic stress. Physiological reactions to stress include increased heart rate, blood pressure, and breathing rate; tensing of the muscles; dry mouth; and shaking, to name a few. In addition to these biological reactions, physical health begins to deteriorate when stress is continually experienced. Ulcers and heart disease may develop, and the immune system can weaken if the stress isn't treated efficiently.

Ulcers and Heart Disease

Ulcers occur when a hole in the lining of the stomach is caused by the release of too much hydrochloric acid. Hydrochloric acid works with enzymes in order to break down food during digestion. Many factors can cause excessive hydrochloric acid release, and stress is one of them. Again, rats were tested using the "warning signal" method before initiating jolts to the rats' tails. And again, the rats that had the good fortune of being warned showed fewer ulcerations than did the rats that were not warned.

Heart disease is another physical ailment that can be brought on by persistent stress. In 1981, the American Heart Association announced that "Type A" behavior should be declared a risk factor in heart disease.

What is Type A behavior?
Type A behavior is the term used to describe individuals who find it extremely difficult to relax. They're competitive on every level (even when playing games with children), experience anger and impatience with people they feel are incompetent, are always under the restraints of time, and continuously push themselves to achieve more.

Some researchers believe that the hostility characteristic exhibited in Type A individuals is the most crucial contributor to heart disease. Learning to slow down, believing in other people's capabilities, and setting realistic goals for oneself can in turn reduce the amount of hostility a person experiences. In some experiments, subjects were told to wait in line, and instead of becoming aggressive (tapping feet, sighing, getting angry at store clerks), were instructed to think about things they don't usually have time to think about or strike up a conversation with the person next to them. Redirecting the energy by turning it into something positive reduces the amount of stress that would normally be amplified by negative reactions to the situation.

The Immune System

Research has shown that stress can suppress the body's immune system, leaving people more open to disease and illness. For example, one study found that the end of important personal relationships through death or divorce can weaken the immune system. College students studying for final exams, for example, are more susceptible to respiratory infections because the body slows down its production of certain agents needed to prevent the illness.

But not everyone's immune system falls prey to stress. People who feel they are in control of their own life and display positive attitudes and take-charge behaviors perform the actions necessary to solve the problems that cause the stress. This may involve seeking help from other individuals or making changes (small or drastic) to alleviate stress.

How Stress Affects Mental Health

Along with physical illness, psychological reactions to stressful events can hinder your ability to think clearly and logically. In a panic, a person might be so caught up in worrying about the repercussions of a negative end result that he or she fails to take the steps needed to cause a positive end result. For example, if a nightclub filled with hundreds of people catches fire and everyone's initial panicked response is to run for the same exit, some people can be trampled on or crushed in the process. Some people worry so much about the possible consequences of a decision that they can't make the decision and it gets made for them. Along with cognitive responses to stress, emotional responses such as anxiety, anger, and depression affect how well you cope with it.

Anxiety

Anxiety is the tense feeling you get when you are worried about bad things that might happen in the future. Anxiety is categorized into two types: objective anxiety and neurotic anxiety. Objective anxiety is what Freud described as a person's realistic approach to the situation causing the anxiety. The person is prompted to act in order to get rid of the anxiety he feels. Neurotic anxiety, on the other hand, is anxiety that Freud believed to be caused by unconscious-driven intentions that the person does not recognize, and therefore is unable to understand or control.

> Anxiety disorders are the most common type of mental illness. According to statistics from the National Institute of Mental Health (NIMH), more than 40 million American adults suffer from at least one form of anxiety disorder. Oddly enough, anxiety disorders are the most undertreated, which could prove why many people take treatment into their own hands by turning to drugs and alcohol.

Anxiety is approached in many ways and is believed to appear in many situations. Fear, worry, dread, and a feeling of urgency are all types of anxiety and exist on many levels, some of which can cause serious disorders, which will be discussed in the next chapter. Causes of anxiety are also approached differently. Freud believed that neurotic anxiety is caused by the id's conflict with the ego and superego, and since this conflict exists on an unconscious plane, the person has no control of it, and therefore experiences feelings of helplessness.

Anger

Anger is a response to stress that often produces some form of aggressive behavior. The frustration-aggression hypothesis presumes that when something hinders your attempts at getting what you want, you become frustrated, an emotion that causes you to act aggressively by trying to injure the person or thing that is preventing you from getting what you want and causing the frustration. Displaced anger occurs when the anger is directed at someone or something that wasn't involved in causing the frustration. A bad day at work may take the form of a verbal argument with family members, and problems in a marriage may emerge as unusual behavior in social situations such as arguing with casual acquaintances or behaving aggressively with co-workers.

Depression

When all sense of hope is lost and the desire to live a full, healthy, goal-oriented life has diminished, depression takes over every aspect of the person's being, including disrupting eating and sleeping habits, thought processes, and the ability to form and sustain positive relationships. While signs of depression itself can be identified, what leads up to the depression and who is more apt to become depressed remains yet to be determined. A combination of events as well as a single experience can cause depression, and all personality types are susceptible.

Types of depression include: major depression, a combination of symptoms that interfere with every aspect of a person's life; dysthymia, a less severe form of depression that is not disabling but still produces feelings of despair; and bipolar disorder, also called *manic-depressive illness*, in which a person experiences an emotional series of extreme highs and lows that are often unpredictable in nature.

Better Ways of Coping with Stress

Think about a period of time in your life when you experienced a lot of stress. Perhaps you were starting a new job or in the middle of a romantic breakup. What strategies did you use to help manage your stress levels? Which techniques did you find the most beneficial? In some cases, you might look back on such an event and think about things you might have done differently in order to deal with the mental and physical stress in a more positive way. You might also look back and see how well certain coping methods worked, which makes it more likely that you will use those same techniques when dealing with future life stress.

Before this chapter examines some of the more efficient ways of coping with stress, let's explore a few of the most unhealthy and unproductive ways of coping with it.

These may include but are not limited to drugs, alcohol, overeating, obsessive shopping, gambling, developing an addiction to television, or expressing anger toward others. While these may temporarily numb or push away feelings of stress, they may end up causing even more stress in the long run. Healthier and more beneficial ways of coping with stress involve identifying the problem and finding a solution that works.

Problem-Solving Approach

Problem-focused coping is when the problem has been determined and the person develops a plan to solve the problem. If a student is told he is about to fail a required class, he works with the professor to find ways that will help him pass the course. This is the most realistic approach to coping with stress and produces the most positive results. On occasions when natural disasters take place, such as hurricanes or tornados, the community works together to solve the stress-causing problems such as sudden homelessness and loss of clothing and food supply.

Emotional Approach

Emotion focused coping is when a person tries to deal with the anxiety indirectly. This can involve turning to alcohol or drugs or just avoiding the situation altogether. The college student who learns he is about to fail the class approaches the situation with apathy and resolves to take the class again next semester rather than put in the effort it will immediately require to pass the class now.

> One common form of emotion-focused coping is avoidance. After you've experienced a stressful situation, you might go out of your way in the future to avoid experiences that are similar.

Positive Psychology and Subjective Well-Being

A wealth of community resources has emerged as the need for them increases. Halfway houses, youth centers, crisis centers, and telephone hot lines are some examples of how the government has put a considerable amount of funding to use in treating mental health issues.

In addition, promoting your own well-being can be as easy as staying in tune with your needs and desires. Know who you are. Accept who you are. Encourage yourself. Help yourself and ask for help when it's needed. Involve yourself.

DISORDERS—
When Thinking and Emotionality Go Awry

THIS CHAPTER WILL TAKE A LOOK at how mental health professionals determine when something is wrong and diagnose a mental disorder. It will also explore some of the major mental disorders affecting our population, including their causes and symptoms. Welcome to the world of abnormal psychology.

What Is Abnormal?

Abnormal psychology is the study of abnormal mental processes and behavior. Abnormal is defined as "not normal," but this definition isn't sufficient in the field of psychology. For one thing, normal is a relative term. For instance, what you consider to be abnormal behavior may be considered normal by your neighbor. Society also has its own standards for normal. A mental health professional must be able to define abnormal behavior and then determine when abnormal behavior constitutes a mental disorder. Not an easy task.

Determining Abnormal Behavior

There are several factors a mental health professional must take into account when trying to determine whether a person's behavior is abnormal. For nearly any type of behavior that you might consider, there is what is called a *normal range*. People may rank either higher or lower than an average set point, but everything that falls within this range is still considered normal. It is when a behavior lies too far outside of this standard range that it may start to be viewed as abnormal or maladaptive.

> Another factor is whether the behavior is distressing to the person. The behavior is only abnormal, however, if the person suffers severe emotional distress or other consequences as a result of the behavior. All people suffer distress from time to time, but this is considered normal. When the behavior becomes extreme or happens on a frequent basis, it is considered abnormal.

One factor is whether the behavior violates cultural standards. Every society has its own set of norms deemed acceptable, and you are expected to conform to those societal norms. Subcultures also have norms; for example, within society in general, wearing extremely baggy pants and bandanas might be seen as abnormal. However, it would not only be considered normal, but would be almost required, in particular subcultures. A behavior that does not conform to the norm of the person's culture is considered statistically abnormal and undesirable. Another factor is whether the behavior is harmful or maladaptive. If the behavior impedes your ability to adjust to the demands of everyday life, it is considered maladaptive. Of course, a behavior that is dangerous and could lead to the harming of oneself or others is considered abnormal.

Other factors determine whether the behavior is irrational, unpredictable, or inexplicable. In these cases, others cannot understand a person's behavior. For instance, someone with anorexia may look as thin as a rail to an outsider, but she believes she looks fat, so she restricts her eating and exercises excessively. This is an irrational behavior that most people cannot understand. Sometimes behavior takes place for no apparent reason. For instance, a person who shouts obscenities at a complete stranger for no apparent reason is considered to be acting erratically. Such behavior is inexplicable and unpredictable and is therefore abnormal.

Making a Diagnosis

Making a diagnosis of mental disorder isn't as easy as just identifying abnormal behavior. Abnormal behavior can be a symptom of a mental disorder, but it does not automatically lead to the existence of a mental disorder. Certainly everyone has behaved irrationally before, but that doesn't mean we all have a mental disorder. These are isolated incidents of a temporary state.

A mental health professional must look at abnormal behavior in terms of length of time and severity. If two or more factors of abnormal behavior apply to a person's behavior, then that warrants a closer look. A person is diagnosed with a mental disorder if the abnormal behavior occurs frequently over an extended period of time and it disrupts a person's normal day-to-day living.

Classifying Mental Disorders

To help identify and diagnose mental disorders, mental health professionals have developed a classification system that describes the symptoms of particular mental disorders. This classification system is found in the *Diagnostic and Statistical Manual of Mental Disorders* (DSM), published by the American Psychiatric Association. This manual contains almost 300 different mental disorders classified in sixteen categories:

Adjustment disorder—A person suffering from this disorder will exhibit an unusually intense or sustained emotional reaction to a change that has occurred in his or her life recently.

Anxiety disorders—The disorders within this category all share a symptom of an extreme fear or anxiety. They include phobias, panic attacks with or without agoraphobia, obsessive-compulsive disorder, and posttraumatic stress disorder.

Delirium, dementia, amnesia, and other cognitive disorders—The disorders within this group are a result of brain damage, including damage caused by degenerative diseases, head injury, stroke, or drug use.

Disorders usually first diagnosed in infancy, childhood, or adolescence—These disorders appear before adulthood and include mental retardation, developmental problems, and attention deficit disorders.

Dissociative disorders—These disorders are characterized by the separation of a person's experience from his conscious memory and include dissociative amnesia and dissociative identity disorder.

Eating disorders—These disorders are characterized by excessive overeating, undereating, or purging as a result of a fear of gaining weight. They include anorexia nervosa and bulimia nervosa.

Factitious disorders—These disorders are characterized by a person's attempt to fake physical or psychological illnesses.

Impulse control disorders—These disorders are marked by an inability to resist an impulse to participate in a behavior that is harmful to oneself or others. These include kleptomania, pyromania, pathological gambling, and intermittent explosive disorder.

Mental disorders due to a medical condition—These disorders are a result of a medical cause, such as a psychotic disorder resulting from epilepsy or a change in personality as a result of a brain injury.

Mood disorders—These disorders are characterized by extreme changes in mood, such as major depression, cyclothymia, dysthymia, and bipolar disorder.

Personality disorders—These disorders are a result of maladaptive patterns that disrupt a person's ability to function in everyday life and/or cause extreme distress. They include narcissistic personality disorder, antisocial personality disorder, borderline personality disorder, obsessive-compulsive personality disorder, and paranoid personality disorder.

Psychotic disorders—These disorders are marked by delusions, hallucinations, or extreme disturbances in thinking (often the sufferer is considered to have lost touch with reality). They include schizophrenia and delusional disorder.

Sexual and gender-identity disorders—These disorders are marked by abnormal behavior regarding sexual functioning. They include sadomasochism, exhibitionism, psychosexual dysfunction, fetishism, and transsexualism.

Sleep disorders—These disorders are marked by a disruption in a person's normal sleeping patterns. They include insomnia, narcolepsy, and sleep apnea.

Somatoform disorders—These disorders are characterized by a complaint of a physical symptom for which no cause can be found. These include hypochondria and conversion disorder.

Substance-related disorders—These disorders are a result of the use of or withdrawal from a drug such as alcohol, caffeine, amphetamines, opiates, or nicotine.

The DSM gives a lot of detailed information concerning each mental disorder to help mental health professionals effectively and accurately diagnose a mental disorder, including symptoms, approximate age of onset (if applicable), prevalence of the disorder, and other pertinent information. The following sections will take a closer look at some of the most commonly known mental disorders.

Anxiety Disorders

As mentioned before, anxiety disorders are one classification of mental disorders. All people feel anxious and fearful sometimes—when you're waiting to get your grade back on that big exam, when you board a roller coaster, or when your mother-in-law comes to visit. However, once a situation like this is over and you realize that you lived through it and are just fine, the anxiety and fear dissipate. For those suffering anxiety disorders, the anxiety and fear doesn't just go away. It may subside for a while, but then suddenly return, or it can hang out in the background, making its mark on the actions and daily life of the sufferer. Forms of anxiety can be general, such as worrying constantly about nearly every aspect of daily life, or very specific such as intense, paralyzing fear of spiders. There are several disorders that fall within this category; let's take a look at a few.

Phobias

Everyone is afraid of something—snakes, heights, public speaking, clowns—but that doesn't necessarily mean that the individual has a phobia. A phobia is an exaggerated and unrealistic fear that incapacitates the sufferer. Some phobias are more severe than others. For instance, you may have a phobia of clowns, but how often are you confronted with a clown? They are pretty easy to avoid, so you don't have to suffer the physiological responses of this extreme anxiety very often (sweating, nausea, trembling, a racing heart, and/or shortness of breath). In order to be termed a *phobia*, the efforts to avoid the feared thing or the response to encountering it must severely impact some area of the person's normal functioning.

> Generalized anxiety disorder is a condition in which a person is continuously anxious or worried for a period of at least six months. The chronic anxiety affects their daily lives and they often physically wear themselves out with worry.

People with social phobia are afraid of situations in which they feel that others may judge them. They aren't easily able to avoid their fear unless they want to skip all their classes, never eat at a restaurant, never go out on a date, and basically avoid all social atmospheres (you can forget about their singing karaoke!). Agoraphobia is even more extreme and is characterized by a fear of being away from a safe place such as your home. It's difficult to imagine being afraid to leave the house, but this is a very real disorder for some.

Panic Disorder

People with panic disorder experience frequent and unpredictable panic attacks. Panic attacks are a period of extreme fear during which the sufferer may feel as though she is dying or going crazy. Panic attacks are often accompanied by shortness of breath, chest pains, dizziness, trembling, and hot and cold flashes. They can last anywhere from a couple of minutes to several hours (though rare). They sometimes seem to appear out of the blue, but they are often first experienced following (sometimes weeks later) a period of heightened stress.

It is possible to suffer a panic attack, or even two or three, without being diagnosed with panic disorder. Many people will have a panic attack now and then, but those with panic disorder suffer them often and change their behavior or restrict their life in some way to avoid another attack. Because panic attacks happen so unexpectedly and are so upsetting, sufferers often become quite anxious, wondering when the next will occur. This in turn increases the stress in the person's life, thus creating another opportunity for a panic attack. It is a very frightening spiral of anxiety and fear and can be disabling.

Posttraumatic Stress Disorder

Posttraumatic stress disorder (PTSD) is an anxiety disorder that develops following a traumatic experience, such as near-death experiences, rape, war, or natural disasters. The symptoms of PTSD include reliving the traumatic experience in dreams or thoughts, irritability, insomnia and hyperalertness, inability to concentrate, depression, and a detachment from others. While these symptoms are typical following any highly stressful event, a person is diagnosed with PTSD when the symptoms persist for at least six months. The onset of the symptoms may immediately follow the event or occur weeks, sometimes even months, later. This isn't to say that you will develop PTSD if you are involved in a traumatic event; some people are able to recover from the event without developing a mental disorder. However, PTSD is considered to be a normal consequence of having experienced severe trauma.

While nearly all people will experience some type of trauma during their lifetime, researchers suggest that only about 8-percent develop PTSD. The factors that influence whether or not a person will develop this disorder include the proximity, duration, and severity of the trauma. For example, soldiers who have spent time in war zones are often at risk of developing PTSD and may experience anxiety and flashbacks due to their experiences. Hypervigilance is another common symptom that is characterized by a constant heightened state of awareness and watchfulness. Sounds that are reminiscent of war experiences, such as the boom of a car backfiring or the sound of planes flying overhead, can trigger flashbacks and cause individuals suffering from PTSD to revert back to actions such as taking cover from enemy fire even though there is no real threat present.

Many students studying abnormal psychology for the first time relate to some of the symptoms of mental disorders and diagnose themselves as having nearly every mental disorder in the book! Don't allow yourself to get swept up along with them. Keep a sense of humor.

Obsessive-Compulsive Disorder

Obsessive-compulsive disorder (OCD) is an anxiety disorder in which a person is stuck in a cycle of repetitive, unwanted thoughts and repetitive, ritualized behaviors. The repetitive thoughts (obsessions) are often an idea or scenario in which the sufferer is in some kind of danger or inflicts danger upon someone else, which is where the anxiety comes from. While these thoughts are frightening and unwelcome, the person can't help but think them over and over. Sufferers are also unable to control the repetitive rituals (compulsions)they perform. While they may seem excessive (such as washing one's hands fifteen times within an hour) even to the sufferer, they are necessary to reduce anxiety.

Adjustment Disorders

There are several types of adjustment disorders, some of which have already been discussed and some of which are a combination of several disorders. The following are the types of disorders and a few of their defining characteristics: adjustment disorder with depression (hopelessness, crying spells), anxiety (nervousness, excessive worry), depression and anxiety (hopelessness, crying spells, nervousness, excessive worry), disturbance of conduct (acts against society such as vandalism, problems in school, problems with the law), and disturbance of emotions and conduct (all of the above characteristics).

Typically, adjustment disorders last no longer than six months unless chronic stress develops and persists—for example, continuous relationship or work-related problems. Often some form of therapy can be helpful, and medication can be prescribed as part of the treatment involved.

Dissociative Disorders

Dissociative disorders involve a break in consciousness in which a person's memories or experience of reality become distorted. One example is known as dissociate fugue, a disorder that is characterized by sudden amnesia and identity confusion. When in a fugue state, a person might suddenly travel long distances from home, wandering through different cities. In some rare cases, people have been known to assume an entirely new identity. One of the most commonly talked about dissociative disorders is known as dissociative identity disorder, but you may recognize it best by its former name: multiple personality disorder. People with this disorder experience major disruptions in memory along with two or more distinct "personalities." However, not all psychologists believe that dissociative identity disorder is real. Some have suggested other mental illnesses such as bipolar disorder, schizophrenia, and borderline personality disorder are often mistaken as dissociative identity disorder.

Mood Disorders

Mood disorders are among the most common types of mental disorders in the United States, impacting nearly 44 million American adults each year. Mood disorders affect a person's mood to the point where it disrupts his life. If your significant other or coworkers tells you that you are moody, don't assume this means you have a mood disorder. Everyone shifts moods from time to time, often due to some kind of stimulus in their environment, such as the bad mood of another. Mood disorders range from extreme depression to extreme mania and last for an extended period of time. A little mood shift here and there, even though it may seem to disrupt your life for the moment (or the lives of others!), is harmless.

Depression

Everyone suffers sadness, and all people experience being in a bad mood, but when you say, "I'm depressed today," that's not the proper description for your suffering. Depression (technically called *clinical* or *major depression*) is not a twenty-four-hour bug. It is a serious mood disorder in which there are severe changes in an individual's behavior, emotion, cognition, and physical functions. This overwhelming feeling of sadness and/or worthlessness must last at least two weeks and disrupt the sufferer's daily life to be diagnosed as depression.

If you suffer several symptoms of depression, it is a good idea to make a visit to your doctor. If you do have depression, he or she can refer you to a mental health professional that can help. It's possible that you may have a physical illness you were unaware of, as many illnesses share a few of the same symptoms as depression.

The symptoms of depression include a feeling of worthlessness, a lack of desire to do anything, even those things you used to love to do, a feeling of overwhelming sadness, thoughts of death or suicide, a lack of energy, changes in appetite (overeating or not eating), changes in sleeping patterns (inability to fall asleep or sleeping a lot more than usual), difficulty concentrating and making decisions, and a lack of desire to be sociable.

Dysthymia

Dysthymia is another mood disorder. Basically it is a lower level of depression. People with dysthymia suffer similar symptoms of depression, such as a change in appetite, a change in sleeping patterns, a feeling of worthlessness or hopelessness, and a low energy level, over the course of at least two years. However, these symptoms aren't constant all the time. The sufferer may have periods during which she feels re-energized and back to normal. Even though the symptoms are milder, dysthymia still disrupts a person's daily life in that it makes activities more difficult to get through.

Bipolar Disorder

Bipolar disorder (formerly called *manic-depressive illness*) is a mood disorder in which an individual suffers severe mood swings between depression and mania, with periods of normalcy in between. The symptoms of depression in bipolar disorder are the same as those for depression discussed earlier. Mania is the opposite of depression. It is a period of extreme exhilaration wherein the individual is full of energy, high self-esteem, creativity, and ambition. Those in manic states feel as though they could conquer the world—quite different from depression. Imagine how exhausting and confusing it must be to alternate between two such states.

Many artists, musicians, writers, and scientists have suffered bipolar disorder and said that they were able to create their best work during the manic periods. Mark Twain was one such creative sufferer.

While it may seem like mania is a good thing, it takes its toll. The individual may suffer restlessness so severe that she may not sleep for days, rapid and dramatic speech (thus the inability to communicate effectively), extreme irritability, the inability to concentrate (thus the inability to finish anything), paranoia, impulsiveness, weight loss, and possibly hallucinations or delusions. Bipolar disorder is diagnosed when a person has a manic episode; otherwise, it would be diagnosed as depression, as the depression side of the disorder is the same as in clinical or major depression.

Cyclothymia

Cyclothymia is a lower level of bipolar disorder. People with cyclothymia suffer mood swings between mania and depression, but they are not as extreme. They will suffer the same symptoms as those with bipolar disorder, but on a milder level. The major difference between one with bipolar disorder and one with cyclothymia is that a person with cyclothymia never experiences a full-blown manic state, nor will he experience a major depressive episode. To be diagnosed, a person must experience these symptoms over the course of at least a two-year period.

Schizophrenia

Schizophrenia is probably the best-known mental disorder, though people often mistakenly confuse it with multiple personality disorder. Someone with multiple personality disorder has two or more personalities that surface; she is still in touch with reality and able to function. Someone with schizophrenia, on the other hand, often loses touch with reality and is unable to carry out many daily activities. Schizophrenia is rather difficult to define accurately as it varies in form and sufferers do not have the exact same symptoms. Even so, mental health professionals have come up with a list of common symptoms of schizophrenia, the most prevalent of which are hallucinations and delusions.

Hallucinations and Delusions

Delusions are false, and often outlandish, ideas that a person believes to be true. These ideas can be anything the imagination can conjure up, from space aliens living in the bathroom sink to rat poison in their ChapStick. Oftentimes, schizophrenics will have paranoid delusions in which they believe someone or an agency such as the government is plotting against them. They will think their phones are bugged, people are following them, and their lives are in danger. Sometimes they will believe they are another person, often someone well known such as Jesus, the president, or a celebrity.

You must understand that as silly as this may seem to you, delusions are as real as the sun to the schizophrenic, and they are just as terrifying as if they were really happening. For instance, one man was hospitalized because he was convinced that the police were after him. He ran from window to window in absolute terror, because he was locked in and was certain that people walking on the hospital grounds were police who were coming to get him. The fact that this wasn't true made no difference to the man; in fact, he understood that other people thought he was crazy, but he believed his worries were true nonetheless.

Hallucinations are false or distorted sensory perceptions that a person believes to be real. These hallucinations can be incredibly vivid and are usually tied to the individual's delusional beliefs. For example, if a woman holds a delusion that she is being persecuted, she may experience terrifying hallucinations in which she is chased, imprisoned, or injured by an angry mob of people.

While schizophrenics see things that aren't there or feel things crawling on their skin, the most common hallucinations those with schizophrenia suffer are auditory; they hear voices. The voices are inside the person's head, but the sufferer believes it is just as real as if someone were standing next to him speaking, because his experience is exactly the same as if someone really were. There could be just one voice or several. The voice may give the sufferer orders or insult him or her. Two or more voices could hold a conversation that completely disregards the sufferer altogether. Regardless of what the voices say, the sufferer believes it is real and often will take the advice or orders of the voices.

> Movies and television shows often portray a schizophrenic as being violent toward others. While violence is a possibility, schizophrenics are more likely to turn the violence toward themselves. Suicide attempts are unfortunately common with schizophrenics.

Disorganization

Other symptoms of schizophrenia include disorganized speech and thought and inappropriate and disorganized behavior. The disorganization of thought manifests itself in speech. A schizophrenic may suddenly begin rhyming or switch from one illogical idea to another without any apparent connection. The sufferer's speech can be scattered and incoherent, unable to be understood. Disorganized behavior can consist of anything from being unable to dress oneself to laughing uncontrollably at a funeral. Disorganized behavior is inappropriate for the occasion or can result in the sufferer's inability to complete an everyday, simple task.

Additional Symptoms

The symptoms already discussed are considered "positive" by psychologists. This isn't to be confused with "good." Positive refers to active symptoms that are added to a person's normal behavior; they are symptoms that healthy people do not display. Negative refers to those symptoms that show a lack in some area—ambition, thought, feeling, behavior, etc. Such symptoms include emotional flatness (when a person does not show any emotion whatsoever), an extreme lack of motivation, withdrawal from society, and impoverished thought and speech.

Schizophrenics may also show changes in emotion. They may suffer extreme mood swings rather abruptly or exaggerate a normal feeling, such as laughing too loudly and too long at a joke. They may also become apathetic toward people they had always been close to.

There are so many symptoms that it wouldn't be possible to list them all here. This is why it is difficult to diagnose schizophrenia. Just as there are no two snowflakes alike, there are no two cases of schizophrenia exactly alike. Mental health professionals must take this very seriously, as it can be a very terrifying and detrimental mental disorder. Fortunately, treatment for schizophrenia has improved over the years. People can now sometimes partially or completely recover from a schizophrenic episode, although others will remain disabled by their condition.

Personality Disorders

As mentioned before, personality disorders are a classification of mental disorders characterized by maladaptive patterns that disrupt a person's ability to function in everyday life and/or cause extreme distress and the inability to get along with other people. As you read, you may recognize someone you know in the symptoms of some of these disorders, but keep in mind that while a person may have some of the symptoms of a mental disorder, this does not necessarily mean he has the disorder itself. So don't go diagnosing your friends with a personality disorder or you just might not have any friends left!

Antisocial Personality Disorder

Probably the best-known personality disorder is antisocial personality disorder. People with this condition will manipulate or exploit others to get what they want, and this behavior if often characterized as criminal. In the past, people have often called people with this disorder *psychopaths* or *sociopaths*, but psychologists now note that each of these represents a distinctly different mental disorder.

The DSM states that in order to diagnose an individual with antisocial personality disorder, he must be at least eighteen years old and have a history of persistent disregard for the rights of other people since at least the age of fifteen. They must also exhibit a history of at least three of seven behavioral problems:

- Impulsive and cannot plan ahead

- Irresponsible and fails to meet obligations

- Repeatedly gets into physical fights

- Repeatedly breaks the law

- Lacks guilt or regret for hurting others

- Deceitful

- Has a reckless regard for his own safety or the safety of others

While genetic factors are thought to play an important role in antisocial personality disorder, the exact cause is still unknown. Unfortunately, this disorder is also one of the most difficult to treat. People with this mental disorder rarely seek treatment on their own, so most are only diagnosed and treated after they have come into contact with the criminal justice system.

Narcissistic Personality Disorder

Narcissistic personality disorder is characterized by self-centeredness, lack of empathy for others, and an exaggerated sense of self-importance. Individuals with this disorder consider themselves to be better than everyone else. They expect everyone else to shower them with attention and favors, though they very rarely, if at all, return the favor. They are self-absorbed to the point where they are obsessed with their own self-importance, brilliance, and power. They are, essentially, in love with themselves.

Narcissism comes from the Greek myth of Narcissus. Narcissus was a beautiful young man who came across his reflection in the water one day. He was so entranced with his image that he fell in love with himself and never left the water's edge. (He was eventually turned into the narcissus flower.)

Borderline Personality Disorder

Borderline personality disorder (BPD) is a personality disorder in which an individual has a history of unstable relationships—one minute the relationship will be passionate and intense as the partner is idealized, but in the next moment, the relationship takes a dive as the partner is suddenly of little or no value. A person with borderline personality disorder is often self-destructive and may threaten to commit suicide. Drugs are sometimes a part of her life. Impulsiveness is also characteristic of this disorder, as is emotional instability.

Causes of Mental Disorders

Now that you've been able to take a closer look at some of the more common mental disorders and have seen how they can be debilitating to a person's life, you are likely wondering what could possibly cause such disorders. There isn't a simple and exact answer for this. Mental health professionals and researchers are constantly studying the causes of mental disorders in an attempt to better understand and treat the disorders.

Biological Factors

Some mental health professionals are of the belief that mental disorders are caused solely by problems in the brain and nervous system. As you know, the nervous system is a delicate and complex system in which there is a constant hum of activity that keeps your body alive and functioning well. If there were to be any damage to or a kink in the brain—the executor of the nervous system—the system could be thrown out of whack, possibly resulting in a mental disorder. For instance, the brain's prefrontal cortex is responsible for impulse control and planning. Should this part of the brain be damaged, a person may suffer impulsiveness and an inability to plan ahead, a symptom of schizophrenia.

> Those researchers who believe biological factors are responsible for the onset of mental disorders have contributed greatly to this field of science, particularly in their development of medications that are sometimes able to allow a person suffering a mental disorder to live a normal life.

These people have also shown that some of the biological factors of mental disorders are hereditary and that some people are more susceptible to particular mental disorders than others. For instance, research has shown that major depression is often a heritable mental disorder. Also, as you've surely heard, addiction is thought to originate in a person's biochemistry, and those with a genetic predisposition to addiction are more likely to suffer an addiction.

Psychological Factors

On the other hand, there are those who believe that psychological factors—such as traumatic experiences, past conflicts, the way parents behaved toward a child, etc.—are responsible for the development of mental disorders. For example, post-traumatic stress disorder is a result of a traumatic experience; it is the body's reaction to and coping mechanism for past events of heightened stress. A mental health professional believing in this theory would focus solely on the traumatic event and its effects in an attempt to help the patient overcome this disorder. Certain phobias, also, have shown that they are a result of psychological factors. For instance, someone with the fear of the number thirteen may have developed the phobia due to societal stimulation or cultural tradition.

Working Together

Many mental health professionals and researchers in the field believe that the causes of mental disorders are found among a combination of biological and psychological factors. For instance, someone may have a genetic predisposition toward a certain mental disorder, such as addiction, but the onset of the mental disorder is triggered by a psychological event, such as being exposed to psychoactive drugs during adolescence. Borderline personality disorder is thought to be based on a problem with the emotion regulation system, so that emotions are experienced much more intensely than normal. Because feelings like frustration, hurt, or anger are so much more powerful even over small things, people with BPD elicit reactions such as "Just get over it"; "You're not that upset"; or "You're just looking for attention." While parents of typical children often teach them how to self-soothe and deal with feelings, parents of people with BPD may not have the skills themselves to deal with extra-intense emotions. After a few years, people with BPD learn to hide their feelings—until they can't anymore, and the pain is simply intolerable. That's when they may hurt themselves, which then starts the consequences all over again. As stated before, the causes of mental disorders are continuously being researched and studied, and treatments are continuing to advance every day.

Understanding and Preventing Suicide

Suicide is a major problem in the United States. Chances are good that you may even know someone who has either committed or attempted suicide. According to the National Institute of Health, suicide was the eleventh leading cause of death in the

United States in 2006, with more than 33,000 people taking their own lives. Experts also suggest that for every death, another twenty-five people try to commit suicide, and it may surprise you to learn that suicide actually outranks homicide as a cause of death. These statistics are even more frightening among teens and young adults; among those age fifteen to twenty-four, suicide is the third leading cause of death.

Risk Factors Associated with Suicide

While the exact reasons why a person chooses to commit suicide vary from one person to the next, researchers have discovered a number of different psychological and environmental risk factors. Recent problems in close relationships, feelings of social isolation, irrational thinking, substance abuse, a family history of suicide, the presence of a firearm in the home and major psychological disorders are all factors associated with an increased risk of suicidal behavior.

People with poor problem-solving skills are also at a greater risk of committing suicide. When faced with a major life problem, rather than looking at the available options and looking for a realistic solution, these individuals may see suicide as the only way to resolve the crisis. For example, a student who fails all of his classes during his first year of college might become so depressed or fear the negative reaction of his parents so much that it seems like death in the only possible option.

How Can People Help Prevent Suicide?

While it is impossible to completely control the behavior of others, there are steps that you can take if you suspect that a friend or loved one is contemplating suicide. First, don't brush off or dismiss the person's suicidal talk by minimizing the situation or trying to paint a rosy picture that "everything is going to be all right." Instead, focus on actively listening to the person's feelings without expressing judgment. Be emotionally supportive, and encourage the person to seek help from a trained mental health professional.

PSYCHOTHERAPY

and Other Approaches to Treatment

PEOPLE SEEK THE ASSISTANCE of mental health professionals for a wide variety of reasons. Not everyone who goes to a therapist has a mental disorder. Many people just need help with various life issues. Now that you are familiar with some of the major mental disorders, let's take a look at some of the approaches used to treat these disorders. Keep in mind that treatments are constantly evolving as new ones enter the scene and older ones are improved upon. This chapter will take a look at both psychotherapeutic and biological approaches to treatment.

Psychoanalysis and Psychodynamic Approaches

Psychoanalysis is a form of psychotherapy in which the therapist delves into the patient's unconscious in an attempt to discover an internal source for the problem at hand. Freud was the father of psychoanalysis, as you've probably guessed. He believed that by talking through a person's dreams and memories, he could tap into the unconscious and determine the inner conflict that was causing the psychological problem. By exposing that source, the patient could then experience emotional release and be free of the problem.

Free Association

In this form of treatment, a patient would meet with his therapist numerous times and simply talk about dreams, emotions, and anything else that came to mind. When you think about this type of therapy, you probably imagine a patient lying on a couch talking about his problems while a therapist sits patiently nearby writing on a notepad. As the patient talks freely, the therapist sits quietly, taking in everything that is said in an attempt to make connections and thus search for the source within the unconscious, a technique known as *free association*.

> Classic psychoanalysis using free association can be rather pricey considering the number of sessions a patient must pay for before the problem can be worked through. While this certainly isn't the only form of treatment available, many people shy away from seeking treatment due to the cost involved.

There is no quick fix involved. Numerous sessions are required, sometimes even years' worth of sessions, before a therapist can delve deeply enough in to the unconscious to produce emotional release. Of course, this emotional release cannot be guaranteed. Because society is "quick-fix" oriented, this form of treatment isn't nearly as popular these days, though it is still the most common portrayal of one seeking help for a psychological problem.

Psychodynamic Therapy

Freud's classic psychoanalysis, though not practiced all too often these days, has evolved into other forms of therapy called *psychodynamic therapy*, which are currently used more often. In psychodynamic therapy, the therapist still attempts to delve into the unconscious to help the patient discover and face the inner conflict that is manifesting itself as symptoms of a mental disorder. However, this form of therapy is more structured to be acceptable to today's quick-fix ideals.

Therapists develop a plan of treatment with their patients, often setting a limit on the number of sessions they will use as well as setting goals for what they want to accomplish. They often guide the patient to discuss a certain topic or emotion, which is much different from the free-association technique used in classic psychoanalysis. In this way, the sessions are more goal-oriented and focused on finding a solution to the problem without having to rifle through the insignificant details of a patient's entire life history.

Transference

One process that is important in both psychoanalytic and psychodynamic approaches is the use of transference, which involves the client unconsciously transferring the emotions and desires she originally associated with another person in her life onto the therapist. The therapist will pay close attention to any emotions that the patient projects onto her and try to associate those feelings with situations or issues in the patient's life. For instance, if you become jealous of the therapist's other patients, the therapist will start to delve into your current relationships with others, searching for that inner conflict that triggered the transference. Or, if you become enraged with your therapist for going on vacation and not being able to keep the regular schedule of sessions, the therapist will try to find out if you have faced rejection or abandonment in your life. Transference is a way to dig up those past conflicts that are affecting your present living.

Medical Approaches

Some mental health professionals take the stand that mental disorders are diseases that must be treated medically. Medical treatments for psychological disorders have actually been around much longer than psychotherapy, although many of these early treatments were based on a very primitive understanding of medicine and the human mind. In recent years, researchers have developed many drugs that are being used to treat the symptoms of mental disorders from schizophrenia to depression. However, drugs aren't always able to fix the problem. In such cases, other biomedical solutions are sometimes sought out, such as brain surgery or electroshock therapy. Following is a look at the drugs that are used to treat mental disorders, as they are the most common form of biomedical treatment.

> Research has found that using a combination of medical approaches and psychotherapy has produced excellent results in the treatment of some mental disorders. For instance, it is common for a mental health professional both to prescribe an antidepressant and to schedule the patient for psychotherapy sessions in the treatment of depression.

Antipsychotic Drugs

Antipsychotic drugs are those that are used to treat psychoses such as schizophrenia. These types of drugs have come a long way since they were first introduced. Earlier drugs such as Thorazine helped dull the symptoms of the mental disorder but produced effects that made it just as difficult for the patient to carry out a normal daily life. Antipsychotic drugs these days are beneficial in reducing or getting rid of hallucinations, delusions, and agitation, allowing patients to live their lives outside of a hospital. New drugs such as Restoril are even able to reduce a schizophrenic's apathy and social isolation.

While antipsychotics work wonders for some people, not all will respond to them. Each case needs to be evaluated on an individual basis. Also, some of these drugs can produce side effects that can be debilitating, such as uncontrollable trembling or disturbances in motor control.

Antidepressant Drugs

Antidepressant drugs are most often used to treat—you guessed it!—depression. However, some of the newer antidepressants are also effective in treating obsessive-compulsive disorder, some phobias, and sometimes anxiety. You've likely heard of at least a few antidepressants such as Prozac, Zoloft, or Paxil. These drugs work by affecting the availability of certain neurotransmitters that are linked to depression and anxiety.

Not all antidepressants will have the same effect on people. For instance, someone who responds well to Zoloft may have shown little or no improvement when using Paxil. Antidepressants also have side effects. While not as severe as those associated with antipsychotics, these side effects can be rather annoying. Common side effects include dry mouth, nausea, headaches, fatigue, blurred vision, weight gain, constipation, and decrease in sexual libido and/or sexual performance.

Saint John's wort, which is an over-the-counter herbal medication, has shown some promise in treating mild forms of depression. However, two large-scale studies found no difference between the herb and a placebo in relieving the symptoms of major depression. If you are considering using this herb, be sure to consult your doctor first.

Antianxiety Drugs

Antianxiety drugs are used in the treatment of anxiety disorders, such as panic disorder and generalized anxiety disorder. Often called *tranquilizers*, these drugs include Valium, Librium, Xanax, Klonopin, and BuSpar. While these drugs can work wonders for those suffering panic attacks that disrupt their daily lives, they can be rather dangerous, as they are highly addictive. They are best used on a short-term basis and patients will need to gradually decrease the dosage to avoid suffering withdrawal and other side effects. Also, while you never want to mix medication with alcohol, this is especially true with antianxiety drugs. The combination can heighten the effects of the alcohol to the point where it is quite possible the person could end up in a coma. Highly effective treatments for phobias, including social phobia, fear of flying, and panic disorders, do exist. A therapist trained in cognitive behavioral exposure–based therapy can often help even severe cases in a relatively short period of time. However, the therapy is intense and scary and requires a significant investment from the client.

Mood Stabilizer Drugs

Mood stabilizers are just as they sound—they are drugs that work to stabilize a person's mood, reducing or getting rid of extreme mood swings. The most common mood stabilizer is lithium carbonate, often used to treat bipolar disorder. Treatment with lithium needs to be monitored closely. If the dose is too small, it may not have any effect; if the dose is too large, it may prove to be fatal. Those taking lithium are required to take toxicity tests regularly. Another problem with lithium is that it can produce side effects such as vomiting, diarrhea, tremors, seizures, and even kidney damage. While lithium has a long history as an effective treatment of mood disorders, there are other drugs being used for mood disorders, such as the antiseizure medications Tegretol and Depakote.

Psychosurgery

Psychosurgery, a method of treatment that involves destroying the part of the brain thought to be responsible for the mental disorder, isn't very common today, but it used to be a popular form of treatment. Psychosurgery began when physician Gottlieb Burckhardt (1836–1907) removed parts of the brain of his schizophrenic patients in the 1890s. While some patients did show calmer behavior following the surgery, some died.

Psychosurgery fell out of favor for some time, but then there was a resurgence in the mid-1930s when prefrontal lobotomies hit the scene. It was discovered that the frontal and temporal lobes controlled aggressiveness and emotional behavior. Holes were drilled into the patient's skull and the nerves connecting the prefrontal lobes were severed or otherwise destroyed. While this operation did reduce the emotional symptoms of mental disorder, it also left most people incapacitated in different ways. Some were unable to make plans and follow through, some became severely withdrawn from society, and some could no longer even care for themselves. Remarkably, the use of this procedure continued for nearly twenty years and tens of thousands of people had the surgery.

> The earliest form of psychosurgery was used on patients suffering from schizophrenia. However, as it gained popularity in the 1900s, it was being used to treat a wide range of mental disorders such as bipolar disorder, obsessive-compulsive disorder, pathological violence disorder, and, of course, schizophrenia.

Such lobotomies are not performed today; however, there is a new form of psycho-surgery that is currently in use. Cingulotomy is a surgical procedure that burns and destroys a small portion of the brain known to be involved in emotionality. This is used as a last resort for those suffering severe obsessive-compulsive disorder and major depression who have not responded to drugs or forms of psychotherapy. Such surgery has not proved to be as debilitating as former psychosurgeries, though many still question the success reports.

Electroconvulsive Therapy

Electroconvulsive therapy (ECT), commonly called *shock therapy*, is a somewhat controversial procedure used to treat those suffering from severe depression with suicidal thoughts who have not responded to drugs or forms of psychotherapy. It is also occasionally used to treat patients with catatonia, mania, or other severe psychiatric illnesses. ECT involves placing an electrode on either side of the patient's head and sending a current of electricity between the two. The current causes the body to convulse for approximately a minute and causes the release of many types of neurotransmitters in the brain. Years ago, the current was so strong and lasted long enough that the body sometimes suffered broken bones from the convulsions. Today, patients are given anesthesia and muscle relaxants so that they are able to sleep through the ordeal without pain or muscular contractions; patients wake up after about ten minutes and may have a headache, but generally the side effects are no worse than those of antidepressant medications. Some patients report short-term memory loss in the day following the procedure, but very few patients have more significant memory loss. When used to treat severe depression, a series of six to ten treatments may be administered over a period of several weeks. Although no one is sure why or how this works, ECT has proved to be effective on almost 70 percent of those undergoing the procedure. Again, this is a controversial procedure. However, it works very quickly, making it a life-saving procedure for extremely suicidal patients. It is often used when someone can't wait or doesn't want to wait the six to eight weeks that antidepressant medications take to start to work. Unfortunately, the effects of ECT tend to be short-lived, with about half of depressed patients experiencing a relapse of symptoms within six months. Because of this, "booster" ECT sessions can be periodically administered.

Humanistic Approaches

The humanistic approach to psychotherapy adopts a philosophy that each person has a desire to be productive, reach her or his goals, and behave in a healthy manner; people are in control of their destiny and, while they are constantly growing, changing, and being affected by outside factors, they maintain the responsibility for their own happiness. Unlike psychoanalysis, humanistic therapists do not try to find hidden or unconscious past experiences affecting the life of the person today. Rather, they concentrate on the here and now, focus on the current situation or problem, and help the patient (or "client," as humanists prefer) work through, make, and feel good about decisions.

> Client-centered therapy is based on Carl Rogers's idea of unconditional positive regard, in which the therapist provides continuous support without attaching any conditions. In this way, the client feels safe and secure in the support provided and is able to build confidence in her ability to solve the problem at hand in the most productive manner possible.

The best-known approach to humanistic therapy is the client-centered therapy strategy developed by Carl Rogers. In this nondirective approach, the client is the focus of the session. He leads the discussion, talking about the situation or problem at hand. The therapist's job is to actively listen to what the client says and show warmth and empathy. The client is the expert on his feelings; the therapist is the sounding board for the client to bounce solutions off of. The therapist must at all times listen with acceptance and not be judgmental in any way, although it is also important that the therapist be honest and genuine in her reactions to what the client is bringing up. In this way, the client is able to build self-esteem and the confidence needed to carry out a solution to the problem. Rogers intentionally used the word *client* rather than *patient* to describe people seeking psychotherapy to emphasize the idea that the individual plays the most important role in his recovery, rather than simply being "cured" by the therapist.

Cognitive-Behavioral Approaches

Cognitive-behavioral approaches to psychotherapy also focus on the "here and now." They are not concerned about what your unconscious may or may not be storing. They want to get right to the point and take action to battle the behavior that is disrupting your daily living. While cognitive therapy and behavioral therapy are technically two separate strategies, they are often combined, as they have the same goal of identifying and changing problematic or self-defeating behaviors. Most believe that thought and behavior feed off each other, and therefore approaches that use both are common in practice.

Behavioral Therapy

Behavioral therapy focuses on tackling the problem behavior itself by finding ways to change or stop the behavior. This type of therapy focuses on the principles of classical and operant conditioning as discussed in Chapter 7. Behavioral therapists employ several different techniques for behavioral therapy, depending on which is considered to be the most effective strategy for the type of behavior.

If you have a phobia, a behavioral therapist would likely consider applying systematic desensitization to help you get over that fear. This technique uses a series of steps to help you create a positive conditioned response to the feared object, eventually helping you to confront your fear while feeling relaxed. For instance, let's say you are deathly afraid of dogs. A behavioral therapist would employ systematic desensitization by teaching you to relax as you gradually face the fear from the mildest form to the most terrifying. In this scenario, you would start out by looking at pictures of cute puppies. Once you are able to view these pictures while relaxed, you would then be shown pictures of smaller yet grown dogs, such as a Jack Russell terrier. From there you would move on to medium-sized dogs such as Border collies. Then you would be shown pictures of large and more aggressive dogs such as rottweilers. The next step would be facing a real dog, though from a safe distance. The ultimate goal is to get you to actually interact with the dog, thus combating your fear and demonstrating that not all dogs are dangerous. All of these steps are done as your body is relaxed. In other words, you will not move on to the next step until you are comfortable and relaxed while in the current step.

> If you have a behavior you are considering getting help for, it is a good idea to keep a record of the problematic behavior; in fact, many therapists request this. Identify the behavior, the rewards of the behavior, and when and where the behavior occurs. From this a therapist has a good starting point on which to build a plan for treatment.

Implosion and flooding are two behavioral therapy techniques in which the patient must face her problem head-on. In implosion, a person is asked to imagine or is shown a picture of the event or object she is afraid of over and over in a safe environment until the fear no longer has such a hold on or power over the patient. Flooding is a technique in which the person is thrown into the situation she fears most—such as an agoraphobic riding on a crowded subway—alongside the safety of the therapist until she no longer feels the panic and anxiety associated with the situation. Both of these techniques focus on immediate exposure, taking away the baby steps of systematic desensitization. The drawback of this kind of therapy is that if the person cannot stay in the intensity of the situation, it can make the fear worse. Most therapists use a combination of education and systematic desensitization, and if done correctly, this treatment is generally highly effective.

Other techniques used in behavioral therapy include skills training, in which the patient is asked to practice a change in behavior in a role-playing situation in preparation for the real event; positive reinforcement therapy, in which the patient is rewarded each time she changes the problematic behavior to a more desired behavior; and aversion therapy, in which punishment, such as electric shock, is used to change a problematic behavior. As you can see, there are several forms of behavioral therapy a therapist may choose from, depending on the severity and type of problematic behavior.

Cognitive Therapy

While behavioral therapy focuses on the behavior itself, cognitive therapy is centered on the thought associated with a particular action. Cognitive therapy employs the premise that rational, realistic, and constructive thinking can reduce the occurrence of or entirely get rid of a problematic behavior. It is also very effective in helping to lessen anxiety or depression that is caused by distorted thinking. Therapists who use cognitive therapy understand that you think before you do, and therefore if you change your thinking, you can change your doing.

One technique used in cognitive therapy is rational emotive behavior therapy, developed by Albert Ellis (1913–2007), in which the therapist counters a patient's unrealistic beliefs or thoughts with rational arguments. Whether the patient is overgeneralizing or catastrophizing, the therapist uses rational thought to make the patient see why her thoughts are irrational and leading to the problematic behavior.

The therapist may also have the patient use rational arguments against herself to better understand the irrational or misinformed beliefs. For instance, the patient is asked to identify the thought leading to the problematic behavior. She is then asked to look at that thought from an outside and objective position, listing rational arguments to dispel that thought or belief.

Whichever technique a therapist finds most beneficial (through rational argument or testing beliefs and thoughts against the evidence), cognitive therapy focuses on the idea that to change a feeling or behavior, one must change the thought process that leads up to that behavior. This is, in effect, a way to head off the problem before it has a chance to affect the patient's life.

What are overgeneralizing and catastrophizing?

Overgeneralizing is taking a thought or belief and irrationally expanding it to areas that would otherwise be unaffected—for instance, believing someone is an entirely evil person just because he made a mistake. Catastrophizing is blowing a small problem out of proportion and turning it into an inescapable disaster—for instance, believing you will be a failure and everyone will hate you if you do not get a perfect score on a test.

Group Therapy

Group therapy in this instance refers to formal therapy in which more than one patient is being treated at a time, such as in couples therapy or family therapy. There are of course several informal group therapies out there that often work as a type of support group in which members suffering from the same type of problem get together and discuss their personal experiences and help each other to find solutions or simply get through the challenges of changing behavior. These groups can be a very powerful form of self-help, as one often encounters people who have lived through the same problem and can offer advice from personal experience as opposed to someone who can understand the problem only from an objective standpoint. People suffering with a problem often feel alone, so one of the greatest benefits of group therapy is that it introduces clients to a peer group that shares the same experiences. Let's take a look at the two most common formal group therapies.

> There isn't one favored approach to treatment for group therapies. Some therapists may utilize psychodynamic approaches, others may use cognitive-behavioral approaches, and some prefer the humanistic approach. Regardless of the approach used, group therapists all have one thing in common: they focus on the unit and each person is treated as a part of that unit.

Couples Therapy

Have you ever heard the saying "There are two sides to every story"? This is also the belief of couples therapists. Often, if a relationship is suffering from arguments that never seem to be resolved, helping just one of the partners is not going to be sufficient in healing the relationship. Therefore, therapists prefer to see both participants in an attempt to look at the issue from both sides and help each understand the other's viewpoint in a rational and formal setting.

Relationships all suffer inevitable conflicts and require a combined effort of both participants; one person cannot bear all the weight. This is where couples therapy comes into play. Since the therapist has no investment in the relationship, she can offer an objective perspective and help weed out the accusations and irrationalities to get to the heart of the matter. The therapist can then help the couple work together to find a way to live with their differences or resolve the conflict.

Family Therapy

It is sometimes recommended that an entire family visit a therapist to seek help for a particular problem. Many people underestimate the influence and effect family can have on a person. The problem of one member can very easily carry over to other members of the family, affecting them in different ways, but affecting them nonetheless. For instance, the eating disorder of a teenager is going to affect not only the teen but the parents and siblings as well. Sometimes problems between the parents are most apparent in the misbehavior of the children, and working on the couple issues resolves the behavior of the child. Other times, the power structure in the family is distorted, and children have more power than the parents, which is not healthy for anyone.

The therapist would help each member recognize the problem for what it is as well as seek out underlying problems that may have contributed to the existence of the problem. The therapist will also help the family recognize and work through the changes that must be made within the unit to best solve the problem at hand. Family dynamics can often be rather complicated and so ingrained in the members that an objective view is sometimes necessary to help the family work together as a unit along the same course of action to face and overcome the problem.

Helping Yourself

Most people have suffered a symptom of a mental disorder at one time or another. This doesn't mean that they have a mental disorder. Not everything can be perfect in your life. Everyone has problems they must deal with, and sometimes they seem overwhelming. Mental health professionals aren't reserved only for those with mental disorders. Anyone can utilize their expertise to help get through a troubling time. Of course, this isn't to say that if you are suffering a troubling time, you have to seek the help of a mental health professional. There are some things you can do to help combat downswings of mental health on your own.

Physical Health

If you are suffering a symptom of a mental disorder, such as loss of appetite, sleeping problems, or mood swings, consider your physical health before assuming it is a mental health problem. For instance, if you seem to be tired all the time lately, take a look at your eating habits. Are you eating healthy foods or junk foods? How often are you eating? Proper nutrition plays a big role in how you feel on a day-to-day basis. Perhaps you have been skipping meals and not acquiring the energy you need to get through the day. Or maybe you are getting your energy from sugar-filled foods, which when the "high" is over cause you to feel even more down and sleepy.

Several symptoms can be attributed to physical problems or changes. For instance, if you suddenly notice you are having muscle twitches, this doesn't necessarily mean you are developing a tick; you could be suffering a vitamin deficiency. Or perhaps you have been quite irritable lately. All that caffeine you are ingesting could be causing you to lose sleep, thus causing you to be more irritable. Whatever the symptom may be, take a look at your physical health. Have you made any recent changes in diet or exercise? Are you suffering any other symptoms? What can you do to improve your physical health?

> There are several physical illnesses that have the same symptoms of mental illnesses. Before you self-diagnose a mental disorder, visit your family doctor and get checked out. While you may just be suffering from a cold, you could have a life-threatening illness. You know your body. If something is wrong, seek professional help.

Talk to Others

When life's troubles get you down or you are facing a problem you just can't seem to solve on your own, enlist the help of trusted family and friends. Sometimes just talking about a problem makes a solution a little easier to see. Or if you are unable to reach a solution on your own, perhaps your confidant will have a suggestion. The two of you could even brainstorm possible solutions and work together to try to see the problem from all angles. Don't be afraid to show emotion. Bottling up emotion and stress only leads to more problems down the road. Sometimes just talking about a problem allows you the emotional release you need to be able to look at the problem more realistically and find a constructive solution.

Embrace Change

Change can be stressful at times and is often unwelcome. However, life throws you in the path of change all the time. If you are able to look at the positive side of change, you can then accept it and make the best of it. Positivity opens the door for optimism, keeps you motivated, and enables you to face your fears. If you find yourself faced with a change and focusing on the negative aspects or possibilities, take the time to create a list of the positive aspects and/or possibilities and redirect your focus.

Celebrate Your Uniqueness

Everyone is unique, whether you try to conform to the ideals of others or rebel against conformity. Once you are able to understand that, it becomes easier to accept yourself as an individual. Too often people place value on themselves according to how they think others view them, even though these thoughts may have no substantial grounding in fact. Accepting yourself and celebrating your uniqueness can only lead to good and positive results. Also, in accepting yourself, it becomes easier to accept others.

Evaluating the Effectiveness of Psychotherapy

After learning about some of the major forms of psychotherapy, you might wonder exactly how effective these techniques are and whether one form of treatment is better than another? Before we answer these questions, it is important to understand that most people simply do not seek professional help. While the National Center of Mental Health estimates that nearly 30 percent of all American adults suffer from at least one mental illness during a given year, only a small portion of these individuals receive treatment. In most cases, people simply continue on with their lives, battling their symptoms on a daily basis with the help of friends and family. So you may wonder, do people who receive psychotherapy recover faster than those who do not?

Researchers have carefully analyzed hundreds of different studies in order to determine the answer to this question. As a result, psychologists have found that psychotherapy is more effective than receiving no treatment. About half of those who receive psychotherapy start to show improvement in functioning and a reduction in symptoms by their sixth session, and more than 75 percent of these individuals are significantly better at the end of six months of treatment.

So is one type of psychotherapy better than others? While some therapeutic techniques are more effective in the treatment of certain disorders, such as the use of cognitive-behavioral therapy to treat phobias, there is not a single proven treatment method that is superior.

CAREERS IN
Psychology

WHEN YOU FIRST PICKED UP THIS BOOK, you may have had a basic idea of what psychologists do. Now that you've explored many of the major subjects studied by psychologists, you probably realize that your initial definition was perhaps a bit limited. While a large number of psychologists do perform therapy and treat psychological disorders, there is actually an astonishing amount of career diversity. In this chapter, you'll learn more about what is takes to become a psychologist as well as some of the other job options available at different educational levels. No matter where your interests lie or what your goals are for the future, there is a specialty area out there that is perfect for you.

How to Become a Psychologist

Having surveyed what psychology is, what psychologists do, and where it all came from, you might be wondering how people get to be psychologists in the first place. There are several routes; but here is the most common one. First, you major in psychology as an undergraduate student, also taking as many natural science, math, and computer courses as you can work in to your schedule. And you make very good grades throughout.

Next, you apply to graduate programs in psychology, many of which also require that you score high on the Graduate Record Exam (GRE). You will also need strong letters of recommendation from faculty members whom you somehow managed to get to know as an undergraduate. Work experience in psychology, especially any research experience that you managed to gain as a lab assistant, helps a lot too. Basically, you do everything you can to prepare yourself and make yourself a strong candidate—competition is fierce and only a very small percentage of applicants are admitted. If you are applying to be a clinical psychologist, it also helps to get volunteer or practicum experience working in human services, such as homeless or domestic violence shelters.

> If you're thinking about earning a graduate degree in psychology, then it is important to take the courses required for entry into most graduate programs. A 1996 survey published in *American Psychologist* listed the top five prerequisite courses: statistics, experimental methods, abnormal psychology, developmental psychology, and personality psychology.

Now comes the really hard part: You have to do the work, and you're likely to find that it's quite difficult and demanding—especially during the first year, which is always the hardest. In all, you have to really want to be a psychologist, and while in graduate school you have to devote your life to it.

If all goes well, you eventually receive your Doctor of Philosophy (PhD) degree or Doctor of Psychology (PsyD), which are the most common types of degrees for psychologists. If your degree is primarily clinical, it probably took you three or four years in the graduate program plus another year of internship in a mental health setting—not counting how much additional time it took you to do your dissertation.

If your degree is primarily experimental, the time was much the same except for the internship. But, especially if your primary interest is research, either clinical or experimental, you'll probably want to continue past the PhD or PsyD with at least a one-year "post doc" to continue your training and help you get established.

Job Options with a Bachelor's Degree in Psychology

Of course, not all psychology majors decide to earn a doctorate degree. In fact, approximately three-quarters of all students who earn an undergraduate degree do not continue on to graduate school. So what kinds of careers do these people have? While the job selection, pay, and opportunities are not as plentiful at the undergraduate level, there are a wide variety of career options for people with a bachelor's degree in psychology.

Some of the most obvious career opportunities are in the health and social services fields. For example, you might find work as a case manager, psychiatric technician, or psychosocial rehabilitation specialist working in a mental health care office, hospital, or school setting. In such positions, you will need to have a great deal of empathy for clients and be capable of juggling the various demands of providing patient care, completing paperwork, and maintaining accurate records. These jobs can be challenging, but truly rewarding if you have a passion for helping people improve their lives and discover their full potential.

How long does it take to become a psychologist?

The amount of time you spend training to become a psychologist depends a lot on the specialty area you choose. If you are interested in becoming a licensed clinical psychologist, you'll need to first earn a bachelor's degree (4 to 5 years of college) before earning a doctorate degree in psychology (4 to 7 years of graduate school). In most cases, you can estimate that it will take between 8 to 12 years to become a psychologist.

It is also important to realize that some of the career options that are open to you may not be quite so evident. Because psychology programs emphasize intrapersonal skills, your background qualifies you to work in jobs that rely heavily on written communication and the ability to work with others. Some jobs in this area include marketing, sales, advertising, and human resources.

Because psychology majors are expected to know a great deal about the research process, jobs that involve collecting data, organizing information, and preparing results are also good matches. This strong research background makes psychology majors well suited to jobs as market researchers, library assistants, probation officers, laboratory assistants, or technical writers.

Job Options with a Graduate Degree in Psychology

If you do decide to continue your education and earn a master's or doctorate degree in psychology, you'll find that job opportunities are much more plentiful. At the master's level, you can find work as a health psychologist, industrial-organizational psychologist, counselor, social worker, or sports psychologist. Earning a doctorate degree is the best way to increase your career options and earnings potential in any given specialty area. For example, while you may be able to start your career as an industrial-organizational psychologist with a master's degree, you will be able to command a much higher salary if you hold a PhD.

A doctorate degree is also necessary if you have an interest in teaching psychology at the university level. While there are some college or university teaching positions available to those with a master's degree, the market tends to be very saturated and competition is fierce. Psychologists working in university settings typically conduct research in addition to teaching classes each semester. If you are considering a future in academic psychology, focus on developing a strong specialty area during your undergraduate and graduate years. Because the competition for teaching and research jobs is so strong, establishing yourself as an expert in a particular area can give you a significant edge in the job market.

> Salaries can vary dramatically based on your specialty area, geographic location, and educational background. According to the U.S. Department of Labor, the average salary for a counseling, clinical, and school psychologists in 2008 was $64,140 annually. The lowest 10 percent earned less than $39,000 a year while the highest 10 percent made more than $149,000 a year. While not common, some of highest paid psychologists can earn over six figures annually.

Of course, teaching at the college level is not the only option for people who earn a graduate degree in psychology. Many psychologists work in applied areas where they directly utilize their knowledge of the human mind and behavior to solve problems or improve people's lives. Clinical psychologists make up the largest employment area within psychology and work to assess and treat clients suffering from psychological distress. Some clinical psychologists work with a wide variety of people, while others specialize in working with a particular group (such as young children or the elderly) or in treating specific types of disorders (such as eating disorders, anxiety, or depression).

One applied specialty area that has garnered a tremendous amount of attention in recent years is known as forensic or criminal psychology. While popular books and television programs often depict forensic psychologists as super-sleuths who use their powers of psychological deduction to hunt down criminals, forensic psychologists actually perform a variety of different functions within the legal system. Some criminal psychologists actually do help investigators solve crimes, but this is not the norm. Many of the people working in this field are actually clinical psychologists, counselors, and school psychologists, but increasing numbers of universities are offering graduate programs specifically in forensic psychology. Typical job duties performed by forensic psychologists include assessing mental competence, investigating cases of suspected child abuse, performing child custody evaluations, and giving expert testimony in court.

While the reality of forensic psychology careers may not be quite as dramatic as it is depicted in the movies and on television, this is still an exciting and dynamic job area with lots of potential for future growth. In addition to having the opportunity to help other people, forensic psychologists have diverse career options and can choose to work in a variety of settings such as in the criminal courts, juvenile justice system, or as a private consultant.

The Job Outlook for Psychology Careers

What does the future hold for psychology careers? Will your chosen specialty area still be in demand by the time you graduate? Fortunately, the U.S. Department of Labor predicts that job growth for psychologists is expected to grow at an average rate over the next ten years. However, they do note that people with doctorate degrees in sought-after specialty areas such as health psychology, school psychology, or counseling psychology will be in the greatest demand.

While strong job growth and demand is expected to be high for certain specialty areas, don't let reports and statistics guide your career decision. Instead, focus on your individual strengths, interests, and goals. After all, if you have a passion for helping people, do you really want to enter a career that requires you to spend hours every day alone in a science lab? If you aren't quite sure where your particular interest lie, then now is the time to start learning more about different career paths and delving deeper into specific topics within psychology. Many colleges and universities offer a "Careers in Psychology" course; in fact, it's often a required class if you are a psychology major. Consider taking this course early in your academic career. By getting an idea of what you'd like to do someday, you'll be able to tailor your course selection and research interests in order to focus on your preferred specialty areas.

Before you make a final decision on your future career, there are a few important questions you need to ask yourself:

Do you like working with others? If you really love talking to people and helping them to solve problems, then a job in clinical or counseling psychology might be an ideal choice for you. However, a career in research might be more appropriate if you prefer not to work directly with clients.

Are you good at math, statistics, and writing? Experimental psychologists spend a lot of time analyzing data and writing up lab results. If you don't enjoy this type of work, you might not be suited to a job in research.

Can you handle stress? Working with clients suffering from mental illnesses can be emotionally draining, so it is essential to learn how to cope with stress and create a division between work and your personal life.

Are you willing to go to graduate school? Some psychology careers, such as clinical or school psychology, require a doctorate degree. Think about whether you are willing to commit the time, energy, and resources necessary for earning an advanced degree before you select a career path.

Psychology for Tomorrow

Over the past 140 years or so, psychology has made remarkable progress. From its rather humble beginnings in Wundt's laboratory to the high-tech brain-imaging techniques used today, psychologists are always finding new ways to learn more about the mind and behavior. Whether you plan on becoming a psychologist or are simply keeping up with the latest scientific findings, you are bound to play an important role in psychology's bright future as a consumer of psychological information, therapist, teacher, researcher, or other whatever area of study you choose.

GLOSSARY OF
Psychological Terms

abnormal psychology
The study of abnormal mental processes and behavior.

agoraphobia
The fear of being away from a safe place, such as your home.

Alzheimer's disease
A degenerative disease that results in the loss of brain cells, typically occurring in the elderly.

amnesia
Loss of memory, whether partially or completely.

anorexia nervosa
An eating disorder in which an individual starves him or herself in order to lose weight.

antianxiety drugs
Drugs that are used in the treatment of anxiety disorders, such as Valium or Xanax.

antidepressants
Drugs that are most often used to treat depression, such as Prozac, Zoloft, or Paxil.

antipsychotic drugs
Drugs that are used to treat psychoses (e.g., schizophrenia), such as Restoril.

anxiety disorders
A category of mental disorders in which all share a symptom of an extreme fear or anxiety. They include phobias, panic attacks with or without agoraphobia, obsessive-compulsive disorder, and posttraumatic stress disorder.

attribution theory
A psychological theory that offers explanations of social or individual behavior.

awareness
How conscious you are of yourself or materials and things within your environment.

behavior therapy
A form of therapy in which conditioning techniques are applied to change or eliminate a problematic behavior.

biological altruism
A selfless act made on the behalf of another in order to attempt to save that person's life, even though your own life may be at risk.

bipolar disorder
A mental disorder in which a person experiences a series of extreme highs and lows that are often unpredictable in nature, formerly called manic-depressive illness, usually occurring over months rather than within one day or week.

brainstorming
A problem-solving strategy in which you come up with as many possible solutions as you can, usually within a certain period of time.

bulimia nervosa
An eating disorder in which an individual eats large amounts of food and then purges in order to lose weight.

catastrophizing
Blowing a small problem out of proportion and turning it into an inescapable disaster.

central nervous system
A system of the body consisting of the spinal column and the brain.

chromosomes
The structures within every cell that carry the genes.

chunk
A unit of information containing smaller bits of information stored in the memory.

cingulotomy
A surgical procedure that burns and destroys a small portion of the brain known to be involved in emotionality. This is used as a last resort for those suffering severe obsessive-compulsive disorder and major depression who have not responded to drugs or forms of psychotherapy.

classical conditioning
The process by which a normally neutral stimulus becomes a conditioned stimulus, eliciting a response in an individual due to its association with a stimulus that already elicits a similar response.

client-centered therapy
A humanistic therapy approach in which the client is the focus of the therapy session.

cognitive processes
Processes (such as thinking, reasoning, remembering, etc.) that allow you to understand your environment and how the environment affects you and in turn how you affect the environment.

cognitive therapy
A form of therapy that employs the premise that rational, realistic, and constructive thinking can reduce the occurrence of or entirely get rid of a problematic behavior.

compliance
Yielding to another person's wishes without modifying your true beliefs.

compulsion:
A repetitive ritual behavior in obsessive-compulsive disorder that is used to reduce anxiety.

conditioning
A learning process in which an environmental stimulus elicits a response, and an individual learns from the association between that stimulus and response. The association is what conditions, or modifies, our behavior and we therefore learn to behave in a certain manner toward the same stimulus in the future.

conscious
The term used to describe your active awareness.

consciousness
Level of awareness.

conventional morality
The second stage of the moral thought process in which adolescents begin to uphold laws because they understand the concept of rules and that they should be obeyed. This is also the stage in which adolescents start doing good out of caring for others.

cyclothymia
A milder form of bipolar disorder. People with cyclothymia suffer mood swings between mania and depression, but they are not as extreme.

deductive reasoning
A form of reasoning that uses premises that guarantee to be followed by a conclusion of truth.

delusions
False, and often outlandish, ideas that a person believes to be true, not consistent with the person's cultural context.

diffusion of responsibility
An event that takes place when a group of people are witnessing the same emergency, yet certain people do not offer assistance because other people are present, therefore diffusing their need to act.

dissociative disorders
A category of mental disorders in which the disorders are characterized by the separation of a person's awareness from his conscious memory. These include dissociative amnesia and dissociative identity disorder.

dysthymia
A less severe form of depression that is not disabling but still produces feelings of despair and pervasive lack of pleasure.

eating disorders

A category of mental disorders in which the disorders are characterized by excessive overeating, undereating, overexercising, or purging as a result of a fear of gaining weight. They include anorexia nervosa and bulimia nervosa.

ego

A component of personality that seeks to gain pleasure; it operates on the reality principle where impulses are controlled when situations aren't favorable for meeting its demands.

electroencephalograph

A device used to measure brain waves, otherwise known as EEG.

event-related potential

Minute electrical changes that are studied to localize brain activity.

explicit memory

The storage location for information you intentionally work to remember.

factitious disorders

A category of mental disorders in which the disorders are characterized by a person's attempt to fake physical or psychological illnesses.

free association

An exercise used in therapy that requires the patient to talk about whatever comes to mind no matter how relevant, nonsensical, or foreign the thoughts sound. This technique, along with dream analysis and childhood memory evaluation, attempt to help patients understand themselves and their actions.

habituation

The most basic form of learning in which an individual turns his attention to new objects and away from already discovered objects.

hallucinations

False sensory perceptions that a person believes to be real.

hypnosis

A procedure meant to create an altered state of consciousness in which a hypnotist suggests changes in feelings, perceptions, thoughts, or behavior of the subject.

id

A component of personality that wants immediate gratification of physical distress such as hunger, thirst, and sexual tension.

implicit memory

The storage location for information you remember but did not intentionally store for future use.

impulse control disorders

A category of mental disorders in which the disorders are marked by an inability to resist an impulse to participate in a behavior that is harmful to oneself or others. These include kleptomania, pyromania, pathological gambling, and intermittent explosive disorder.

inductive reasoning
A form of reasoning that uses premises to predict an outcome or conclusion that is probably true, though there is a possibility the conclusion is false.

long-term memory
The memory that stores all information the mind wishes to keep for the long term, information that may be retrieved and used in the future.

major depression
A mood disorder involving interruptions in an individual's behavior, emotion, cognition, and body function.

mania
A period of extreme exhilaration wherein the individual is full of energy, high self-esteem, creativity, and ambition.

menopause
A time of physical change in women (typically during middle adulthood) in which menstruation ceases and the ovaries stop producing estrogen.

mnemonics
Strategies, such as a rhyme or formula, that are used to improve the memory and help you retain and retrieve the information by making use of the information already stored in your long-term memory.

mood disorders
A category of mental disorders in which the disorders are characterized by extreme changes in mood, such as major depression, cyclothymia, dysthymia, and bipolar disorder.

mood stabilizers
Drugs that work to stabilize a person's mood, reducing or getting rid of extreme mood swings.

operant conditioning
A process by which an individual's response is followed by a consequence (either positive or negative) and that consequence teaches her either to repeat the response or to decrease its occurrence.

overgeneralizing
Taking a thought or belief and irrationally expanding it to areas that would otherwise be unaffected.

panic disorder
An anxiety disorder in which an individual suffers recurring panic attacks.

personality disorders
A category of mental disorders in which the disorders are a result of maladaptive patterns that disrupt a person's ability to function in everyday life and/or cause extreme distress. They include narcissistic personality disorder, antisocial personality disorder, and paranoid personality disorder, as well as borderline personality disorder, obsessive-compulsive personality disorder, and avoidant personality disorder.

phobia
An exaggerated and unrealistic fear that incapacitates the sufferer.

postconventional morality
The third stage of moral thought in which an adolescent will act according to his or her own basic ethical principles.

posttraumatic stress disorder
An anxiety disorder that develops following a traumatic experience, such as near-death experiences, rape, war, or natural disasters. The symptoms of PTSD include reliving the traumatic experience in dreams or thoughts, irritability, insomnia, inability to concentrate, depression, and a detachment from others.

preconscious
The part of the mind that stores memories that you do not have a use for at the present moment but that you can retrieve in the future if needed.

preconventional morality
The first stage of the moral thought process in which a child will obey the rules and choose to do right only to avoid punishment or gain a reward for acting "good."

psychological altruism
A selfless act made for the benefit of another that does not reward you in any way.

psychosurgery
A method of treatment that involves destroying the part of the brain thought to be responsible for the mental disorder.

psychotic disorders
A category of mental disorders in which the disorders are marked by delusions, hallucinations, or extreme emotional disturbances (often the sufferer is considered to have lost touch with reality). They include schizophrenia and delusional disorder.

reference group
Groups we identify with when we need to understand our own opinions and analyze our behavior or reactions to situations.

reinforcement
Rewards and punishments.

REM sleep
A stage of sleep in which your brain is just as active as it is when you are wide-awake during the day.

repressed memory
A memory that has been involuntarily pushed to the unconscious and that the individual is unaware of.

schemata
Cognitive structures stored in memory that are abstract representations of events, objects, and relationships in the real world.

schizophrenia
A mental disorder in which an individual loses touch with reality, suffers hallucinations and delusions, and is unable to carry out many daily activities.

scripts
Schemata or abstract cognitive representations of events and social interactions.

self-perception
A theory that concludes that we make the same judgments about ourselves, use the same processes, and make the same errors as we do when making judgments about others.

sensory memory
The memory that briefly stores incoming impressions.

sexual and gender-identity disorders
A category of mental disorders in which the disorders are marked by abnormal behavior regarding sexual functioning. They include sadomasochism, exhibitionism, psychosexual dysfunction, fetishism, and transsexualism.

short-term memory
The memory that deals with only the present time. It stores everything you are conscious of at the moment.

sleep disorders
A category of mental disorders that are marked by a disruption in a person's normal sleeping patterns. They include insomnia, narcolepsy, and sleep apnea.

somatoform disorders
A category of mental disorders that are characterized by a complaint of a physical symptom for which no cause can be found. These include hypochondria and conversion disorder.

stimulants
Drugs that speed up the activity in the central nervous system. Stimulants include, but are not limited to, cocaine, methamphetamine hydrochloride (speed), and amphetamines (uppers).

stimulus generalization
Occurs when an individual has the same conditioned response to a stimulus that is similar though not the same as the conditioned stimulus.

stress
A condition in which extreme pressure, hardship, or pain is either suddenly experienced or built up over time.

stressors
Those stimuli that produce stress.

subconscious
The part of the mind that handles the information and mental processes needed to perform routine activities that do not require conscious thought.

substance-related disorders

A category of mental disorders in which the disorders are a result of the use of or withdrawal from a drug such as alcohol, caffeine, amphetamines, opiates, or nicotine.

superego

A component of personality that censors and restrains the ego, makes value judgments, sets standards, and weighs consequences.

transference

The process of transferring one's emotions toward a figure from one's past onto another person, often a therapist.

trial and error

A problem-solving strategy in which an individual tries out several solutions until she or he finds the correct one.

unconscious

The part of the mind that stores those memories we are unaware of.

RESOURCES

<u>Online Psychology Resources</u>

About.com Psychology
http://psychology.about.com

American Psychological Association
www.apa.org

Amoeba Web
www.vanguard.edu/faculty/ ddegelman/amoebaweb

Association for Psychological Science
http://psychologicalscience.org

PsychCentral
http://psychcentral.com

Social Psychology Network
www.socialpsychology.org

<u>Mental Health Websites</u>

Medline Plus
www.nlm.nih.gov/medlineplus/ mentalhealth.html

National Alliance on Mental Illness
www.nami.org

National Institute of Mental Health (NIMH)
www.nimh.nih.gov/index.shtml

National Mental Health Association
www.nmha.org

Further Reading

Abnormal Psychology: An Integrative Approach, by David H. Barlow and Vincent Mark Durand.

Biological Psychology, by James W. Kalat.

Diagnostic and Statistical Manual of Mental Disorders, by American Psychiatric Association.

Doing Psychotherapy, by Michael Franz Basch.

Exploring Psychology, by David G. Myers.

Forty Studies that Changed Psychology: Explorations into the History of Psychological Research, by Roger R. Hock.

Genetics of Mental Disorders: A Guide for Students, Clinicians, and Researchers, by Stephen V. Faraone, Ming T. Tsuang, and Debby W. Tsuang.

Mental Disorders in Older Adults: Fundamentals of Assessment and Treatment, by Steven H. Zarit and Judy M. Zarit.

Mental Health Disorders Sourcebook, edited by Karen Bellenir.

Obsessive-Compulsive Disorders: A Complete Guide to Getting Well and Staying Well, by Fred Penzel.

Personality: Theory and Research, by Lawrence A. Pervin, Daniel Cervone, and Oliver P. John.

Psychology, by David G. Myers.

Publication Manual of the American Psychological Association, by the American Psychological Association.

Social Psychology, by Robert A. Baron, Nyla R. Branscombe, and Donn Byrne.

Understanding Psychotherapy, by Michael Franz Basch.

What's Going on in There?: How the Brain and Mind Develop in the First Five Years of Life, by Lise Eliot.

When Someone You Love Has a Mental Illness: A Handbook for Family, Friends, and Caregivers, by Rebecca Woolis.

INDEX

ACKNOWLEDGMENTS

I would like to thank my parents for all of their help while I was pursuing my education and career. Many thanks to all of my readers at *http://psychology.about.com* for their endless fascination with the mind and behavior. Thanks to Brett Palana-Shanahan at Adams Media for starting me on this path. A very special thanks to Madaleine Burry and the wonderful staff and writers at About.com for their support and guidance over the last five years. I would especially like the thank my awesome husband, Richard, without whom this book would not have been possible.